THE COLLAPSE
OF COMMUNISM IN
THE SOVIET UNION

THE COLLAPSE
OF COMMUNISM IN
THE SOVIET UNION

William E. Watson

Greenwood Press Guides to
Historic Events of the Twentieth Century
Randall M. Miller, Series Editor

Greenwood Press
Westport, Connecticut • London

Library of Congress Cataloging-in-Publication Data

Watson, William E.
   The collapse of Communism in the Soviet Union / William E. Watson.
     p. cm.—(Greenwood Press guides to historic events of the
twentieth century, ISSN 1092–177X)
   Includes bibliographical references and index.
   ISBN 0–313–30162–X (alk. paper)
   1. Soviet Union—Politics and government—1985–1991. 2. Russia
(Federation)—Politics and government—1991– 3. Post-communism—
Russia (Federation) I. Title. II. Series.
DK288.W38   1998
320.947—dc21   97–40857

British Library Cataloguing in Publication Data is available.

Library of Congress Catalog Card Number: 97–40857
ISBN: 0–313–30162–X
ISSN: 1092–177X

First published in 1998

Greenwood Press, 88 Post Road West, Westport, CT 06881
An imprint of Greenwood Publishing Group, Inc.

Printed in the United States of America

∞

The paper used in this book complies with the
Permanent Paper Standard issued by the National
Information Standards Organization (Z39.48–1984).

10 9 8 7 6 5 4 3 2 1

Front cover photo: Workers loosen the cable used to remove a statue of Lenin. Reuters/
Corbis-Bettmann.

Back cover photo: Ronald Reagan and Mikhail Gorbachev in front of St. Basil's Cathedral,
May 31, 1988. Courtesy of the Ronald Reagan Library.

Contents

Series Foreword

As the twenty-first century approaches, it is time to take stock of the political, social, economic, intellectual, and cultural forces and factors that have made the twentieth century the most dramatic period of change in history. To that end, the Greenwood Press Guides to Historic Events of the Twentieth Century presents interpretive histories of the most significant events of the century. Each book in the series combines narrative history and analysis with primary documents and biographical sketches, with an eye to providing both a reference guide to the principal persons, ideas, and experiences defining each historic event, and a reliable, readable overview of that event. Each book further provides analyses and discussions, grounded in both primary and secondary sources, of the causes and consequences, in thought and action, that give meaning to the historic event under review. By assuming a historical perspective, drawing on the latest and best writing on each subject, and offering fresh insights, each book promises to explain how and why a particular event defined the twentieth century. No consensus about the meaning of the twentieth century emerges from the series, but, collectively, the books identify the most salient concerns of the century. In so doing, the series reminds us of the many ways those historic events continue to affect our lives.

Each book follows a similar format designed to encourage readers to consult it both as a reference and a history in its own right. Each volume opens with a chronology of the historic event, followed by a narrative overview, which also serves to introduce and examine briefly the main themes and issues related to that event. The next set of chapters is composed of topical essays, each analyzing closely an issue or problem of interpretation introduced in the opening chapter. A concluding chapter suggesting the long-term implications and meanings of the historic event brings the strands of the preceding chapters together while placing the event in the larger historical context. Each book also includes a section of short biographies of the principal persons related to the event, followed by a section introducing and reprinting key historical documents illustrative of and pertinent to the event. A glossary of selected terms adds to the utility of each book. An annotated bibliography—of significant books, films, and CD-ROMs—and an index conclude each volume.

The editors made no attempt to impose any theoretical model or historical perspective on the individual authors. Rather, in developing the series, an advisory board of noted historians and informed high school history teachers and public and school librarians identified the topics needful of exploration and the scholars eminently qualified to examine those events with intelligence and sensitivity. The common commitment throughout the series is to provide accurate, informative, and readable books, free of jargon and up to date in evidence and analysis.

Each book stands as a complete historical analysis and reference guide to a particular historic event. Each book also has many uses, from understanding contemporary perspectives on critical historical issues, to providing biographical treatments of key figures related to each event, to offering excerpts and complete texts of essential documents about the event, to suggesting and describing books and media materials for further study and presentation of the event, and more. The combination of historical narrative and individual topical chapters addressing significant issues and problems encourages students and teachers to approach each historic event from multiple perspectives and with a critical eye. The arrangement and content of each book thus invite students and teachers, through classroom discussions and position papers, to debate the character and significance of great historic events and to discover for themselves how and why history matters.

The series emphasizes the main currents that have shaped the modern world. Much of that focus necessarily looks at the West, especially Europe and the United States. The political, commercial, and cultural expansion of the West wrought largely, though not wholly, the most fundamental changes of the century. Taken together, however, books in the series reveal the interactions between Western and non-Western peoples and society, and also the tensions between modern and traditional cultures. They also point to the ways in which non-Western peoples have adapted Western ideas and technology and, in turn, influenced Western life and thought. Several books examine such increasingly powerful global forces as the rise of Islamic fundamentalism, the emergence of modern Japan, the communist revolution in China, and the collapse of communism in eastern Europe and the former Soviet Union. American interests and experiences receive special attention in the series, not only in deference to the primary readership of the books but also in recognition that the United States emerged as the dominant political, economic, social, and cultural force during the twentieth century. By looking at the century through the lens of American events and experiences, it is possible to see why the age has come to be known as "The American Century."

Assessing the history of the twentieth century is a formidable prospect. It has been a period of remarkable transformation. The world broadened and narrowed at the same time. Frontiers shifted from the interiors of Africa and Latin America to the moon and beyond; communication spread from mass circulation newspapers and magazines to radio, television, and now the Internet; skyscrapers reached upward and suburbs stretched outward; energy switched from steam, to electric, to atomic power. Many changes did not lead to a complete abandonment of established patterns and practices so much as a synthesis of old and new, as, for example, the increased use of (even reliance on) the telephone in the age of the computer. The automobile and the truck, the airplane, and telecommunications closed distances, and people in unprecedented numbers migrated from rural to urban, industrial, and ever more ethnically diverse areas. Tractors and chemical fertilizers made it possible for fewer people to grow more, but the environmental and demographic costs of an exploding global population threatened to outstrip natural resources and human innovation. Disparities in wealth increased, with developed nations prospering and underdeveloped nations starving. Amid the crumbling of former European colonial empires, Western technology, goods, and culture increasingly enveloped the globe, seeping into, and undermining, non-Western cultures— a process that contributed to a surge of religious fundamentalism and ethno-nationalism in the Middle East, Asia, and Africa. As people became more alike, they also became more aware of their differences. Ethnic and religious rivalries grew in intensity everywhere as the century closed.

The political changes during the twentieth century have been no less profound than the social, economic, and cultural ones. Many of the books in the series focus on political events, broadly defined, but no books are confined to politics alone. Political ideas and events have social effects, just as they spring from a complex interplay of nonpolitical forces in culture, society, and economy. Thus, for example, the modern civil rights and women's rights movements were at once social and political events in cause and consequence. Likewise, the Cold War created the geopolitical framework for dealing with competing ideologies and nations abroad and served as the touchstone for political and cultural identities at home. The books treating political events do so within their social, cultural, and economic contexts.

Several books in the series examine particular wars in depth. Wars are defining moments for people and eras. During the twentieth century war became more widespread and terrible than ever before, encouraging new efforts to end war through strategies and organizations of international cooperation and disarmament while also fueling new ideologies and instruments of mass persuasion that fostered distrust and festered old national rivalries. Two world wars during the century redrew the political map, slaughtered or uprooted two generations of people, and introduced and hastened the development of new technologies and weapons of mass destruction. World War I spelled the end of the old European order and spurred communist revolution in Russia and fascism in Italy, Germany, and elsewhere. World War II killed fascism and inspired the final push for freedom from European colonial rule in Asia and Africa. It also led to the Cold War that suffocated much of the world for almost half a century. Large wars begat small ones, and brutal totalitarian regimes cropped up across the globe. After (and in some ways because of) the fall of communism in eastern Europe and the former Soviet Union, wars of competing cultures, national interests, and political systems persisted in the struggle to make a new world order. Continuing, too, has been the belief that military technology can achieve political ends, whether in the superior American firepower that failed to "win" in Vietnam or in the American "smart bombs" and other military wizardry that "won" in the Persian Gulf.

Another theme evident in the series is that throughout the century nationalism has continued to drive events. Whether in the Balkans in 1914 triggering World War I or in the Balkans in the 1990s threatening the post–Cold War peace—or in many other places—nationalist ambitions and forces would not die. The persistence of nationalism is yet another reminder of the many ways that the past becomes prologue.

We thus offer the series as a modern guide to and interpretation of the historic events of the twentieth century and as an invitation to consider how and why those events have not only defined the past and present but also charted the political, social, intellectual, cultural, and economic routes into the next century.

Randall M. Miller
Saint Joseph's University, Philadelphia

Preface

The essays and documents contained in this volume seek to explain the decline and fall of a superpower and its ruling party. For well over half a century the Soviet Union (1917–1991) was one of the most powerful empires in history. At its height, it consisted of 15 national republics spanning 13 time zones. The Soviet Union also possessed an external empire of client states in Europe (through the Warsaw Pact) and a number of overseas clients that were, to one degree or another, dependent on Soviet Communism for their survival. The Communist Party, its general secretary, and its Politburo determined the Soviet Union's political, economic, and military destiny for over seven decades. The reform of the system undertaken by General Secretary Mikhail Gorbachev (1985–1991)—perestroika—was intended to make the Soviet system profitable and popular. However, hard-line party opposition to the reform process led to the unsuccessful coup of August 1991 that hastened the demise of the party and the Soviet Union itself.

The search for ultimate causes of the collapse of Communism in the Soviet Union is aided by substantial contemporary source material, written by proponents of reform as well as by opponents. In addition, there has already been considerable contemporary analysis of the event by other historians and political scientists. The narrative overview (Chapter 1) in this volume explains in broad terms the collapse of Communism, through the end of the Soviet government and its replacement by the Commonwealth of Independent States (CIS). Chapters 2–4 explore three important themes discussed in the overview: the evolution of Mikhail Gorbachev's perestroika reform policies; the costly Soviet imperial legacy and the 10-year Afghan War; and the rise of nationalism and the breakup of Soviet unity. These subjects merit further attention because they can be isolated as specific but interrelated causes of Soviet decline.

Chapter 5 discusses contemporary post-Soviet Russia and explores the problems faced by the Russian Federation government of Boris Yeltsin in the attempt to establish a democratic capitalist system, after 70 years of Communist totalitarian rule. Contemporary problems include lingering internal imperial dilemmas and a declining economic infrastructure, both inherited from the Soviet system; an inability to assert power over (and collect taxes from) the distant provinces; growing corruption within the economy from organized crime; and the possible resurgence of Communism. The prospects for the return of Communism are discussed.

The Biographies section reviews the careers of individuals involved in the decline and fall of Soviet Communism—including the last four Soviet leaders, whose policies inadvertently led to the collapse of the system; the principal opponents of reform; the leaders of the August 1991 coup attempt; the first post-Soviet leader of Russia; and the first post-Soviet Communist Party leader in Russia.

The Primary Documents section illustrates the reform attempt by Mikhail Gorbachev and his trailblazing economic advisors; party opposition to the reforms; the August 1991 coup attempt; and the subsequent collapse of the party and the Soviet Union. Documents relating to the August 1991 coup attempt, and the resistance to coup, are included at length because a familiarity with the events of August 19–21, 1991, is essential to understanding why the Communist system subsequently collapsed. Important documents about the fall of the party and the end of the Soviet Union have been included, as well as documents about the creation of the Commonwealth of Independent States. The hope is that students will find these helpful in their research activities and classroom discussion.

I would like to express thanks to Randall M. Miller of Saint Joseph's University and Barbara A. Rader of Greenwood Publishing Group, for their helpful suggestions and patience; to Alexander Valentinovich Riasanovsky of the University of Pennsylvania, for many years of guidance and friendship; to Martin Sixsmith for his generous grant of permission; to John H. Ahtes, Rev. J. Francis Watson and Filmic Archives; and to my wife, Debra, to whom this volume is dedicated.

Chronology of Events

1917

The 300-year rule of Romanov dynasty ended with abdication of Tsar Nicholas II during the February–March revolution. Provisional Government lasted from February to October (November, new style) 1917. In October–November the Bolshevik revolution led by Lenin (Vladimir I. Ulyanov) established a Communist state (named the Union of Soviet Socialist Republics, or USSR, in 1922). Cheka, or Soviet political police, was created to enforce the regime's totalitarian policies.

1918

Constituent Assembly, a popularly elected legislative body, met for only one day in January; was broken up by Lenin because Bolsheviks were only a minority of the body.

1918–1920

Russian civil war, a Communist "Red" victory over non-Communist "Whites," in which some two million Russians perished. Tsar Nicholas II and his family were executed by Bolshevik "Reds" in July 1918.

1921

Gosplan, the state economic planning commission, was created; directed the Soviet economy for almost 70 years, emphasizing heavy industrial production.

1921–1928

New Economic Policy (NEP), Lenin's successful experiment with capitalism, ended under Stalin in 1928.

1924

Death of Vladimir Lenin. Rise of Joseph Stalin.

1928–1932

First Five-Year Plan. Beginning of collectivization.

1932–1933

"Terror Famine" in which some five million Ukrainians perished.

1936–1938

Show trials of party members whom Stalin perceived to be his rivals (about one million were purged). Purges in the Red Army officer corps through 1941 took about 80,000 lives.

1941–1945

World War II, called The Great Patriotic War by the Russians. At least 20 million Soviet citizens of all nationalities perished.

1950

Creation of Sino-Soviet Pact, an alliance between the Soviet Union and the newly formed People's Republic of China under Mao Zedong.

1950–1953

Korean War, in which Soviet forces played a small role; nevertheless the war heightened Cold War tensions between the USSR and the United States.

1953

Death of Stalin. Rise of Nikita Khrushchev.

1955

Creation of the Warsaw Pact (a military alliance among the Soviet Union, Poland, East Germany, Hungary, Czechoslovakia, Romania, and Bulgaria), which was intended to provide a united front against the capitalist countries of NATO, the North Atlantic Treaty Organization (the United States, Canada, Iceland, the United Kingdom, France, Portugal, Italy, Belgium, the Netherlands, Luxembourg, Denmark, and Norway).

1956

Khrushchev's destalinization in USSR. Whereas under Stalin the Soviet government had total and absolute control, under destalinization its narrow and primary focus was to end domination of the Communist Party by the political police. Hungarian revolt of October–November was brutally crushed by Red Army.

1957

Small man-made mechanical spacecraft *Sputnik* was launched, demonstrating Soviet scientific prowess. However, the secret Kyshtym nuclear disaster in the Urals demonstrated the government's lack of safety concerns for citizens.

1962

Novocherkassk incident (in which dissatisfied Soviet workers rose up against the party) was brutally crushed. Cuban missile crisis (October) brought the world to the brink of World War III.

1964

Forced retirement of Khrushchev. Rise of Leonid Brezhnev.

1967

Yuri Andropov became head of KGB, the Soviet political police.

1968

Czechoslovakian revolt, called Prague Spring, was crushed by Red Army in August.

1972

SALT I, first Strategic Arms Limitation Treaty between USSR and United States, was signed; it attempted to limit overall numbers of nuclear weapons and establish testing rules, but it failed to provide adequate verification procedures.

1978

Election of Pope John Paul II, a pope from Poland, an Iron Curtain country, caused alarm in the Kremlin that Vatican would serve as a NATO Cold War "listening post" and that religion and nationalism might become agents of anti-Soviet agitation within Warsaw Pact nations.

1979

SALT II, second Strategic Arms Limitation Treaty between USSR and United States, was signed. Soviet invasion of Afghanistan in December began 10-year Afghan War, which renewed Cold War tensions.

1980–1981

Solidarity labor movement, founded by Lech Walesa, became legal in Poland, serving as a means of dissent against Soviet domination until it was outlawed in 1981.

1982

Death of Brezhnev. Rise of Yuri Andropov.

1983

Soviet plane shot down a South Korean passenger liner (KAL 007) in September, exacerbating Cold War tensions. U.S. invasion of Grenada (a Soviet client) in October made Soviets wary of U.S. intentions.

1984

Death of Andropov. Rise of Konstantin Chernenko.

1985

March   Death of Chernenko. Rise of Mikhail Gorbachev. Beginning of perestroika reform era.

1986

April   Beginning of glasnost. Chernobyl nuclear disaster spread dangerous pollution throughout Ukraine, Belarus, and western Russia.

1987

July–August   Gorbachev wrote *Perestroika*, a book outlining his ideas for reform.

December   Washington Summit. INF (Intermediate Nuclear Forces) Treaty was signed, reducing nuclear threat between Warsaw Pact and NATO nations.

1988

January   Law on State Enterprises was enacted, granting control of salaries and leadership to workers' collectives, and declaring the Soviet state no longer responsible for debts of economic enterprises.

February   Nagorno-Karabakh troubles began in the Caucasus as a civil war between Armenia and Azerbaidjan over control of an ethnic Armenian enclave within the Azeri republic.

March   Nina Andreeva's letter, published in the newspaper, *Sovetskaya Rossiya*, was taken as a hard-line manifesto against perestroika.

October   Electoral Law established a new principle of multi-candidate elections to newly formed Congress of People's Deputies, as well as term limits for deputies (another first for the Soviet Union).

December   Gorbachev delivered a speech at UN, outlining Warsaw Pact troop reductions and end of Soviet involvement in Afghan War.

1989

February   Soviet withdrawal from Afghanistan, 20,000 Soviet soldiers had been killed in the 10-year conflict.

March   Elections to Congress of People's Deputies.

July   Commission on Economic Reform was established; explored ways to reform Soviet economy.

October   Beginning of anti-Soviet movements in Warsaw Pact nations; Gorbachev pledged not to intervene.

November   Fall of Berlin Wall, symbol of Cold War.

December   Malta Summit, in which Mikhail Gorbachev and U.S. president George Bush declared Cold War over.

1990

February   Communist Party of the Soviet Union (CPSU) monopoly ended when Article 6 of USSR constitution was dropped. Article 6 had guaranteed the political monopoly of the CPSU within the USSR.

March–May   Baltic republics (Estonia, Latvia, and Lithuania) declared independence.

May   Boris Yeltsin was elected chairman of Supreme Soviet of the Russian Republic.

July   Yeltsin resigned from CPSU at 28th Party Congress. The 500 Days program for economic reform was drawn up.

1991

January   Vilnius Massacre, in which Interior Ministry troops killed Lithuanian civilians.

June   Election of Boris Yeltsin as president of Russia.

August 19–21   Unsuccessful coup attempt against Gorbachev by his hard-line subordinates.

August 23   Yeltsin outlawed CPSU on Russian soil.

August 24   Gorbachev resigned as CPSU general secretary and dissolved CPSU.

December 8   Minsk Agreement was signed, ending the USSR and replacing it with Commonwealth of Independent States (CIS) as of December 25. Russian Federation is largest member of CIS, encompassing the former Russian Soviet Federated Socialist Republic.

1992–1993

December–October   Yeltsin struggled with Russian Parliament over the pace of economic reform in the Russian Federation.

1994–1996

Chechen War (December 1994 to August 1996) in which Chechniya sought to break free from Russian Federation; 30,000 casualties occurred, mainly civilians.

1995

December   Communists won 22 percent of Russian parliamentary seats; many citizens were dissatisfied over Yeltsin's handling of Chechen War and economic reforms.

1996

April   Russia and Belarus agreed to establish a military and customs union, leading to Western concern over revival of Soviet Union.

June   Yeltsin narrowly won Russian presidential election primary; had to prepare to face a Communist candidate in the runoff.

July Yeltsin decisively defeated the Communist opponent in presidential election runoff.

1997

May New NATO treaty was agreed to by Yeltsin; NATO membership was granted to three former members of Warsaw Pact: Poland, Czech Republic, and Hungary. Russia was granted a voice in NATO affairs.

October Communists in parliament failed to gain sufficient support to force a vote of no-confidence in Yeltsin's government.

THE COLLAPSE OF COMMUNISM IN THE SOVIET UNION EXPLAINED

1

Narrative Overview

The Soviet Union was created in October 1917 by a small but devoted band of revolutionaries whose beliefs and goals were shaped by the writings of Karl Marx. Marx (1818–1883) considered the Industrial Revolution to be an era of increasing social and economic injustice, and he was opposed to the accumulation of wealth by capitalist means. Believing his theories to be the solution to global injustice, he advocated revolution by the proletariat (industrial working class) against its alleged exploiters, the bourgeoisie (capitalist class). He predicted that a clash between proletariat and bourgeoisie was imminent and unavoidable, and that the new political, economic, and social order created by the "dictatorship of the proletariat" would be truly egalitarian and communist in nature.

In many European countries Marx gained followers who tended to call themselves Communists. Nineteenth-century Russia, however, was largely agrarian and did not have a sizable proletarian population. Marx believed at first that preconditions for a proletarian revolt in Russia would not develop for hundreds of years. To his surprise, however, Russian radicals were won over to the Communist cause. These radicals were disillusioned with the autocratic tsarist system in part due to the poor conditions of the Russian peasantry, who were liberated from serfdom only in 1861.

THE BOLSHEVIKS

The Bolshevik Party grew out of the first Russian Communist movement of the 1880s, the Emancipation of Labor, which was founded by George Plekhanov. Vladimir I. Ulyanov, who used the assumed name of Lenin, rose to the leadership of the Bolshevik faction of the party that was determined to bring on a revolution against the ancient regime of the tsars. Marx's stress on the role of the proletariat was altered by Lenin so that in Russia, the Bolshevik leaders (most of whom, ironically, came from a bourgeois background) would bring on the revolution through the activities of a group of full-time (in some cases even salaried) agitators. Lenin also altered Marx's "dictatorship of the proletariat"—the socialist state that would be created following the revolution—into a "dictatorship of the proletariat and peasantry," given the almost ten-to-one ratio of peasants to industrial workers in Russia.

When the failures of the Russian army in World War I and the Rasputin Scandal caused the tsar to step down in March 1917, members of the Duma (parliament) formed a democratic Provisional Government. The Provisional Government lost the support of many citizens because it kept Russia in the war, promised to repay the tsarist debt (in order to receive Western assistance), and only slowly began to introduce economic and political reforms. The Bolsheviks overthrew the Provisional Government in October (new style, November) 1917 with the support of weary soldiers who flocked to support the revolutionary Soviet of Workers' and Soldiers' Deputies in Petrograd. Lenin disbanded the democratically elected Constituent Assembly in January 1918, because the Bolsheviks held only about one-quarter of the seats. During the subsequent history of the USSR (Union of Soviet Socialist Republics, 1917–1991), the Communists relied on pseudo-democratic processes such as local and national elections; but until the Gorbachev era in the late 1980s, there was only one legal party operating within the system and only one name appearing on the ballot. The democratic centralism of Lenin changed very little during the subsequent 61 years of rule by the next five men who succeeded him—Stalin, Khrushchev, Brezhnev, Andropov, and Chernenko.

THE COMMUNIST PARTY

The Soviet Communist regime was completely dominated by the party, and in a peculiar sense the Soviet state arose from the party. The party infiltrated the army and created numerous "social organizations" to influence many aspects of daily life among the population. Possessing massive police powers, the state efficiently and violently removed all opposition. During the first seven years of its existence, however, the state made tentative and even contradictory economic changes. The confiscatory program of peasant grain by the Soviet government during the Civil War period—"War Communism"—was replaced by Lenin's New Economic Policy (NEP), which encouraged small-scale capitalism in both manufacturing and agriculture.

STALIN

Despite the clear economic progress made in Russia because of the NEP, the program was abandoned by Stalin following Lenin's death in 1924. Stalin's "Socialism in One Country" emphasized heavy industrialization and collectivization in agriculture that brought about significant results in iron, steel, coal, and oil production, and the bringing of electricity to much of the country. The massive command economy created by Stalin was headed by Gosplan, the state planning commission that set quotas for all items produced by Soviet workers.

This progress in economic production was attained at a great price in human lives and in the morale of the work force, as tens of millions of Soviet citizens died in Stalin's purges and in the network of concentration camps called the Gulag Archipelago. Stalin made a critical error in overemphasizing large-scale production ("gigantism"), because key support industries such as spare parts were not given appropriate attention by Soviet planners. Stalin's rule (1924–1953) lasted beyond World War II into the early years of the Cold War, and his emphasis on the production of conventional military items and on nuclear weapons drained the Soviet economy to the point that it was unable to meet routine demands for housing, transportation, food, and health care. Stalin's legacy to future generations of Soviet leaders was the authoritarian one-party political system and an overemphasis on military hardware, which the Soviet economy found itself increasingly strained to produce.

Stalin also presided over the creation of an external Soviet empire in eastern Europe when the Red Army occupied Poland, East Germany, Czechoslovakia, Hungary, Bulgaria, and Romania (the countries of the future Warsaw Pact after World War II). These states, which became client regimes dependent on Moscow, were economically drained by the USSR from 1945 to 1950 to help bolster the war-ravaged Soviet economy. In time, however, they were guaranteed certain economic and military subsidies from the USSR—such as guaranteed purchases of their products at artificially high prices, and cheap weapons systems.

KHRUSHCHEV

When Stalin's successor, Nikita Khrushchev (1953–1964), began to follow a policy of "destalinization," his main goal was simply to end the the terrorizing of the Communist Party by the political police, which had been common during the Stalin years. Khrushchev's destalinization speech, delivered before the Twentieth Party Congress (February 24–25, 1956), actually did not promise much in the way of reform. He wanted to restore, or "rehabilitate," the reputations of individuals within the party whose careers and lives had been ruined by Stalin's "cult of personality." Nevertheless, in the years immediately following Stalin's death, some citizens hoped for a change in the system or simply a change in the style of government. (This was evident, for example, in Ilya Ehrenburg's 1953 play entitled *The Thaw*.) There had been a hope that the change in leadership would result in a change in economic and political priorities—the end of the Cold War and the bloated Soviet military budget—so that the government would ease its grip on virtually every aspect of life and then the material prosperity of Soviet citizens might improve.

Not only was the Khrushchev regime uninterested in granting freedoms within the Soviet Union itself (consider, for example, the persecution of Boris Pasternak in 1957 for writing *Dr. Zhivago*), but the Soviet leaders also carefully watched for signs of independence within the Warsaw Pact nations and promptly crushed them (as in Hungary in November 1956). The year 1957 was important for Soviet science and a vindication for Khrushchev of his technological expenditures: in that year the Soviets began their ICBM (Inter-Continental Ballistic Missile) program and launched *Sputnik* (the world's first artificial satellite).

Realizing the propaganda value of *Sputnik*, Khrushchev was primarily interested in gaining a strategic advantage over the United States and the North Atlantic Treaty Organization (NATO). He announced in 1961 that the Soviet Union would increase its assistance to developing Third World countries, and he presided over two critical moments in the Cold War—the Berlin crisis (the Soviet-American confrontation over the status of Berlin, 1960–1961, which resulted in the construction of the Berlin Wall by the Soviets) and the Cuban missile crisis (the Soviet-American confrontation over the placement of intermediate-range nuclear missiles in Cuba by the Soviets in 1962, which almost caused a nuclear war between the superpowers). Khrushchev's greater interest in Soviet global strategy led to internal crises, including crop failures in Ukraine and worker unrest in Novocherkassk on the Don River. His blustery attitude earned him so many enemies within the Soviet regime that he was removed from power and forced to retire in 1964.

BREZHNEV

Khrushchev, who ironically was accused of creating his own "cult of personality," was replaced by Leonid Brezhnev (1964–1982). During the Brezhnev years, the Soviets spent even more of their resources on foreign policy. Warsaw Pact subsidies were only a part of these expenses, as Brezhnev also paid for several tens of thousands of Cuban troops and thousands of Warsaw Pact technicians to do his bidding in the Third World and create a new group of overseas client regimes. The goal now was to alter the global balance of power in favor of Soviet Communism at the expense of both the NATO countries and the People's Republic of China.

This policy was referred to as the Brezhnev Doctrine. Cuba and Vietnam were non–Warsaw Pact proxy regimes that were particularly close to the USSR and that received large subsidies from Moscow during this time.

Brezhnev was willing to use Soviet troops openly on two occasions to further his foreign policy interests—during a tentative revolt against Soviet control in Czechoslovakia (the "Prague Spring" of 1968), and in supporting Communist allies in Afghanistan in 1979 (precipitating a 10-year war). Both operations ultimately were disastrous to the global image of the USSR that Brezhnev was trying to promote.

Brezhnev wanted to be recognized as a promoter of détente, a global balance of power. Therefore he negotiated two Strategic Arms Limitation Treaties (SALT) with the United States in 1972 and 1979. Among the issues covered by the treaties were testing rules and anti-ballistic missile systems (ABMS), but the treaties ultimately accomplished nothing because of the problems posed by mutual verification procedures. The fact that Brezhnev was willing to negotiate the SALT treaties with the United States was ironic because he outspent Khrushchev on the Soviet intercontinental, intermediate, and submarine-launched arsenals. In fact, it was only during his tenure that the USSR finally reached nuclear parity with, and even surpassed, the United States in several critical nuclear weapons categories.

The Brezhnev years were also a time of a pronounced growth in the Soviet government bureaucracy. Party membership grew during Brezhnev's tenure; consequently, so did the number of individuals for whom the party had to find employment and housing. Along with the increase in party size came an increase in the number of vacation residences and government pensions. Along with the "perks and privileges" of party membership, however, came opportunities for further exploitation of the system. Corruption by Brezhnev's party cronies was rampant in the late 1970s and early 1980s. One of the more notorious instances (which was hushed up until after Brezhnev's death) involved his own daughter, in the so-called Moscow Circus Case that involved illegal currency speculation and diamond smuggling. Many Soviet citizens came to identify the Brezhnev years with stagnation and corruption.

ANDROPOV

Many cases of corruption under Brezhnev were investigated through KGB chief Yuri Andropov. Andropov had been the Soviet ambassador to Hungary in 1956, and he presided over the destruction of the Hungarian resistance. He rose to become KGB head in 1967 and was charged by Brezhnev with maintaining the policy of not interfering too openly in the affairs of the party, which had been the trend since Khrushchev's destalinization policies of the mid-1950s. He also became a member of the

Politburo. This arrangement was convenient for corrupt officials as long as Brezhnev was well, but there were a few revelations of corruption in the months when the general secretary's health declined, and then quite a few following his death. Andropov's political power was based in part on the information that he might use against his rivals. Consequently, he was chosen to become the new general secretary.

Only 10 days after Brezhnev's death, Andropov commented publicly that "the USSR should make use of the experience of friendly socialist countries." This statement contained the coded message that reforms were going to occur. He spoke of "the force of inertia, the old habits" that caused "narrow departmental attitudes and parochialism" within the Soviet leadership. Many bureaucrats were concerned when Andropov stated that he wanted to relate the compensation and official status of Soviet managers to their work performance, because this had not been done much during the Brezhnev era. In 1984, however, Andropov became ill and died of diabetic complications before he could initiate the reforms. The younger generation of party members actually welcomed the idea of change, because the morale of the Soviet work force and the "true believers" within the party ranks had fallen as a result of the stagnation and corruption during Brezhnev's tenure.

Cold War tensions increased during Andropov's illness. A South Korean commercial airplane (KAL 007) was shot down by a Soviet warplane on September 1, 1983, because it had strayed into Soviet airspace. All 269 passengers (including some Americans) were killed in the incident. The Soviets at first denied that one of their planes had shot down KAL 007, and then they refused to allow American and Japanese teams to search the area in the Pacific where the plane went down. They later admitted that one of their planes was in fact responsible for the downing, but they claimed that KAL 007 had been on an espionage mission.

The United States responded by stating that an American electronic reconnaissance plane of the same type as KAL 007 (a Boeing 747) had been flying within 75 miles of KAL's flight path. As a result of the incident, U.S. president Ronald Reagan suspended planned Soviet-American talks on transportation issues and the opening of an American consulate in Kiev. Soviet foreign minister Andrei Gromyko was denied permission to fly in to airports in New York and New Jersey by the governors of those states, and he had to cancel a speech planned for September 17 at the United Nations. Soviet strategic insecurity was heightened in October when U.S. forces invaded the Caribbean island of Grenada and overthrew its Communist regime, which the Kremlin had hoped might become another Soviet client. Although it is unclear how Andropov might have responded to these crises had he been well, the Kremlin leaders (both conservatives and reformers) were unnerved that Cold War incidents of such importance occurred at this time.

When Andropov died in February 1984, the reform-minded younger generation was disappointed in the choice of Konstantin Chernenko to succeed him. A 72-year-old Brezhnev protégé, Chernenko sought to uphold his mentor's political style. However, the reformers knew that their time would come, given Chernenko's advanced age, and it was no surprise when Chernenko died in 1985. The man chosen to succeed him was Brezhnev's former minister of agriculture, 54-year-old Mikhail Gorbachev.

GORBACHEV

Gorbachev and his supporters believed that immediate reforms of the country's economy and political landscape were necessary to prevent the collapse of the Soviet system. His program was called perestroika (restructuring). It involved taking measures to make the Soviet Communist system both profitable and popular. The corruption of the Brezhnev era was to be eliminated by dismissing incompetent and criminal bureaucrats. Gorbachev outlined the scope of his reform program in 1987 in a book entitled *Perestroika*, which was intended for domestic and foreign audiences. He stressed the urgency of perestroika: "[a]ny delay in beginning perestroika could have led to an exacerbated internal situation in the near future"; and he suggested that a future consisting of the Brezhnev-style status quo would lead to "serious social, economic and political crises." Few apparatchiks (let alone Western observers) envisioned any possible internal threat to the Soviet system, given the party's political monopoly, the loyalty of the Soviet military, and the coercive power of the KGB (the Soviet political police). From Gorbachev's perspective, however, the entire system was being weakened and drained by the bloated and corrupt bureaucracy, inefficient manufacturing and agricultural infrastructures, and the overly large military budget.

Gorbachev appointed like-minded reformers to key positions in the Politburo and publicly revealed shortcomings in the economic infrastructure. He discussed this in a general way in his book, but his spokesmen began making specific admissions about deficiencies in manufacturing techniques, transportation, and storage, which amounted to millions of rubles each year in revenue losses for the USSR. The government tolerated new publications that revealed prior cases of repression and corruption on the part of government officials. This policy of political openness, called glasnost, facilitated a reevaluation of Soviet history. For example, dissident historian Roy Medvedev published articles in November 1988 and February 1989 that revealed in detail the numbers of victims of Stalin's purges (some 20 million people had been killed and 20 million others were otherwise repressed by the regime). Such numbers previously had been rejected by Soviet leaders. The notable exception to glasnost was

Gorbachev's initial silence about the 1986 Chernobyl nuclear disaster in Ukraine.

An unexpected result of glasnost was an increase in ethnic and national consciousness among the minority populations of Soviet states in Central Asia, the Caucasus, and the Baltic region. When the government relaxed its control over the press, it became possible for minority groups with grievances against the regime to express their discontent openly. Details of the Stalinist repressions of minority nationalities in the 1940s were revealed in the glasnost press, and long-standing quarrels between minority groups were revived.

Interethnic riots occurred from 1986 to 1989 in the urban areas of Kazakhstan, Tajikistan, Kirghizstan, and Uzbekistan, and beginning in 1988 an extremely bloody civil war broke out in the Caucasus between Armenians and Azeris over control of an ethnic Armenian enclave called Nagorno-Karabakh, located within the borders of Azerbaidjan. From 1988 to 1991 the conflict caused the loss of thousands of lives and prompted tens of thousands of citizens to migrate. Despite the deployment of military and Interior Ministry units to the region, Gorbachev was utterly incapable of restoring order. Full-fledged independence movements got under way in all three Baltic republics in the fall of 1988, and in the Caucasian republic of Georgia in early 1989. In each case, "national fronts" were created to try to bring about a separation from the union. Gorbachev resorted to violence against civilians in Georgia in April 1989 and in Lithuania in January 1991.

The Gorbachev regime also sustained a great deal of criticism in the glasnost era for the Afghan War, which had been initiated by Brezhnev in December 1979. The Afghan Muslim resistance fighters, or *mujahidin*, received enough assistance from Islamic and Western countries (who wanted to prevent the expansion of Soviet Communism) to ensure that the Soviet military could not win a decisive victory in the country. The Soviets suffered some 2,000 deaths per year in the war, fully half of them during Gorbachev's tenure. Gorbachev's various political tactics in Afghanistan failed, as did the Soviet military strategy (e.g., replacing the Soviet puppet Babrak Karmal with another man, Muhammad Najibullah). Informal veterans' organizations called Afghan Clubs appeared and became clearinghouses for information about the war to the general public. Gorbachev decided to withdraw from Afghanistan in 1988 when it became clear that he needed public support for his planned economic and constitutional reforms.

YELTSIN

In the fall of 1989, Gorbachev created a Reform Commission to outline the alteration of the Soviet economy, which was led by an economics professor named Leonid Abalkin. The "Abalkin Program" consisted of a staged shift away from the command economy of the past, and toward economic competition by state-owned companies—with an alteration of the pricing system (which kept some items priced too low and others too high). Gosplan (the state planning commission that set quotas) was not eliminated, but it had to compete in the realm of ideas with the Reform Commission.

In the spring of 1990, yet another group formed to discuss altering the economy—the Presidential Commission, led by Stanislav Shatalin. One of the driving forces for change was Boris Yeltsin, whom Gorbachev appointed as secretary of the Central Committee of the party, first secretary of the Moscow branch of the party, and also a candidate member of the Politburo. Yeltsin openly criticized the Gorbachev administration for the slow pace of reform in 1988 and was subsequently removed from his positions of power. Thereafter elected as a parliamentary representative for Moscow in 1989, he was next elected president of the Russian republic in 1990 on a platform of faster-paced economic change.

Yeltsin gathered together his own group of economic reformers, including the Russian republic's deputy prime minister for economic reform, Gregory Yavlinsky, and Minister of Finance Boris Federov. Yeltsin's declaration of the Russian republic's "state sovereignty" in June 1990 indicated that he was going to push for changes on a republic-wide level that could serve as a model for the union. Gorbachev met with Yeltsin and the more radical reformers in July and formed the Shatalin Group. They fostered a 500-Day Program of market reform consisting of privatization, creation of a genuine market economy, and granting of more power to the union republics in a new union treaty. (The new treaty would supersede the exploitive arrangment that the Bolsheviks had inherited—and augmented—from the tsarist system.)

REFORMS UNDER GORBACHEV

Gorbachev's economic reform involved a decentralization of the political system. The constitutional reforms he initiated were intended to make Soviet politics more democratic. He believed that he needed the support implied by popular mandate to push through his economic reforms. The first of these changes was a 1988 electoral law that granted multicandidate elections and established term limits. This was followed in 1989 by legislative change revamping the Supreme Soviet (to give it more real power) and creating a new parliamentary body, the Congress of Peoples' Deputies. Members of the Congress were elected according to similar-sized local districts, comparable-sized administrative units, and party-dominated "social organizations." In February 1990, Gorbachev shocked the party (as well as the rest of the USSR and the world at large) when he announced that the Soviet constitution would be altered to remove Article 6, which had guaranteed the party's political monopoly. To minimize the subsequent lessening of his powers as general secretary of the party, he also created a new executive presidency.

Gorbachev's internal reforms were linked to his foreign policy, because the Cold War defense expenditures had sapped the ability of the system to meet the needs of ordinary citizens. Unlike his predecessors, Gorbachev admitted that the escalating arms race was linked to the lack of consumer goods and the poor quality of life for average Soviet citizens. Several summit meetings between the USSR and the United States occurred between the fall of 1985 and the summer of 1991 for the purpose of easing international tensions between the superpowers. The Afghan War was only one of the reasons for the perceived need for such meetings between Gorbachev and his American counterparts (Presidents Ronald Reagan and George Bush). American research into anti-ballistic missile systems had expanded considerably into the Strategic Defense Initiative (SDI), to which the Soviet economy would be hard-pressed to respond. If the Soviet economy were to rise to that next level of defense expenditures, Gorbachev feared that perestroika would be impossible.

The first summit meetings between Gorbachev and Reagan took place in Geneva, Switzerland, in November 1985, and in Reykjavik, Iceland, in October 1986. They occurred at a time when it was too early in Gorbachev's career to make significant changes in policy regarding Afghanistan or the long-standing Warsaw Pact–NATO standoff in Europe. Likewise, Reagan was not interested in making concessions to the ideological enemy whom he had referred to as "the evil empire" in March 1983. However, in a speech at the celebrations commemorating the seventieth anniversary of the Bolshevik revolution (November 8, 1987), Gorbachev stated that because an alliance between the Soviet Union and capitalist countries had been possible during World War II, when each side was threatened by fascism, perhaps another alliance would be possible in the present: "Does this not suggest a lesson for the present, for today's world which faces the threat of nuclear catastrophe?" Only two months after this speech, Gorbachev and Reagan signed the Intermediate Nuclear Forces (INF) Treaty at the Washington Summit. This was followed by the April 1988 talks in Geneva about Afghanistan and Gorbachev's stunning speech in December 1988 at the UN when he stated that he would withdraw Soviet troops from Afghanistan (he had actually started this the previous May) and that he also would reduce the number of Soviet troops and tanks in the Warsaw Pact countries.

By the fall of 1989, glasnost had spread to the Warsaw Pact countries. Despite the fact that Soviet puppets occupied the upper level of the hierarchy in each client state, mass independence movements began to arise throughout the Warsaw Pact that fall. They would test the limits of perestroika in the way that Hungary had tested Khrushchev in 1956 and Czechoslovakia had tested Brezhnev in 1968. Given Gorbachev's economic priorities, however, he had no more interest in keeping Soviet troops in the Warsaw Pact than he did in Afghanistan. He hoped that Communist parties would be popular enough in each of the Warsaw Pact countries that they could hold on to power in popular elections. Poland had most recently challenged the Soviet status quo in eastern Europe. Solidarity (the popular Polish non-Communist labor movement that was created in 1980) had survived Soviet attempts to crush it, and in June 1989 it formed the basis of the opposition to Communism in that country when it defeated the Communists in elections.

THE BEGINNING OF THE END

A broad-based anti-Soviet movement began in all the Warsaw Pact countries in October 1989, and Gorbachev allowed it to grow. Perhaps he underestimated the force of nationalism and the popular disregard for Soviet authority in these countries, but he was determined that Warsaw Pact Communists had to win the support of their own people to maintain power, without Soviet assistance. Gorbachev regarded the Warsaw Pact as expendable because the strategic dividends that the USSR received from control of these countries were not worth the cost of the subsidies they received from the USSR in the era of perestroika. By late October, Hungary and East Germany were caught up in the move away from the Soviet external empire. Gorbachev's spokesman, Gennady Gerasimov, told Western reporters on October 25 that Gorbachev had adopted the "Sinatra Doctrine" (in reference to singer Frank Sinatra's theme song, "My Way"). He said that the Warsaw Pact regimes were "doing it their way" and that "the Brezhnev Doctrine is dead."

Beginning on November 9, 1989, the most important symbol of the Cold War—the Berlin Wall—was torn down. That December, the world watched in awe as Communism was repudiated in each of the Warsaw Pact countries. Almost every former client state underwent a transitional period in which Communist reformers or non-Communists made the change from Soviet client to free state, a process that lasted for varying lengths of time. The exception was Romania, which seemed to be resistant to change until December 17, when Nicolae Ceaucescu (who had been in power for 24 years) faced a mass uprising. It culminated with the execution of Ceaucescu and his wife on Christmas Day, and television coverage of his corpse in order to induce his followers to surrender. This footage, along with television coverage at the Berlin Wall, symbolized the ending of an era—caused by Gorbachev's reforms. At the Malta Summit in December 1989, Gorbachev and U.S. president George Bush formally announced that the Cold War was over.

Gorbachev received criticism from the reform wing of the party, which wanted him to step up the pace of domestic reform within the USSR, and also from the anti-reform wing of the party, which sought to maintain the political, social, and economic privileges of party membership. Although party membership peaked at 19 million in the Gorbachev era, several million members who were frustrated by the slow pace of reform resigned from the party. Even Boris Yeltsin resigned in July 1990. The anti-reform faction of the party made its position clear as early as March 1988, when a letter from a Leningrad chemistry teacher was published in *Sovetskaya Rossiya*. The author, Nina Andreeva, claimed to speak for many party members who were unhappy with the move toward reform. She criticized the reevaluations of the Soviet past that characterized much of the glasnost press, and she implied that the attacks on Stalin's legacy were particularly unpatriotic. She attacked the spirit of reform and complained about "militant cosmopolitanism" (a term used in anti-Semitic contexts during the Stalin period). Politburo member Yegor Ligachev also spoke out on behalf of the hard-line anti-reform segment of the party and seemed willing to take any opportunity to criticize other, more radical, reformers until he retired in August 1990.

A number of Gorbachev's appointees received direct calls for their resignation from the reform wing of the party because of the slow pace of reform. One of those to suffer a politically inspired demotion or premature retirement was Prime Minister Nikolai Ryzhkov, whose official duties were cut back in December 1990 (he subsequently had a heart attack and resigned). Gorbachev then cautiously chose a number of individuals of moderate or conservative background in order to satisfy those within the government and party who feared that the reform could no longer be contained.

Fear of a conservative backlash was one of the reasons for Gorbachev's violent crackdown in the Baltic region in January 1991. Nevertheless, in the summer of 1991 he negotiated a new union treaty, which would have had the result of further decentralizing the Soviet government in order to help bring about the market economy that had been promised to the citizenry. The reformers were still optimistic and felt that their ideas had the momentum of history on their side. In July, however, Foreign Minister Eduard Shevardnadze resigned suddenly, claiming that he feared an impending dictatorship. His fears were not unfounded. Unbeknownst to Gorbachev and Yeltsin, a coup was being prepared against them at precisely that moment.

THE AUGUST COUP

Gorbachev went on vacation to the Crimea in August and was prepared to sign the new union treaty upon his return. However, a number of anti-reform members of Gorbachev's government took measures when he left that they hoped would put an end to perestroika. They ensured that they had the support of a number of military officers loyal to the anti-reform defense minister, Dmitri Yazov, and proceeded to place Gorbachev under house arrest on August 19. An eight-man committee then declared over television that Gorbachev was ill and unable to perform his duties as president of the USSR. The committee also declared the beginning of a six-month national state of emergency and proclaimed a curfew in Moscow. The principal coup plotters were Defense Minister Yazov; Vice President Gennady Yanaev (who was now declared president); Prime Minister Valentin Pavlov; Interior Minister Boris Pugo; the KGB chief, Vladimir Kryuchkov; the deputy chairman of the USSR Defense Council, Oleg Baklanov; the chairman of the USSR Peasants' Union, Vasili Starodubtsev; the president of the Association of State Enterprises, Alexander Tizyakov; and the speaker of the Supreme Soviet, Anatoly Lukyanov.

A few Gorbachev supporters in the Kremlin, however, benefited from disorganization among the coup plotters and managed to contact several military commanders by telephone and convince them to remain loyal to Gorbachev. Many officers in the army (particularly the junior officers) were not in favor of the coup. Yeltsin's headquarters in the Russian Parliament building became the public center of resistance to the coup, and his aides established a radio station in the building with which to make appeals to the public. He also was able to establish telephone contact with U.S. president Bush and the heads of the other republics. Yeltsin declared the coup illegal, and he urged the citizenry and the military to remain loyal to Gorbachev. He also demanded an immediate medical inquiry into Gorbachev's health. He knew that he had the support of the Moscow police force and several military units. His example was followed by the leaders of the Ukrainian, Moldavian, Kazakh, and Uzbek republics. Yeltsin contacted the heads of most of the republics, and they assured him that they backed Gorbachev and not the so-called Emergency Committee.

Meanwhile, tens of thousands of individuals rallied around the Russian Parliament building in Moscow and began erecting barricades. Strikes broke out in opposition to the coup in Siberia, and large protests were organized against the coup in Leningrad and Kiev. Fearing the rise of a resistance movement in the Baltic region, the coup plotters dispatched troops to Estonia, Latvia, and Lithuania.

The European Union cut off $1 billion in food and technical assistance to the USSR, fearing that the coup might mean a return of the Cold War. The United States and NATO cautiously watched the use of force to crush anti-coup activities in the Baltics and feared that similar force might be used in Moscow. This concern stemmed from their anticipation of a resumption of global Cold War conflicts if the hard-liners eliminated Yeltsin and his supporters.

The night of August 20 was the turning point in the coup, as the Emergency Committee gave orders for military units to sweep away Yeltsin's supporters from the streets of Moscow and for the KGB Alpha Team to storm the Russian Parliament building. Although three protesters were killed that night in clashes with the military, the army essentially refused to obey the committee's orders. Most significant, the KGB Alpha Team refused to attack Yeltsin's position at the Parliament building. From that moment, the coup began to fall apart. Gorbachev was freed from captivity and allowed to return to Moscow early on August 22. The coup plotters were placed under arrest and charged with treason. Pugo committed suicide rather than surrender. It was revealed subsequently that both Pavlov and Yanaev had been drunk for much of the time during the coup, and Pavlov afterwards had to be hospitalized. Each of the plotters faced the death penalty, but they were all freed after the collapse of the USSR because Yeltsin did not want to give them a national forum on which to air their grievances.

DISSOLUTION OF THE SOVIET UNION

Even though his defiance to the coup was theoretically on behalf of Gorbachev, it was apparent that Yeltsin emerged as the genuine hero of the ordeal. Following his return to Moscow, Gorbachev stated that he would immediately revamp the party and purge it of the hard-liners who had supported the coup. Yeltsin took the bold step on August 23 of outlawing the activity of the CPSU (Communist Party of the Soviet Union) within the borders of the Russian republic. It soon became apparent to Gorbachev that a large number of party members had supported the coup. Yeltsin made him read out loud in a meeting of the Congress of Peoples' Deputies the minutes from a meeting of his subordinates that showed almost all of them to be in support of the coup. On August 24, after Yeltsin's authorized state funerals of the three protest victims, Gorbachev made the stunning announcement that he would step down as general secretary of the party and would dissolve it. That same day, Yeltsin—and not Gorbachev—accepted the declarations of independence of Estonia and Latvia (the declarations actually had been made the previous week). Ukraine also announced an upcoming referendum regarding independence. Yeltsin proclaimed August 22 a national holiday, renamed the square outside of the Russian Parliament building "Victory Square," and restored the pre-Soviet Russian tricolor flag and national anthem.

With the de facto independence of Russia from the union and the end of the CPSU, the USSR was no longer viable. Negotiations then got under way to dissolve the Soviet Union and officially grant independence to the

15 republics of the union: Russia, Ukraine, Belarus, Moldavia, Estonia, Latvia, Lithuania, Georgia, Armenia, Azerbaidjan, Kazakhstan, Turkmenistan, Uzbekistan, Kirghizstan, and Tajikistan. The treaty signed on December 8 in Minsk, Belarus, ended the USSR and replaced it with a new entity, the Commonwealth of Independent States (CIS). The pact became official on December 25 when Gorbachev resigned as head of the Soviet Union. The 74-year Soviet experiment was over.

2

The Evolution of Perestroika

One of the principal doctrines of Soviet leaders, put forth from the moment Lenin took power in 1917, was that the Soviet citizenry could expect the party to bring about in the near future a utopian "dictatorship of the proletariat and peasantry" in which the economic and social injustices of the tsarist era would be corrected. This would be accomplished by state control over the "means of production" and by coercion. However, as Lenin, Stalin, and Khrushchev presided over the Russian Civil War, World War II, and the early crises of the Cold War, respectively, the party rank-and-file realized that fulfillment of the utopian promise made in 1917 would be postponed.[1] Faced with a chronic shortage of housing and consumer goods, the Soviet public could only hope that better circumstances might prevail in the future.

The Communists had faced opposition to their policies as early as Lenin's time. The Civil War (1918–1920) would not have occurred without the presence of a large number of dissatisfied non-Communists in the country. Lenin's experiment with small-scale capitalism, the New Economic Policy (1921–1928), was successful precisely because the peasants and small entrepreneurs had monetary incentives. Many of the millions of people whom Stalin "purged" and sent off to the Gulag Archipelago in the 1930s were peasants opposed to forced collectivization. By 1940, however, with all of Stalin's real and perceived opponents having been removed, there was no hope of a successful opposition group forming within the Soviet Union. During World War II the Germans found among their Eastern Front POWs (prisoners of war) about 50,000 soldiers of the Red Army who were willing to fight against Stalin. These men became the so-called army of General Andrei Vlasov. However, Vlasov went down in defeat just as surely as Hitler's Wehrmacht, the army of the Nazi German regime, in 1945. Hundreds of thousands of Soviet ethnic minorities such as the Volga Germans, the Crimean Tatars, the Chechens, and the Ingushes died during the war at Stalin's orders, just because of his suspicion that they might attempt to link up with Hitler's forces. In the climate of recovery through the 1950s, even after the death of Stalin in 1953, there were simply no possibilities of reform.

DESTALINIZATION

With Khrushchev's destalinization policies in 1956, however, the Soviet system faced an important crossroads. Khrushchev openly criticized Stalin's "cult of personality" and his use of terror against the party that had resulted in the purging of party members (no mention was made of the many millions of other nonparty victims of Stalin). Destalinization signaled a lessening of the hard-line party control over the artistic, educational, and scientific establishments within the Soviet Union, and the end of the terrorizing of the party by the political police. The numbers of victims of the regime sent off to the Gulag Archipelago dropped significantly as well. But destalinization did not mean the end of the authoritarian one-party state, or of the use of terror against dissenters.

Khrushchev faced a circumstance in June 1962 that no Soviet leader had faced since the time of the Civil War. Workers in the town of Novocherkassk on the Don River were told that their wages were going to be lowered and that food prices were going to be raised. A spontaneous revolt occurred in which the local headquarters of the Communist Party was attacked. Militia units were called out, and between 70 and 80 workers were killed. The government made sure that henceforth there would not be a double dose of such bad news delivered so openly to workers. Khrushchev was removed from office in 1964, not because of the Novocherkassk incident but because of the demoralizing loss of national prestige in the Cuban missile crisis and the growing rift with the People's Republic of China. (Khrushchev was also accused of creating his own "cult of personality.") Party leaders still equated the internal success of the Soviet Union with Cold War successes abroad.

MILITARY SUPERPOWER

In the 1977 Soviet Constitution, Leonid Brezhnev engineered the combination of the positions of chairman of the CPSU and president of the USSR, officially making him head of the state apparatus as well as the party apparatus. The position of party chair had been his springboard to power, just as it had been for Khrushchev and Stalin. During the Brezhnev era (1964–1982) the Soviet Union developed into a military (although not an economic) superpower. By 1980, thanks to Brezhnev's defense expenditures, the Soviet nuclear arsenal surpassed that of the United States and its NATO allies in several categories (including "megatonnage," that is, total destructive capabilities). Economic subsidies to client regimes, as well as indirect foreign intervention in the Third World, gave the Soviet Union a host of global allies to enhance its standing in the eyes of its citizens.

THE NEED FOR REFORM

By 1980, however, many younger, more practical party members began to worry about the country's bloated bureaucracy and the revelations of corruption among Brezhnev's close associates. The hopes for a better future, held by many party members through the early 1960s, began to give way in the late 1970s to a more realistic assessment that the Soviet system was in need of reform. There was a public recognition of this as early as 1982, when in an address to the Central Committee of the party Yuri Andropov spoke of "the force of inertia, the old habits," and the need "to improve the entire sphere of guidance of the economy."[2] There existed in the USSR tens of thousands of high-ranking party officials, known by the somewhat derogatory term *apparatchiks*, who received substantial benefits in return for their loyalty—such as the best housing (including vacation residences), education, employment opportunities, and access to scarce consumer goods. Andropov began investigating a number of corruption cases, and as the former KGB head he had presided over the investigation of the so-called Moscow Circus Case involving Brezhnev's own daughter. Andropov's tentative move toward reform, however, was cut short when he died of diabetic complications in 1984. He was succeeded by Konstantin Chernenko, a 72-year-old Brezhnev protégé who had no domestic or foreign policy vision beyond maintaining the status quo. He was infirm and had been elevated simply because he was next in the line of succession. It surprised few observers when he died in March 1985.

Many younger party leaders recognized the need to promote one of their own so that a reform of the system might be possible. These younger party members had grown up during an era of Cold War comparisons between the Soviet and American economies. As a result of their knowledge of the world beyond the USSR, they realized that claims of economic superiority made by the Soviet government in the later Stalin years and in the Khrushchev years were untrue. Their interest in reform stemmed in large part from the hopes raised by Khrushchev's destalinization in the 1950s.

This generation received its chance just hours after Chernenko's death, when the 54-year-old Mikhail Gorbachev was elected. He had been minister of agriculture under Brezhnev, but he was not a member of Brezhnev's inner circle. Within a month after coming to power, Gorbachev launched an ambitious reform program. He began to fill the Politburo with supporters who would back the changes he planned to introduce. He wanted to make the Soviet economy more successful, but unlike the tentative changes of the system attempted by Khrushchev and Andropov, Gorbachev also wanted to eliminate what he regarded as unnecessary coercive elements of Soviet power. The reform program, called perestroika (restructuring), involved a fundamental changing of the economy and the governmental system. A crucial part of the program was glasnost (political openness).

GLASNOST AND PERESTROIKA

Gorbachev provided examples of glasnost in the admissions he made regarding economic and societal shortcomings of the Soviet system in his book *Perestroika*, published in 1987 for domestic and foreign consumption. He spoke of the system's unwillingness to change owing to "inertia" (as Andropov had done), and of the "[p]ropaganda of success" that had misled previous Soviet leaders. He admitted that the Soviet regime had "failed to use to the full the potential of socialism." Gorbachev cited Soviet shortcomings in housing, foodstuffs, transportation, health, and education. He also spoke of the need for Soviet leaders to understand the opinions and concerns of the citizenry. Writing in his book that perestroika was "an urgent necessity arising from profound processes of development within our socialist society," Gorbachev managed to convince many of the younger generation of party members that there was an aspect of inevitability to the changes he began to initiate.[3]

Over the next few years, official spokespersons for the regime became very specifc about the kind of economic problems that the USSR faced. In mid-April 1988, government spokesmen admitted that 20 million metric tons of grain were lost each year in the Soviet system owing to improper storage and transportation. They also admitted that more than 20 billion rubles (equivalent to $35 billion American) were lost each year owing to shoddy workmanship and antiquated methods of transportation and storage.

The economic reforms urged by Gorbachev were called "market socialism." The underlying concepts of the reform were shaped by the economist Abel Aganbegyan, who wrote in 1988 that "the existing system of management is out of date and acts as a brake on the development of the economy."[4] He proposed that the central planning system be altered so that government ministries would no longer closely regulate economic enterprises, and that regional managers play a more important role. He also advised that the structure of rates and wages be reformed to reflect more realistically the demands of a market economy. This was similar to Lenin's New Economic Policy, and it offered the hope of improving productivity and morale among the Soviet work force.

However, the Soviet command economy was set too rigidly in what both Andropov and Gorbachev referred to as "the old habits" to change as rapidly as many consumers expected. Gorbachev's economic spokesmen talked of the availability of new consumer goods in the near future. But the public at large was greatly disappointed by the early results of Gorbachev's so-called 500 Days economic reform launched in August and September 1990, and demonstrations were held to show Gorbachev that a good many citizens were opposed to the end of the limited guarantees of the past.

Some of the loudest voices raised in the late 1980s were those of citizens who were in favor of the increased democratization of Soviet society. A host of new periodicals appeared in the country, such as the appropriately named *Glasnost*, in which common citizens and liberal party activists vented their frustrations against the regime. Private citizens as well as government officials released a torrent of information regarding cases of corruption and repression. Gorbachev's supporters reevaluated Soviet history to attempt to convince the undecided public that perestroika was worth the present struggle, lest the system revert to the terror of the Stalin era or the stagnation of the Brezhnev era. Yevgeny Yevtushenko wrote an article for *Moscow News* in July 1988 whose title reflected the views of many citizens: "Time That the Silent Majority Was Heard." He explained that a "party of non-party people" was engaging in a "struggle against the dark ghosts of the past," and that "[t]he aim is to achieve a way of life in our country in which we will not be ashamed of a single queue [waiting line]."[5] Dissidents who had been kept in psychiatric facilities, as well as victims of the Gulag Archipelago, were restored to acceptability in the manner of Khrushchev's "rehabilitations" of party members in the 1950s.

An important exception to glasnost was the handling of the April 1986 Chernobyl nuclear plant disaster in Ukraine, in which an explosion caused a significant and widespread leak of radiation. Gorbachev first tried to suppress news of the disaster, as his predecessors had done in similar circumstances. Owing to the rise in the Soviet public's expectations regarding government disclosures, Gorbachev was compelled to prosecute some of those involved in the disaster. His later attempts to rationalize the initial government coverup harmed his credibility.

Gorbachev altered the Soviet constitution in 1988, 1989, and 1990, seeking to transfer the power traditionally held by the CPSU to the Soviet state. The cumulative effect of these changes was to democratize the Soviet constitution. Soviet electoral law was changed first, when in 1988 multicandidate elections for a forthcoming legislative body, the Congress of Peoples' Deputies, were sanctioned by law. The term limits established for the body were the first in Soviet history (two consecutive five-year terms). Significant parliamentary reform occurred in 1989 when the Supreme Soviet, whose proceedings previously were a mere formality, was given real power as its members were elected from the Congress. The Congress deputies were elected from three categories: one-third from similar-sized electoral districts; one-third from administrative units, according to size of the unit (union republics, autonomous republics, autonomous regions, and autonomous districts); and one-third from the party-dominated "social organizations."

In 1990 the strongest shock rocked the party: Article 6 of the Soviet constitution was altered so that the party no longer held authority over the state government apparatus. It would now be legally possible for other political parties to operate within the Soviet system. Gorbachev stated bluntly in February, when the constitution was amended, that the CPSU would "struggle for the status of the ruling party within the framework of the democratic process by giving up any legal and political advantages."[6] The office of president was made more important than it had been previously (and thus more important than general secretary of the party). Henceforth, Gorbachev used the title of president rather than general secretary, which seemed to imply to some disillusioned party members that the party only served as a means to Gorbachev's personal goals. With his pledge to eliminate the party's monopoly on power, together with talks on a new union treaty that would decentralize the Soviet state, Gorbachev was putting himself on a collision course with those party members who longed for the stability of the Brezhnev era. Besides, perestroika was not bringing prosperity to Soviet citizens.

The core ideology of the Communist leadership changed little since the creation of the USSR. The citizenry, however, was conditioned by a succession of leaders from Lenin to Gorbachev to expect not capitalist-style prosperity, but certain material dividends in return for their sacrifices and their pledge of loyalty to the system. Despite the NEP, Stalin's heavy industrialization and collectivization projects, and Khrushchev's destalinization, the Soviet public at large knew that only the closed aristocracy of Soviet Communism, the apparatchiks, had achieved a lifestyle of material decency comparable to that of people in the capitalist countries. Gorbachev's perestroika policies aimed to even out the benefits available within the Soviet economy. What Gorbachev did not know was that the institutions of Soviet totalitarianism had become so rigid that an attempt to change them in a fundamental way would ultimately bring about their collapse.

NOTES

1. Even Stalin spoke of a utopian future, which would be created when the USSR could "overtake and surpass these [capitalist] countries also in technique and economic structure." See his November 1928 speech to the Plenum of the Central Committee in Joseph V. Stalin, *Leninism*, vol. 2, ed. J. Fineberg (New York: International Publishers, n.d.), p. 72.

2. Yuri V. Andropov, *Selected Speeches and Writings* (Elmsford, NY: Pergamon Press, 1983), p. 9.

3. Mikhail S. Gorbachev, *Perestroika* (New York: Harper and Row, 1987), pp. 21, 17.

4. Abel G. Aganbegyan, *The Economic Challenge of Perestroika*, ed. Michael B. Brown (Bloomington: Indiana University Press, 1988), p. 20.

5. Yevgeny A. Yevtushenko, "Time That the Silent Majority Was Heard," *Moscow News* (July 1988), p. 7.

6. Quoted in Craig R. Whitney, "Renouncing the Revolution's Holy Writ," *New York Times* (Sunday, February 11, 1990), p. 1E.

Leonid Brezhnev and Nikita Khrushchev. Reproduced from the collections of the Library of Congress.

3

The Brezhnev Doctrine and the Afghan War

During its 74-year existence the Soviet Union consisted of both an internal and an external empire. The union itself was an empire of nations forcibly attached to Russia and held together by the Russian-dominated party (the Communist Party of the Soviet Union) and the Russian-dominated military. During the end of World War II and the years immediately following that conflict, Stalin acquired control over a large extent of territory in eastern Europe, some of which had previously been ruled by the tsars. The Baltic states (Estonia, Latvia, and Lithuania) were incorporated into the Soviet Union as national republics, whereas client regimes were established in Poland, East Germany, Hungary, Czechoslovakia, Bulgaria, and Romania—countries that in 1955 formed the Warsaw Pact. Through direct intervention and the cultivation of local Communist parties, the Soviets controlled the economic, political, and military structures of the Warsaw Pact countries. Any signs of rebellion were put down with massive force, as was the case in Hungary in 1956 and Czechoslovakia in 1968. Once the dividing line (which British prime minister Winston Churchill called the Iron Curtain) had been drawn between Soviet-dominated states and the outside world, both the Soviets and their adversaries in the U.S.-dominated NATO alliance believed that only a World War III could alter the global balance of power.

Fearing that further Soviet expansion might provoke World War III, Stalin had backed down from the Berlin blockade (1948–1949) and did not actively support Kim Il-Sung, the Communist dictator of North Korea, in the Korean War (1950–1953). Similarly, Khrushchev (1953–1964) pulled back from the Cuban missile crisis in 1962 out of fear of war with the United States. As late as 1962, the Soviets and their Warsaw Pact allies were outmatched by the United States and its NATO allies in terms of nuclear delivery systems, which both sides regarded as critical to their success in future conflicts.

CREATING A SPHERE OF INFLUENCE

Khrushchev fell from power in 1964, partly as a result of political repercussions from backing down to the United States in 1962. Beginning in the Brezhnev era (1964–1982), however, Soviet leaders stepped up their support of Communist causes in the Third World in order to alter the global balance of power in their favor while still trying to avoid a direct confrontation with NATO. The Soviets did this by sending subsidies to their client regimes, especially the Warsaw Pact countries and those that served as Soviet proxies. Beginning in 1974, for example, Cuba provided over 40,000 troops (equipped and paid for by the Soviets) who were employed in creating and propping up Communist client regimes in three African coastal countries (Angola, Mozambique, and Ethiopia). This facilitated the projection of Soviet naval power far from Soviet home territory by providing reliable supply and repair facilities. By the early 1980s, Cuba received subsidies totaling approximately 2.3 billion rubles a year from Moscow. Less strategically significant than Cuba, the Communist Sandinista regime in Nicaragua, by comparison, received only 171 million rubles a year from Moscow. The Soviets also sent thousands of civil and military advisors from the USSR and the Warsaw Pact (many from East Germany) to provide technical assistance to their Third World clients.

Brezhnev viewed Southeast Asia as an area of strategic interest to the Soviet Union for purposes of projecting power and stemming American involvement in the region. Beginning in 1965, during the Vietnam War the Soviets increased support to the North Vietnamese by providing more conventional weaponry as well as anti-aircraft defenses. Learning from the lessons of the Korean War, in which American air superiority played a large role, Brezhnev provided the North Vietnamese with radar facilities (manned by Soviet technicians) and anti-aircraft missile batteries. Moreover, growing Soviet influence in Southeast Asia was partly responsible for an inconclusive Sino-Soviet border dispute in 1969. Following the American withdrawal from South Vietnam in 1973, the North Vietnamese conquered South Vietnam in 1975, and the neighboring countries of Laos and Cambodia also fell under Communist rule. The Pathet Lao, who had won in Laos, were Soviet clients, but the brutal Khmer Rouge in Cambodia were Chinese clients. The Soviets directly backed a 1979 Vietnamese invasion of Cambodia that overthrew the Khmer Rouge and also gave the Soviets a strong hand in Southeast Asia. The Vietnamese provided the Soviet fleet with crucial ports near the juncture of the Pacific and Indian

Oceans, thereby enhancing Soviet power projection. In return, Vietnam received over one billion rubles a year in subsidies from Moscow.

Brezhnev also regarded the Middle East as critical to Soviet global strategy. He provided direct assistance to Communist rebels who took over South Yemen in 1969, and who in turn provided the Soviet fleet with a friendly port of call on the Indian Ocean. South Yemen was regarded by the Western powers as a potential springboard for Soviet power into the oil-producing Gulf region of the Arab Middle East. Brezhnev similarly backed the Baathist (Islamic Socialist) regimes in Syria and Iraq, providing weapons that he knew would be tested against the American weapons used by the Israelis.

While he was achieving many of his strategic objectives, Brezhnev was also advocating policies of détente with the United States. He wanted to limit the NATO response to his foreign policy initiatives and his nuclear buildup. The United States regarded détente as a means to prevent the USSR from gaining a strategic global advantage. The failure of each side to provide adequate verification procedures in the two Strategic Arms Limitation Treaties (SALT) in 1972 and 1979 was a sign of mutual insecurity between the superpowers. The Soviet invasion of Afghanistan in December 1979 seriously threatened détente. The United States regarded Soviet intervention in Afghanistan as a serious challenge to the stability of U.S. interests in southern Asia; in protest, Congress suspended consideration of the ratification of SALT II.

THE INVASION OF AFGHANISTAN

Although Afghanistan is not located in the Middle East, it is an Islamic country important to Soviet global strategy because of its location along the Soviet Central Asian border. A mountainous, landlocked, and geographically remote country, its population has traditionally consisted of over 20 ethnic and linguistic groups organized along tribal lines but who are solidly Sunni Muslim. The majority population is ethnic Afghan, whereas other large groups—Uzbeks, Turkomen, Kirghiz, and Kazakhs—are Turkic groups linked historically and culturally to the Muslim populations of the former Soviet Central Asian republics. Imperial Russian expansion into Turkic Central Asia in the eighteenth and nineteenth centuries first brought Afghanistan to the attention of Russian leaders. The conquest of the Kazakh steppe (1730–1846) by Russian troops was followed by the capture of the great trade cities of Turkestan (1865–1884). The conquest of Merv in 1884 brought Russian troops into territory claimed by the amir (native ruler) of Afghanistan.

Russian expansion into Turkestan occurred almost simultaneously with the British conquest of the Indian subcontinent (1690–1858), and Afghanistan became trapped between competing Russian and British imperialism.

The British fought two Afghan wars (1839–1842 and 1878–1879) and held the upper hand until 1919, when a jihad (holy war) proclaimed by Amir Amanullah forced them to end their involvement in the country. Amir Amanullah signed a Treaty of Friendship with the Bolsheviks in 1921 and used it to prevent further British encroachment. Turkic Muslims fleeing from Bolshevik rule in Central Asia found refuge in Afghanistan, but Bolshevik leaders decided not to regard that as a provocation.

Amanullah sought to modernize his country, and he established a constitution in 1923. A Council of State was created and many reforms were undertaken in the government, the economy, and the educational system. Amanullah proclaimed himself king in 1926, initiating the constitutional monarchy period of Afghan history that lasted until 1973. Although beset by assassinations and coups in the late 1920s, the Afghan monarchy engaged in progressive policies of modernization and maintained a nonaligned position in relation to the great powers. Nonaggression pacts were signed with the Soviet Union in 1931 and 1955, and the Soviets provided several loans for Afghan development projects (especially road construction). In 1964 a two-house parliament was created, and its members were elected by universal suffrage in October 1965.

In January 1965 the country's first Communist party emerged, called the People's Democratic Party of Afghanistan (PDPA). Almost from the beginning it was divided into two factions reflecting social divisions within the country. Parcham (meaning "banner") was a moderate reformist faction consisting of an urban intelligentsia, led by Babrak Karmal. Khalq (meaning "people") was less sophisticated, openly Marxist, and consisting of a less wealthy rural intelligentsia, led by Nur Muhammad Taraki. By 1968 the two factions had their own Central Committees that claimed the right to speak for the PDPA as a whole. Together, both factions of the PDPA numbered in the low thousands. Khalq had approximately two-thirds of the total PDPA membership.

The constitutional monarchy period of Afghan history ended in 1973 when King Muhammad Zahir was overthrown by his premier, Muhammad Daoud, who was supported by reform-minded army officers, the emerging middle class, and a majority of the nation's intelligentsia. Daoud tried to establish a moderately progressive, nonaligned republic. At first he viewed the PDPA favorably, but in the mid-1970s he saw both Parcham and Khalq as threats to his regime and began repressing them. The Soviets engineered the cooperation of Parcham and Khalq in the period 1976–1977. In April 1978 the PDPA staged a coup against Daoud and founded the Democratic Republic of Afghanistan (DRA). The DRA signed a 20-year treaty of friendship with the Soviet Union. Taraki was the theoretical head of state, but his subordinate, Hafizullah Amin, held the real power. Amin undertook immediate and sweeping reforms that challenged many of the country's cultural traditions. By doing so, he angered so many Afghans that by the summer of 1978 a three-way civil war developed between Khalq, Parcham, and Muslim resistance fighters called *mujahidin* (holy warriors).

In spring 1979 the *mujahidin* killed several dozen Soviet advisors in Herat. The Soviets were quite distressed by the turn of events in Afghanistan. They feared possible U.S. intervention, which, although unlikely, they felt might be possible because Amin had once studied in the United States and might have made important contacts with Americans. The Soviets clearly hoped to gain Afghanistan as a client state. Their interest in the country was partly based on Afghanistan's location along their own border, and partly because it would put them within striking distance of the Persian Gulf and India. The Soviets accordingly arranged the assistance of Parcham to plan a coup against Amin in September 1979 and get Karmal and Taraki to reconcile. In the confusion Taraki, not Amin, was killed. The regime continued to fragment.

Brezhnev then consulted with three Politburo members—Andrei Gromyko, Mikhail Suslov, and Dmitri Ustinov—and decided on a course of direct military intervention. On December 24, fully 70,000 Soviet troops began crossing into Afghanistan while DRA troops stood down, believing the invasion to have been ordered by their own government. Amin was killed in an assault on his palace, but Khalq was not eradicated. Parcham leader Karmal was placed in control of a Parcham-Khalq coalition. Soviet motorized rifle divisions and paratroop regiments were deployed in cities throughout the country: Kabul (where Soviet headquarters was located), Bagram, Faizabad, Ghazni, Kandahar, Kunduz, Herat, Mazar-I-Sharif, Sherbghan, and Shindand. They never held more than 20 percent of the country.

Within two months the Soviets had unexpected difficulties in the ranks—Central Asian Muslim troops who refused to regard the Afghan Muslims as their enemies had to be sent home. Army service was traditionally viewed as a sure means of linguistic and cultural Russification, but feelings of ethnic consciousness were hard to overcome among the Muslim conscripts. These troops were replaced by ethnic Slavic soldiers from the western part of the Soviet Union. By February 1980 the total number of Soviet troops in Afghanistan was about 90,000. At the same time (February) a strike began in Afghan cities in protest to the presence of Soviet troops; the strike was suppressed with large numbers of Afghan deaths. In the spring another series of protests was also crushed by force, including the shooting of Afghan schoolgirls. Such outrageous actions emboldened the *mujahidin* to step up their resistance to the Soviet presence. They resented the fact that their occupiers were non-Muslim, and particularly that they were atheistic. The Soviets came to use a variety of nonconventional tactics to subdue the *mujahidin*-held countryside, including poison gas, napalm, and booby traps.

The world's reaction to the invasion and the use of such policies was justifiably harsh: a condemnation by the United Nations, U.S. withdrawal from the 1980 Olympic Games in Moscow, and suspension of future U.S. grain sales to the Soviet Union. The United States and NATO regarded the invasion as a serious challenge to détente. The *mujahidin* received assistance in the form of arms, food, and medicine from other Sunni Islamic nations such as Pakistan (where some 3.5 million Afghan refugees fled during the 10-year war), Saudi Arabia, and several Persian Gulf states, as well as from Shiite Iran. The United States sent a great deal of assistance, directly and indirectly (sometimes through Muslim third parties). *Mujahidin* units supplied by the U.S. Central Intelligence Agency operated out of Pakistan. Even the Communist People's Republic of China sent assistance to the *mujahidin*, fearing the growth of Soviet dominance in Asia was against China's own interests. China was particularly wary when the Soviets annexed part of the strategic Wakhan corridor, located on the border with the Soviet Union, Pakistan, and China.

Throughout the 10-year war, much of the combat between Soviet forces and the *mujahidin* was of short duration—ambush and search-and-destroy missions. However, Soviet casualties totaled about 2,000 deaths per year. By 1984 Soviet combat personnel in Afghanistan numbered about 120,000, and they had already sustained 10,000 deaths and 40,000 wounded since the start of the war. Soviet policies in the country remained uniform during the period of transition from the death of Brezhnev in 1982 through the tenure of Yuri Andropov (1982–1984) and Konstantin Chernenko (1984–1985).

Mikhail Gorbachev at first followed the same policies and even ordered the bombing of Afghan refugee camps in Pakistan (which had been identified by Soviet intelligence as *mujahidin* bases). At the Twenty-Seventh Party Congress in 1986, however, Gorbachev referred to the Afghan War as a "bleeding wound." Privately, Gorbachev had already concluded that the war was unwinnable. The Soviet public already knew a great deal about the war. Veterans organizations called "Afghan Clubs" formed for mutual assistance purposes, but they also became unofficial centers for the dissemination of information about the war to the Soviet public at large. The relatively open press of glasnost also made it more difficult to suppress the bad news coming from Afghanistan.

The Soviet press had experimented in printing stories about Afghan War veterans in 1984. Many stories were about the difficulties in readjustment when the Soviet soldiers returned home. Ostensibly, this was to generate popular support for the veterans and, it was hoped, for the war effort as well. But the idea backfired, and public opinion intensified against, not for, the conflict. Glasnost created an atmosphere in which the Soviet citizenry could express opinions about a broad range of issues, including Afghanistan. If Gorbachev was truly serious about glasnost, he could not ignore the facts that Afghanistan appeared to be the most important current policy issue in the view of many Soviet citizens, and that many Soviet citizens wanted a change in official government policy.

In May 1986, Gorbachev engineered the removal from power of Afghan leader Babrak Karmal and his replacement by Muhammad Najibullah, formerly the head of Khad, the Afghan intelligence agency. Najibullah tried to appease his opponents by calling his government "Islamic" and by repairing mosques, but these policies had no effect on the *mujahidin*. The war continued along its natural course for another year and a half until Gorbachev announced that he wanted to end Soviet involvement in the conflict. He signed the Geneva Agreement in April 1988, stating his intention to withdraw Soviet troops from Afghanistan. He followed this with a December 1988 speech before the United Nations in which he pledged to initiate a reduction in Soviet military personnel, linking the involvement of Soviet troops in the Afghan War and the deployment of Soviet forces within the Warsaw Pact.

As a consequence of the Afghan War, the morale of the Soviet armed forces was the lowest in the history of the USSR. Alcoholism and drug abuse were widespread throughout the ranks in the occupation forces in Afghanistan. In their desperation, some Soviet addicts who could not locate any alcohol consumed jet fuel instead and died. A few Slavic soldiers even defected to the *mujahidin* and eventually provided Western intelligence sources with details of the morale problems facing the Soviet army.

The war also had become a personal liability for Gorbachev and a threat to the success of perestroika. He actually began withdrawing Soviet forces from Afghanistan in March 1988, prior to his UN speech. By February 1989 almost all Soviet combat personnel had been withdrawn from the country, with only a few Soviet military and civil advisors remaining. Soon after the Soviet withdrawal, however, *mujahidin* forces partitioned the country among themselves. In 1996, rebels from the religious group Taliban from the south of Afghanistan seized Kabul. To demonstrate the total failure of Communism in their country, they killed Najibullah and hung him from a lamp post in Kabul.

The invasion of Afghanistan was the last significant operation of the Brezhnev Doctrine, and it was also the costliest. Because it involved Soviet troops rather than Cuban or Warsaw Pact forces, the attention of the world was focused directly on the USSR's expansionist goals. It also cost Brezhnev's successors a great deal in terms of domestic support, as Soviet casualties mounted each year. Even though Gorbachev at first tried to maintain control over Afghanistan, the failed operation ultimately provided him with a clear example of why Soviet policies needed to be oriented away from the Brezhnev Doctrine and toward perestroika.

Ronald Reagan and Mikhail Gorbachev in front of St. Basil's Cathedral, May 31, 1988. Courtesy of the Ronald Reagan Library.

4

Nationalism and the End of the Soviet Empire

One of the results expected by Russian Communists following the Bolshevik revolution was the emergence of a new sense of national consciousness that would outweigh the older, ethnic-national identities among the populations of the empire. Lenin encouraged a nonethnic sense of national identity through allegiance to the party and the union, and his successors promoted the same idea for over 70 years. However, Soviet leaders misjudged the strength of nationalism among the USSR's minority populations, and even among ethnic Russians. Consequently they were unprepared when the forces of nationalism pulled apart their vast multiethnic empire in the 1980s.

THE PERSISTENCE OF ETHNICITY

During the Afghan War the Kremlin leadership was surprised by the poor performance of Turkic Muslim conscripts from the Central Asian republics, because military service was traditionally regarded as one of the most effective agents of Russification in the Soviet system (second only to public education). Individuals from a non-Russian background who wanted to become professional soldiers had to acquire fluency in the Russian language and adopt (or adapt themselves to) ethnic Russian social customs. The fact that some units sent to assist in the pacification of Afghanistan preferred to spend time with their own ethnic comrades and coreligionists was evidence that 70 years of Soviet political control and Communist indoctrination policies directed from Moscow had not overcome ethnic consciousness and religious sentiment among the minority Muslim populations.

Most officers in the Soviet military were of an ethnic Russian background, and the Strategic Rocket Forces were exclusively from the Slavic republics. Some 90 percent of the Soviet General Staff and the members of the Ministry of Defense were ethnic Russians. Lenin had complained about Russian partiality within the Communist Party in the early 1920s. However, party membership (numbering 19 million in the mid-1980s) was always mainly Slavic. In the 1980s ethnic Russians made up 60 percent of party members, Ukrainians made up 16 percent, and 3.8 percent were from Belarus. There were always only a few members from the non-Slavic areas. Leadership positions in the party were overwhelmingly held by ethnic Slavs—Russians held 70 percent; Ukrainians, 15 percent; and Belarussians, 5.2 percent. As in the military, a non-Russian who sought to rise in the party needed to be fluent in Russian and able to conform to Russian social customs.

The official doctrine of the party and the state, articulated in Article 70 of the 1977 constitution, was that the Soviet Union was a "multi-national state" and a "voluntary association of equal Soviet Socialist Republics." Although Western critics pointed out the almost complete monopoly of political power was held by Russians within the Soviet federal system, defenders of the system argued that the Russians had been the largest group to participate in the October 1917 Revolution when the Bolsheviks took over and that ethnic Russians made up 50 to 60 percent of the total Soviet population. The Soviet justification for an internal imperial policy (i.e., the forced union of ethnically non-Russian republics with Russia) was to foster "proletarian internationalism."

THE REPUBLICS AND THE UNION

Each republic within the union theoretically had the right "to secede from the USSR," according to Article 72 of the 1977 constitution. However, only those individuals among the ethnic minorities who had proven their loyalty to the state by means of party membership and adherence to all the party's official positions rose to leadership on the republic-wide level. Within each republic, the KGB vigorously watched for signs of growing nationalism as well as ideological dissent.

Each republic was provided with an administrative apparatus that fostered a peculiar sense of national identity. However, this identity was as dependent on Moscow as was the republic's economy. The Kremlin leadership encouraged a kind of dual allegiance in the republics—directed toward their loyal national minority clients and toward themselves. This dual allegiance needed to be directed equally toward the national republic and the union. The constituents of the republic theoretically shared a common language, culture, and religion (as members of a "nation"), which may or may not have been linked historically to Russia. In order to foster allegiance toward the union, Soviet leaders sometimes promoted industrial growth in areas that needed financial investments. Kazakhstan, for instance, was the site of large-scale development twice in the 1950s—the Virgin Lands program and the Soviet space program. Infusions of state funds usually occurred in areas inhabited by ethnic Russians. Twenty-four million ethnic Russians resided outside of the Russian Federated Socialist Republic, mainly in urban settings. At the time of the breakup of the union (1991), the population of Kazakhstan was 42 percent Russian and that of Ukraine was 22 percent Russian.

Within the republics, the types of potential conflict were between Russians and minority groups and between two different minority groups. During World War II, Stalin decided that some minority groups were dangerous to the Soviet war effort. He feared that some groups that were chafing under Soviet rule might seek independence by linking up with advancing Nazi forces. He deported large numbers to Central Asia, including two million Volga Germans, 400,000 Chechens and Ingushes from the Caucasus, 200,000 Crimean Tatars, and 95,000 Kalmyks, also from the Caucasus. A significant proportion (at least several hundred thousand) perished on forced marches or shortly after their arrival in Central Asia.

COERCION IN UKRAINE

The most drastic hardship to befall a national minority group at Stalin's hands occurred in Ukraine, where the population resented the fact that their short-lived independence following World War I was stifled by the Red Army during the Civil War (1918–1920). When Ukrainian peasants resisted collectivization, Stalin took advantage of a poor harvest and used the political police to aggravate the famine by prohibiting supplies from getting in and by preventing anyone from leaving the affected areas. Between five and six million Ukrainians perished as a result in 1932 and 1933.

The coercive nature of Soviet Russian rule in Ukraine can be measured by examining how the Russian language was imposed on the population. By the mid-1980s, over 50 percent of the schoolchildren in Ukraine were enrolled in Russian language schools. As for all minority groups, fluency in Russian was essential for those who wanted to advance into higher education. Ukrainian doctoral candidates were required to write dissertations in Russian rather than Ukrainian. It was forbidden to read the works of certain Ukrainian authors, including a number from the tsarist period, because the Soviet regime feared it might provoke nationalism among Ukrainian readers. Moreover, the Soviet regime imprisoned authors of any ethnic background whom it regarded as hostile to the union. Other populations were also affected by linguistic Russification. In the Islamic areas of Central Asia and the Caucasus, the Arabic alphabet used by the Muslim populations was translated into Latin characters by 1934 (as in Turkey), and into Cyrillic by 1940. The Soviets believed that the common use of the Cyrillic alphabet throughout the USSR would enhance a sense of national unity and bring the Caucasian and Turkic Muslim populations closer to the Slavs.

Two Soviet leaders came from Ukraine—Khrushchev and Brezhnev. Khrushchev enlarged the size of the Ukrainian republic by adding to it the Crimean peninsula, largely inhabited by ethnic Russians at that time. The population of the Ukrainian Soviet Socialist Republic (as well as in the post-Soviet state) is largely Roman Catholic, but it includes a substantial minority of Orthodox Ukrainians as well as Orthodox Russians. Most of the republic's Catholic churches were closed during the early years of Soviet rule. Some were converted into Orthodox churches. Catholicism was regarded by Soviet leaders as more dangerous to the union than Russian Orthodoxy, because of the traditional dominance of the Orthodox Church by the state in Russia and because of the international nature of Catholicism.

CHERNOBYL NUCLEAR DISASTER

In April 1986 an accident at the Chernobyl nuclear facility spread poisonous radiation throughout Ukraine and into Belarus. The Number Four reactor exploded during a test in which the cooling equipment had been turned off. Low-level officials apparently had known for some time that the Number Four reactor was defective, but nothing had been done about it. About 100,000 people were evacuated from the region surrounding the facility within a week of the accident. However, evacuations did not begin until almost 36 hours after the disastrous explosion. Four thousand people died within five years. Tens of thousands more were exposed to significantly high levels of radiation and may eventually develop cancer as a result. As many as 140,000 people who were evacuated had to be resettled elsewhere because their homes had been irradiated.

Information about the explosion was suppressed by the government for some time (despite glasnost), but the population at large learned about the disaster through informal means. As a result, Gorbachev's policy of glasnost was discredited because of the Kremlin's failure to disclose fully what it knew about the problem—until a domestic and foreign outcry forced Gorbachev's hand. He then appointed the world-renowned chess expert Anatoli Karpov as head of a Chernobyl Assistance Group and asked the UN Atomic Energy Commission to undertake a study. Western environmentalists criticized this approach to the crisis as inadequate. Gorbachev had chosen Karpov because he had a "name recognition" quality that he felt would legitimize his inquiry.

A gigantic concrete "sarcophagus" was constructed over the reactor to try to contain the radiation, but it began to leak in 1991. Eventually Chernobyl's director, Viktor Bryukhanov, and chief engineer, Nikolai Fomin, were convicted of negligence and sent to prison. Also, the Ukrainian premier, Alexander Lyashko, was removed from office for incompetence owing to his mishandling of the disaster relief operations. Gorbachev's domestic image was severely harmed by the incident. In fact, rumors circulated in Ukraine that the population was being experimented upon by the Kremlin. The entire Ukrainian environment suffered, along with the rest of the Soviet Union, from the callous disregard of the Kremlin leaders. Roman Szporluk, a historian, has commented that thanks to many years of Soviet rule, "the entire Ukraine is an ecological disaster area."[1]

What made the Chernobyl crisis unique was not so much that the Soviets tried to cover up an environmental disaster, but that they were unable to do so. Previous disasters had evoked little concern outside the areas of the incidents, because the Soviets successfully suppressed the news. For example, the Kremlin presided over a nuclear disaster in 1957 at Kyshtym in the Urals when approximately 30 villages were contaminated as a result of the early Soviet nuclear effort. The Soviets also detonated some 470 nuclear weapons in Kazakhstan at the Semipalatinsk test site between 1949 and 1989. Several thousand Kazakh and Russian civilians who lived nearby were consequently irradiated, and there have been numerous instances of birth defects among the bewildered and demoralized population. Misguided Soviet irrigation policies on Kazakhstani cotton farms have taken water away from the Amu Darya and Syr Darya Rivers, which traditionally fed the Aral Sea. As a result, the Aral (formerly the world's fourth largest inland sea) has lost almost 60 percent of its volume and 30 percent of its size. Some environmentalists predict that it will disappear by 2010. The Warsaw Pact countries also suffered in ecological terms from Soviet economic development and exploitation. Industrial pollutants poisoned as many lakes and rivers within the Warsaw Pact countries as in the Soviet republics.

POLITICAL PROBLEMS IN EASTERN BLOC NATIONS

The Soviet Union also had political problems with its client states in eastern Europe. Despite (and in some ways because of) the Soviet heavy hand in eastern Europe, nationalism was an important factor within the Warsaw Pact countries since the late 1940s. Yugoslavia's break with Moscow in 1948 was caused by Josip Broz Tito's, the Yugoslav Communist dictator, brand of nationalism more than by ideology. Nationalism was the critical element behind the Hungarian uprising of 1956 and the Czechoslovakian uprising of 1968. Romania under Nicolae Ceaucescu was considered to be the potential maverick of the Warsaw Pact, following a more independent foreign policy than other members.

Poland was the site of the largest and most important anti-Soviet mass movement—in the form of the labor union known as Solidarity. The movement was bolstered in large part by the Roman Catholic Church, which had 20 million active members in Poland and whose spiritual head, Pope John Paul II, had been a Polish cardinal before being elected pope in 1978. John Paul visited Poland in 1979, and the enormous turnout at his public appearances was an embarrassment to the Polish Communist government.

Solidarity was formed in Gdansk in August 1980 and was led by an electrician named Lech Walesa. Walesa mobilized the Polish work force to demand better wages and conditions in a manner that (ironically) seemed very Marxian. However, there were also moral and reformist overtones to Solidarity's influence; this can be observed in the decline of alcohol consumption in Poland by one-third during the 16-month period during which Solidarity was in operation legally. Its 10 million members represented 80 percent of the Polish work force. The Brezhnev administration found the very existence of Solidarity to be distressing. From the Kremlin's perspective, rampant Catholicism was dangerous enough, given Poland's proximity and historical ties to Catholic Lithuania and Ukraine.

As Solidarity appeared to be on a collision course with the Soviet-backed Polish government, Brezhnev made a warning in his February 1981 address to the Twenty-Sixth Party Congress in Moscow that he would not tolerate "counterrevolutionary" actions undertaken in Poland by "opponents of Socialism, supported by outside forces." This was a reference to the possible use of Soviet forces to suppress Solidarity if the Polish government of General Wojciech Jaruzelski failed to act decisively (with the examples of Hungary in 1956 and Czechoslovakia in 1968 looming large). The Soviets regarded the Catholic Church as one of the main pillars of support for Solidarity, and they believed that Pope John Paul II—the pope from behind the Iron Curtain—was a threat to the stability of the *pax Sovietica* in central and eastern Europe. The *pax Sovietica* can be compared with the *Pax Romana* of ancient Rome. Both Rome and the USSR imposed brutal and thorough systems of law and order on their conquered territories. John Paul II was a clear foe of Communism within his native country and within the world at large. Consequently, both the Soviet and Bulgarian intelligence agencies engineered the attempted assassination of the pope by a Turk in Rome on May 13, 1981.

Solidarity proclaimed at a national congress in September 1981 that the workers in other socialist states should follow its example and create independent labor unions. With this, the Polish government was forced to respond, lest Soviet forces intervene in the near future. Jaruzelski declared martial law on December 13 and outlawed Solidarity. Hundreds of thousands of resentful Poles left the Polish Communist Party over the next few years (800,000 left from 1980 to 1983). The threat of Soviet intervention altered the course of Polish history, but the experience of Solidarity had shown that there was indeed some rust on the Iron Curtain, and that—if given the opportunity—the Warsaw Pact states would cease being Soviet clients. The events in Poland were watched closely within the USSR's own minority republics, whose populations had likewise not forgotten their own sense of national consciousness.

THE EFFECT OF GLASNOST ON THE SOVIET REPUBLICS

Glasnost ushered in an era of increasing conflict over ethnic territorial rights within the Soviet republics. For decades, Soviet leaders had forced ethnic minorities to put aside their interethnic conflicts in the name of "proletarian internationalism" and for the sake of the union. Age-old conflicts were, in the words of Roy Medvedev, a historian on Afghanistan, "suppressed and unmentioned" by the Kremlin.[2] Glasnost inadvertently provided the means for unspoken discontent among ethnic minorities to become articulated in the policies of individual political factions or of governing bodies of the national republics—often at the expense of the union. Of the approximately 100 ethnic groups in the USSR, 24 consisted of at least one million members. Many of these were not happy with the status quo. Gorbachev seemed unable to please any of the discontented minorities. Even though a crisis in one republic usually emerged from a unique set of circumstances, the glasnost press coverage of the event would indirectly intensify ambitions for independence within other republics. Anti-foreign riots broke out periodically in parts of economically disadvantaged Central Asia in the 1980s—Dushnabe, Tajikistan (June 1986); Frunze, Kirghizstan (October 1986); Tashkent, Uzbekistan (December 1988); Ferghana, Uzbekistan (May–June 1989).

In a praiseworthy effort to eliminate dishonest politics from Soviet life, Gorbachev removed from office the Kazakh party chief Dinmukhamed Kunayev, a corrupt Brezhnev appointee, in December 1986. Brezhnev had been so close to Kunayev that he appointed him to be a member of the Politburo in 1971 (Brezhnev was once the first secretary of the Kazakh Central Committee). Gorbachev's choice as replacement was Gennady Kolbin, an ethnic Russian. Many Kazakh party apparatchiks owed their careers to Kunayev's 26-year tenure and saw the change in the republic-wide leadership as the end of their personal success.

They consequently encouraged anti-Soviet and anti-Russian hatred among the Kazakhs, and on December 17 and 18, 1986, a large riot erupted in Alma Ata. Buildings housing the Kazakh Central Committee were attacked, as was the Alma Ata Prison. Some 1,700 people were injured, and 2,400 were arrested as Interior Ministry troops were called in to crush the riot. A special Soviet inquiry subsequently found that there was widespread discontent in the republic stemming from the population's dissatisfaction with Soviet rule. A number of Kunayev's cronies were investigated, but they in turn complained of interference by "foreign" judicial officers. The unrest in Central Asia, although having no direct bearing on events elsewhere, was followed by unrest among the Muslim population of the Republic of Azerbaidjan in the Caucasus.

In Azerbaidjan, another Brezhnevite Politburo member, Gaidar A. Aliyev, felt politically overlooked by Gorbachev, and he retired in 1987. His apparatchik followers, however, began agitating against the union and in favor of Azeri nationalism. The bloodiest ethnic clash in the late Soviet period broke out in Azerbaidjan in February 1988, between Shiite Muslim Azeris and Orthodox Christian Armenians. The Kremlin was concerned because there were about 14 million Shiite Azeris residing in Iran who could easily become a political and military problem for Soviet troops if they decided to intervene on behalf of their ethnic comrades.

Armenians traditionally accounted for only 8 percent of the Azerbaidjan republic, but they were a majority in an autonomous region called Nagorno-Karabakh (which had been removed from Armenia and added to Azerbaidjan in 1923). In February 1988 the ethnic Armenian Nagorno-Karabakh Regional Committee voted to secede from the Republic of Azerbaidjan and join the Armenian republic. Mass demonstrations in support of the annexation occurred in Yerevan, Armenia's capital. An Armenian Union of National Self-Determination was formed, and several prominent Armenian intellectuals visited Gorbachev in Moscow. The Kremlin tried to placate both Armenia and Azerbaidjan, but it only perplexed both sides by seeming to promise simultaneously that Nagorno-Karabakh could join Armenia and also remain within Azerbaidjan.

In March 1988, Azeri mobs made brutal attacks on Armenians in Sumgait, an industrial town north of Baku. Local Azeri authorities did nothing while over 30 Armenians were butchered, dozens of women were raped, and several hundred others were seriously injured. Azeri party officials in Sumgait actually tried to cover up the extent of the massacre. In time, the Sumgait party secretary, mayor, and police chief were all removed from their positions because of criminal negligence. However, the official Communist Party newspaper, *Pravda*, only published a brief and stilted account of the events, which enraged Armenians throughout the union. The Sumgait incident led to an undeclared war between Armenians and Azeris that Gorbachev was unable to suppress despite a declaration of martial law within the two republics.

The Supreme Soviet of the USSR rejected the Armenian claim on Nagorno-Karabakh, and *Pravda* articles openly criticized the members of the Nagorno-Karabakh Committee. When a powerful earthquake killed some 100,000 Armenians on December 7, sympathy may have motivated the Kremlin's next move. In January 1989, Gorbachev authorized a special status for the disputed region. A Russian, two Armenians, and an Azeri served on a special commission as leaders who had a large number of

Soviet troops at their disposal. The commission lasted only until September, when the Azeris carried out a rail blockade of Armenia, trying to starve the weakened republic into submission.

Meanwhile, a new non-Communist Azeri nationalist group called the Popular Front was created in 1990 and plotted to act against the Armenians and Russians residing in Baku. Consequently, Azeri mobs attacked Armenian civilians and Russian military families in the city. Gorbachev sent several thousand troops to put down the unrest and evacuate the city's Armenian and Russian families. Azeri mobs also shot at the troops. The troops reciprocated and killed over 100 Azeris. In the 1990 elections, however, the Communists were decisively victorious over the Popular Front in Azerbaidjan, and former Politburo member Aliyev was elected to parliament. Azerbaidjan remained an international embarrassment to Gorbachev because it demonstrated to the world how miserably Communism had failed to eradicate notions of political independence and religious sentiment within the national republics. At the time of the collapse of the union in 1991, at least 1,500 people had died in the conflict, and 230,000 Armenians and 70,000 Azeris were uprooted from their homes.

The Republic of Georgia was also the scene of violent political and ethnic clashes in the late Soviet period. Two minority groups, the Abkhazians and the Ossetians, wanted to secede from Georgia and join the Russian republic, even though most Georgians wanted Ossetia and Abkhazia to remain within Georgia and for Georgia to secede from the USSR. Georgian nationalism emerged as a mass movement in February 1989, when 15,000 protesters marched in Tbilisi on behalf of the republic's independence. The march took place on the anniversary of the republic's incorporation into the union. Although about 200 marchers were taken into police custody, the Kremlin was unable to stem the spread of nationalist sentiment within the republic.

On April 9, 100,000 demonstrators marched, demanding the right to secede from the union and keep Abkhazia within Georgia. Interior Ministry units attacked the demonstrators, and 16 civilians were reported to have been killed. Eduard Shevardnadze, the foreign minister of the Soviet Union and an ethnic Georgian, went to Tbilisi to appeal for calm as armored units of the Soviet army entered the Georgian capital. On April 14 the Georgian party's first secretary and the republic's prime minister both resigned. Subsequently the Georgian parliamentary commission, which investigated the events of April 9, concluded that the attack on civilian protesters by Interior Ministry troops was "a preplanned mass massacre, committed with special cruelty."

Meanwhile, in the Baltic republics of Estonia, Latvia, and Lithuania, mass demonstrations commemorating the anniversary of the 1939 Nazi-Soviet Pact (August 23) occurred in 1987 and 1988. The Pact had set the conditions for the Soviet annexation of the republics, which was a clear violation of their territorial integrity. Resentment of the annexations simmered for 50 years. The Western-oriented, Lutheran Estonians and Latvians and the Roman Catholic Lithuanians also resented the presence within their republics of a large number of ethnic Russians, mainly military personnel and their families.

In October 1988 full-fledged independence movements were begun with the creation of National Fronts in all three Baltic republics. The National Fronts demanded the restoration of national languages and pre-Soviet national flags and anthems—symbols of national autonomy—as well as economic independence (including control of natural resources) from Moscow. In a ground-breaking move, the Estonian Supreme Soviet proclaimed its independence on November 16, 1988. The republic's new constitution stated that Soviet law could apply within the republic only if it did not conflict with Estonian law. Latvia and Lithuania did the same in 1989, with Lithuania proclaiming its independence on May 18 and Latvia on July 28. Lithuania's constitution asserted the supremacy of the republic's law within its borders along the lines of Estonia; Latvia cautiously took a middle course in which the republic's law and the union's law would be regarded as coequal, but in the event of a conflict between the two, Soviet law would prevail. A Council of Popular Fronts moved to link the three republics economically. But when the Estonians began to discuss ethnic qualifications and residency requirements for citizenship, the republic's Russian population began to pressure the Kremlin to bring a halt (at least temporarily) to such actions.

Gorbachev, however, was powerless to stop the drive for independence in the Baltics completely, and he authorized the use of brute force early in 1991 to restrain the rebellious national republics. Armored units under the command of Interior Minister Boris Pugo attacked a large group of protesters at the Vilnius television station on January 13, killing 14 and injuring many more. The fact that the attack occurred so openly and at the television station showed that the assault was intended to send a message to the other Baltic republics and to any other independence-minded national republic. Lithuanian president Vytautas Landisbergis called for a plebiscite with which, on February 9, Lithuania declared itself to be "free and democratic." The so-called Vilnius Massacre cost Gorbachev dearly in the arena of global public opinion and at home, and it hastened the breakup of the Soviet empire.

REVIVAL OF RUSSIAN NATIONALISM

In addition to the nationalism expressed in the minority national republics, Gorbachev had to deal with a revived Russian nationalism. Signs of a new Russian nationalism first emerged in the mid-1960s, when an organization formed called the Rodina (meaning "Motherland") Club. Its members emphasized the Russian nature of the union and glorified the legacy of the Stalin era, a time of economic expansion and military success. However, it would not be until 1982 when a nationally significant non-Soviet variant of Russian nationalism appeared in the form of Pamyat (meaning "Memory"). Originally, Pamyat members wanted to preserve the cultural legacy of Russia's pre-Soviet period. The Soviet regime had done great damage to the cultural artifacts from the era of the tsars, especially those associated with the Russian Orthodox Church. Many churches were demolished to make way for Stalinist architecture (considered to be very ugly) or were transformed into museums or warehouses. In the 1930s, Stalin sold icons (painted religious images) and other sacred objects to foreign collectors.

Pamyat achieved prominence in the glasnost era. On May 6, 1987, the organization's head, Viktor Vasiliev, led 6,000 supporters on a protest march in Moscow, demanding that the regime rebuild churches that had been destroyed by previous Soviet leaders. Members met with Mayor Valery Saikin and the first secretary of the Moscow party, Boris Yeltsin. Within a year, Pamyat membership peaked to a high of 90,000. Three factions had developed by 1989. One consisted of Vasiliev's followers; another was largely comprised of intellectuals (led by a man named Sychov); the third (led by a man named Smirnov-Ostashvili) spouted anti-Semitic propaganda and saw a conspiracy in the shift toward market forces under Gorbachev. Pamyat split apart into constituent factions in 1989, but it had achieved the result of making it possible to view Russian nationalism apart from the union. The organization led the way toward the emergence of a right-wing faction of the Communist Party called the Rossiya (meaning "Russia") Club in October 1989, which was supported by literary apparatchiks such as the Writers' Union of the Russian Republic and the editors of *Sovetskaya Rossia*.

A critical part of perestroika involved changing the USSR's global military and economic policies. Gorbachev had stated in his December 1988 speech to the United Nations that the USSR was planning to withdraw some military units from Warsaw Pact countries. These plans were put into effect in the fall of 1989 when Poland, East Germany, Hungary, Czechoslovakia, Romania, and Bulgaria were allowed to break from direct Soviet influence. Soviet military forces were withdrawn, and economic subsides from Moscow were stopped. The experience of the Warsaw Pact countries had the unintended result of helping to fan the nationalist movements within the Soviet republics and thereby hasten the demise of the Soviet system.

No Soviet leader from Lenin to Gorbachev was able to replace the preexisting nationalist sentiments held by the minority populations in the Soviet empire (or held by the ethnic Russians themselves) with a new national identity based on the Communist idea of proletarian internationalism. Soviet leaders denied the validity of the very concept of nationalism apart from the union. The failure of the Kremlin to recognize the power of national sentiment in the Soviet external empire in eastern Europe led to upheavals within the Warsaw Pact as early as the mid-1950s. The failure of Soviet leaders to heed the warning signs provided by their Warsaw Pact client regimes indicated that they were likewise unprepared for the upsurge of nationalism within the USSR, inadvertently brought on by glasnost in the 1980s.

NOTES

1. Roman Szporluk, "The National Question," in Timothy J. Colton and Robert Levgold, eds., *After the Soviet Union* (New York: Norton, 1992), p. 104.

2. Roy Medvedev and Guilietto Chiesa, *Time of Change* (New York: Pantheon, 1989), p. 184.

5

Russia after the Collapse of Communism

The democratic system that replaced Soviet Communism in Russia has been threatened by several factors, including national minority unrest, relations with neighboring states in the Commonwealth of Independent States (CIS) that contain Russian minority populations, and a struggling capitalist economy that is troubled by corruption. Post-Soviet Russia is a federation with a population of 150 million, over 80 percent of whom are ethnic Russians. It resembles the former Soviet Union in its multinational character, with 27 percent of its area consisting of 22 non-Russian autonomous republics and 10 autonomous regions. Most of the republics and regions are located in Siberia; the largest republic, Yakutia, accounts for almost 18 percent of the land mass of the Russian Federation. Yakutia, like several other autonomous republics, has vast natural resources, including petroleum, diamonds, and gold. The individual national-ethnic populations, however, are extremely small compared to the number of Russians in the federation. Boris Yeltsin presided over the drafting of a federation treaty that was signed on March 31, 1992, by all but two of Russia's autonomous republics. The dissenters were the largely Muslim republics of Tatarstan and Chechniya (called Ichkeria by the Chechens). Both republics contain petroleum deposits vital to the federation. Tatarstan is surrounded by other Russian territory and has not asserted its claim to independence.

THE WAR IN CHECHNIYA

Chechniya is located in the northern Caucasus, and its proximity to other Islamic nations helped spur a full-fledged independence movement

Ronald Reagan and Mikhail Gorbachev during Reagan's visit to the USSR on June 1, 1988. Courtesy of the Ronald Reagan Library.

that began in December 1994. When Yeltsin sent troops into Chechniya, rebels led by Dzhokar Dudayev made use of the mountainous terrain and irregular tactics to offset their numerical disadvantage. The geography of the Chechen War seemed to be similar in many ways to that of the Afghan War—with fighting on rugged terrain that favored Russia's opponent both tactically and logistically. Because the Russian Federation inherited its attitudes toward warfare and its military hardware from the Soviet army, its commanders were more prepared to do battle in a linear confrontation on terrain resembling the northern European plains than in a mountain war of ambushes and search-and-destroy missions.

The Chechen soldiers were also able to blend back into the civilian population the way the *mujahidin* had done in Afghanistan. As the war dragged on, Chechen soldiers began wearing Islamic symbols on their clothing and appealed for help from Muslims from other Islamic nations. Russian troops occasionally shelled civilian areas in order to flush out the rebels, and the Chechen capital of Grozny was wrecked in the fighting. The rebels attacked civilians who were opposed to them in Chechniya, as well as Russian civilians living near the border in the town of Budennovsk. In January 1996 they took Russian hostages in the town of Pervomaiskoye. The Chechen rebels also attacked each other, and two Chechen commanders, Salman Radayev and Zelimkhan Yandarbiyev, were killed by rivals rather than by Russian troops. The Russians managed to kill Dudayev in an air strike in April 1996 and got the Chechens to sign a treaty in late August. According to the provisions of the treaty, Russian troops would withdraw from the region, but the question of Chechen independence was to be deferred for five years (the withdrawal was completed in late January 1997).

The war cost some 30,000 lives (mainly civilians) and caused 500,000 people to become refugees. The war became a political liability for Yeltsin in the months preceding the 1996 presidential election, and politics rather than enemy military strategy forced him to push for the treaty. Chechniya is the most extreme case of the territorial-national problems that the Russian Federation inherited from the imperial Soviet and tsarist systems, but it may foreshadow future conflicts as other groups seek independence.

RELATIONS AMONG THE STATES OF THE CIS

Another concern of the Russian Federation government is its relationship with its colleagues in the CIS. After the breakup of the Soviet Union, the Soviet armed forces were divided among the USSR's 15 successor states, but the Soviet nuclear arsenal went to only four of those states— Russia, Belarus, Ukraine, and Kazakhstan. The Belarus nuclear weapons have been placed voluntarily under Russian control, and in 1995 Russia and Belarus signed an agreement that created a military and customs union between the two nations. The two governments also pledged to work toward a joint constitution and monetary system. In an example of post-Soviet cooperation, the armies of Kazakhstan, Kirghizstan, and Uzebekistan send troops to train jointly with Russian units.

The Ukrainian-Russian relationship has been strained over Ukrainian president Leonid Kravchuk's decision to keep some of the Soviet nuclear weapons. Also at issue has been the status of the Crimean peninsula (the location of an important tourist industry), whose population is ethnically Russian but who were incorporated into Ukraine by Khrushchev. Under pressure from the United States, Ukraine agreed to relinquish control of two-thirds of its nuclear weapons to Russia. Since independence Ukraine has become the third largest recipient of U.S. foreign aid and has tried to appease the United States, which fears the wide dispersion of Soviet nuclear weapons. Its government, however, wants to maintain control of a small nuclear arsenal as a deterrent to possible future Russian aggression. Although it has kept control of the Crimean peninsula, Ukraine has relinquished control of the strategic Sevastopol naval base to Russia. Therefore, Russia is also appeased because it still can project its power into the Black Sea.

Ukraine is still energy-dependent on Russia, and several other republics have signed treaties extending ties with Russia because they are energy-poor (Belarus, Kazakhstan, and Kirghizstan). The Russian Federation has cautiously watched the calls for unity among some Central Asian republic leaders, such as Uzbek president Islam Karimov, who fosters the idea of a unified Islamic Turkestan. President Sapurmurad Niyazov of Turkmenistan, however, has been the most vocal opponent of the concept, fearing a loss of autonomy.

The Yeltsin regime has been more concerned with the plight of ethnic Russians living in the other CIS republics, which some Russians refer to as the "near abroad." In the Central Asian, Baltic, and Caucasian republics, the linguistic Russification of the tsarist and Soviet regimes was reversed after independence in 1992. Ethnic Russian settlers now face the choice of learning the language of the dominant group and accepting a minority status, or repatriating themselves to the Russian Federation. Many have chosen to emigrate to Russia, and this has caused a "brain drain"—especially in the Central Asian republics, whose new official languages frequently lack the terminology necessary for many modern scientific and technical occupations.

Questions about the status of the Russians in Ukraine and Moldova have caused the Yeltsin regime much distress, given the fact that these are more substantial populations living in close proximity to Russia. Ukraine's population is more than one-fifth ethnic Russian, but the struggle for civil rights there, which many Russians in the federation anticipated, has not materialized. Roughly 93 percent of the Ukrainian population voted for independence, with many ethnic Russians voting in favor alongside their Ukrainian comrades. The linguistic differences between Ukrainian and Russian are small, compared to the differences between the East Slavic dialects and the Central Asian or Caucasian languages. About one-sixth of the population of Moldova (the former Soviet republic of Moldavia) is Russian, and there is also a sizable Ukrainian population, but the dominant group is Romanian. Moldova was the scene of a violent post-Soviet conflict in 1992, and Russian troops stationed in the republic were accused by Romanians of taking up the cause of the Russians. However, there also have been a few cases of Central Asian republics requesting Russian military assistance to put down local uprisings. The Yeltsin regime has attempted to delay the incorporation of the Baltic states into the European Union (the descendant of the Common Market, and one of the world's most important trading blocs), but they already have been tentatively accepted as members, and they receive a great deal of economic assistance from the Scandinavian countries.

PROBLEMS IN THE NEW CAPITALIST ECONOMY

The transition from the command economy of Communism to capitalism has not been easy in Russia or any of the post-Soviet republics. The new capitalist economy of the Russian Federation is dominated by wealthy elites with ties to the power structures of the Soviet past. Many individuals have tried to carve out personal fiefdoms from the vast Russian market. There have been many cases of Russian firms cooperating with, and being infiltrated by, organized crime gangs. The result has been the stifling of competition. Many of these corrupt business elites refuse to obey the tax laws of Yeltsin's federal government and tend to invest their profits abroad (as much as $80 billion in 1994 alone). Smuggling and extortion are rampant, and contract killings of uncooperative business rivals or investigative journalists have become commonplace. Many of the several thousand banks created since 1992 have failed because of corruption, resulting in lost savings by depositers. The central government is troubled by both massive inflation and a poor cash flow (fully one-half of the country's cash supply is in U.S. dollars). The government controls only about 15 percent of the gross domestic product.

An increasing number of firms have found it difficult to pay wages. In fact, Russian companies were unable to pay $9 billion in wages to workers in 1996. They are hindered by the fact that many consumers (especially of fuel products) are unable to pay their bills on time. The decaying Soviet-era manufacturing, agricultural, and transportation infrastructures are not being upgraded rapidly enough to accommodate the demands of the new economy. The Russian oil and gas industries are also declining, even though there are untapped reserves of these products in Siberia from which future generations of Russian citizens could benefit.

Although some Russians have managed to adapt and even thrive in the new economy, many others have experienced a lowering of their expectations for prosperity. The area where economics-inspired desperation is potentially most dangerous is in the Russian nuclear industry. The United States has spent over a half-billion dollars to help guard weapons-grade nuclear material in post-Soviet Russia. The NATO countries and Japan also have subsidized the salaries of nuclear technicians throughout the CIS. The purpose of this assistance is to prevent the sale of weapons-grade uranium and plutonium to terrorist groups—a valid concern, given the wage payment problems that these technicians would otherwise face (there were four publicized interceptions of such material in Europe in 1994).

The unstable nature of the economy has been affected by the unstable nature of the post-Soviet Russian political system. Even though Yeltsin has been voted into office in public elections and has ruled according to the current constitutional law, he has been accused by his domestic critics (ironically, often Communists) of engaging in unfair tactics—such as intimidating his opponents in an authoritarian style reminiscent of late tsarist-style politics, and manipulating the electoral system. Although he won easy approval for his 1993 presidential referendum, which expanded his powers, it was found that over 9 million votes had been falsified.

Yeltsin's first serious political clash was with the Russian Parliament, which contained a number of former Communists who still favored a slow transition from state-owned to private-owned enterprises in the new Russia. By December 1992, Yeltsin's quarrels with parliament had become so bitter that he threatened to disband it. Yeltsin claimed that many parliamentarians were committed to delaying or stopping the reform process. The dialogue between the president and the parliament became so bitter that Yeltsin finally used military force and ordered artillery to be fired on the parliament in October 1993 to crush his parliamentary adversaries.

THE NEW POLITICS

A bewildering number of political parties have emerged in Russia following the collapse of Communism. Several parties have stated goals of reacquiring the lost parts of the former internal empire of the tsars and Soviets (the "near abroad") and slowing or ending the transition to a market economy. The Liberal Democratic Party of Russia, led by Vladimir Zhirinovsky, is actually a fascist party with goals of territorial expansion beyond the "near abroad" into the former Warsaw Pact countries and even Alaska (which was sold by Tsar Alexander II to the United States in 1867). Although opinion polls taken before the 1995 parliamentary elections showed that about 10 percent of the population supported Zhirinovsky, his party did not fare well in either the parliamentary elections or the 1996 presidential elections.

The Communist Party of the Russian Federation (CPRF), formed after the breakup of the CPSU, contains some half-million members, many of whom are older former apparatchiks who feel threatened by market reforms and democracy. Led by Gennady Zyuganov, the CPRF has stated that it seeks the end of capitalism and a "voluntary" restoration of the former union between Russia and the "near abroad." The CPRF won 22 percent of the seats in Russia's 1995 parliamentary elections, showing that the breakup of the Soviet empire and the end of the economic and social guarantees of the past had stimulated the supporters of the old order.

The 1996 presidential elections were a referendum on Russia's turn toward capitalism and democracy. Yeltsin's tenure up to that point was regarded by members of the CPRF (and by many others in the country) as the cause of economic chaos and the political disintegration of a once-great nation. Yeltsin's health also became a political issue, as his coronary artery disease was seen by his rivals as an explanation for his apparent inactivity and the failure to bring about widespread prosperity. In February 1996 opinion polls showed that Zyuganov then held a strong lead— 14 percent to Yeltsin's meager 4 percent. In fact, Yeltsin also trailed at that point behind the reformist economic specialist Gregory Yavlinsky (11 percent), who had been his deputy prime minister for economic reform during the last days of the USSR. In an interesting development, Mikhail Gorbachev decided to run against both Yeltsin and Zyuganov although Russian opinion polls suggested that he had almost no popular support. A large number of citizens blamed him personally for the country's economic woes, and he seemed to have more admirers in the West than in the Russian republic.

By the time of the first round of presidential elections in June, however, thousands of Yeltsin's political appointees had gotten organized and managed to mobilize a large bloc of voters. The state-controlled television and radio stations ran commercials that reminded the public of Yeltsin's important role in the nation's transition from Communism to democracy. American political strategists were secretly brought in to help Yeltsin's campaign by Felix Braynin, a Belarussian immigrant to the United States and a Yeltsin supporter. They used polls and voter focus groups to help Yeltsin's daughter and campaign manager, Tatiana Dyachenko, guide the campaign.

Seventy-three million citizens voted in the June election, and Yeltsin received 35 percent of the vote. Zyuganov, however, got 32 percent, with the former general and moderate reformer, Alexander Lebed, coming in third with 14.7 percent. The economist Yavlinsky only received 7.4 percent, the fascist Zhirinovsky got 5.8 percent, and Gorbachev got a mere 0.52 percent. Because of the narrow margin of Yeltsin's victory over Zyuganov, a runoff election would have to be held in July. Yeltsin forged an alliance with Lebed and thereby gained the support of many of his backers. Lebed had a significant following due to his ultra-nationalist stance and his populist hard-line approach to the economy (privatization with the maintenance of some social guarantees of the past). He also played an important role in ending the unpopular war in Chechniya.

In the runoff campaign, Yeltsin's supporters emphasized the tragedies of Russia's Soviet past in many of their commercials on television and radio, linking Zyuganov with the repressive Soviet system. Yeltsin won a decisive victory in the runoff election because his campaign caused the voters to fear a return to the totalitarianism of the past if Zyuganov and the CPRF were to win. The assistance of American professional campaign strategists and pollsters was an important element in Yeltsin's victory, and if this information had been revealed during the campaign, Zyuganov might have convinced many voters that Yeltsin was a pawn of foreign interests.

CURRENT PROBLEMS IN RUSSIA

The Yeltsin administration faces the very problems that plagued it prior to the 1996 election: the economic and political instability of the federation. First Deputy Prime Minister Anatoly Chubais has taken steps to create an enforceable tax code, so that the regime can acquire much-needed revenue. His co–first deputy prime minister, Boris Nemtsov, has sounded a populist appeal on behalf of Yeltsin's government to silence the regime's populist critics such as Lebed (whom Yeltsin removed from power shortly after the victory over Zyuganov). Yeltsin's health problems continued to pose a dilemma after the election, and subsequently he survived heart bypass surgery. Chubais and Nemtsov are considerably younger than both Yeltsin and Prime Minister Viktor Chernomyrdin, and they would be in a position to continue Yeltsin's privatization policies in the future.

The stability and growth of the economy is dependent on the political success of the federation. Yeltsin's skillful diplomacy that brought an end to the Chechniya crisis, and his decisive electoral victory over the Communists, have provided a favorable climate for foreign investments. To underscore the peace with Chechniya, Yeltsin signed a treaty in May 1997 with Chechen president Aslan Maskhadov, which, like the 1996 treaty, does not explicitly acknowledge Chechen independence but is likely an intermediary step toward the complete autonomy of Chechniya in the future. Yeltsin also signed a treaty in May 1997 in which he gave his qualified assent to the incorporation into NATO of Poland, Hungary, and the Czech republic (all former members of the Warsaw Pact). While pledging to cooperate with NATO in the future, Yeltsin has made it known that he is opposed to the use by NATO units of former Warsaw Pact facilities. NATO knows, however, that Russia lacks the capacity to prevent their use, and it remains to be seen whether NATO will consult with Russia as it indicated it would. Yeltsin knows that Russia cannot afford a conflict with NATO at a time when the country is in need of financial assistance from the Western nations.

Prospects for Russia's future depend on several factors: the maintenance of the free market, the stability of the institutions of political democracy, and the ability to sustain a peaceful transition of power. Despite his peculiar characteristics as a politician, Yeltsin has helped to develop Russia's evolving democratic-capitalist system. This system, despite its flaws, is still more tolerable to more citizens than the totalitarianism of Soviet Communism.

Biographies of the Collapse of Communism

Abel G. Aganbegyan (1932–   )

Abel G. Aganbegyan is an economic specialist whose ideas of reforming the Soviet economy greatly influenced Mikhail Gorbachev's perestroika program.

Born in Tbilisi (capital of the Soviet Republic of Georgia) on October 8, 1932, he received undergraduate and doctoral degrees in economics from the State Institute of Economics in Moscow in the 1950s. Aganbegyan began working in the general economics department of the USSR Council of Ministers' State Committee for Labor and Social Problems in 1955, and he joined the CPSU one year later. He rose quickly through the committee's hierarchy, becoming sector head and deputy head by 1961. He became the director of the Siberian branch of the USSR Academy of Sciences in 1966 (a position he held until 1985). Joining the faculty of Novosibirsk State University in 1968 as professor of economics, he came to believe that the Soviet economy did not perform well because of flaws in the planning system, and that the Soviet system was in need of drastic change.

As editor of *Eko*, the widely read journal of the Siberian branch of the Academy of Sciences, Aganbegyan gained a large following among younger, reform-minded economists. His views on economic reform received a great deal of official attention. He wrote and lectured extensively on the need for changes in wages and government subsidies. Aganbegyan suggested that the Soviets eliminate subsidies for all but education, elder health care, and book publishing.

Mikhail Gorbachev attended many of Aganbegyan's seminars and was won over to the idea of economic reform thanks to his coherent arguments. When Gorbachev became general secretary, he brought in Aganbegyan as an official advisor. Aganbegyan's 1987 book, *The Economic Challenge of Perestroika*, explained the need for reform and the policies that underlay perestroika. He advocated a departure from the command economy and a return to the economy of the NEP period. He suggested that a market economy and socialist planning were compatible, but he worded his reform plans in ambiguous language out of fear that the hardline faction in the CPSU would target him as a "counterrevolutionary." Aganbegyan's plans called for a reform of the pricing and credit systems toward intra-enterprise and regional self-financing. He also suggested that wages throughout the Soviet Union be determined by local and regional managers, rather than by Moscow. The book had a significant impact on other economists, and it motivated reformers within the government to initiate more sweeping changes.

In 1987 Aganbegyan devised a three-year plan, the New Economic Mechanism, to reform the economy. His ideas provided the basis for the January 1988 Law on State Enterprises, which granted control over salaries and leadership to workers' collectives and established that the Soviet state was no longer responsible for the debts of economic enterprises within the USSR.

Aganbegyan's influence, however, was gradually overshadowed by other economists (such as Stanislav Shatalin) who were advocates of more radical market reform within the Soviet economy. The material benefits of Aganbegyan's reforms would have taken far longer to evolve than the immediate results demanded by the public. In the calls for swift market reform by Shatalin and others, Aganbegyan's gradual approach to change was thus perceived as overly tentative. Aganbegyan predicted in 1987 that the first substantive results would be seen only by the year 2000 if his model were put into practice. Following his loss of influence, Aganbegyan became the rector of the Academy of the National Economy.

Nina A. Andreeva (1938–   )

Nina Andreeva achieved national prominence when her anti-perestroika letter was published in the newspaper *Sovetskaya Rossiya* in 1988. It was considered to speak for the conservative wing of the party and revealed much about Gorbachev's opposition.

Andreeva was born in 1938 in Leningrad, where her father worked at Leningrad's port and her mother was a mechanic in the city's Kirov plant. Andreeva became a chemistry teacher at the Leningrad Technical Institute. She joined the CPSU in 1966 and had a generally unspectacular career until the publication of her letter.

Andreeva supported the hard-line position of the party and rejected perestroika and glasnost because she felt these policies undermined Soviet institutions and Soviet greatness. When she first submitted the letter, it was rejected, but it was reworked and expanded to include more criticisms of perestroika. It was finally published when Gorbachev was out of the country, and many observers speculated that Yegor Ligachev might have been involved in drafting the letter and placing it (she quoted a speech he gave at the February 1988 plenary session of the Central Committee). The letter appeared in *Sovetskaya Rossiya* on March 13, 1988, under the heading "I Can't Forgo My Principles."

In the letter she chastised her students for not appreciating the Soviet achievement and for reevaluating the heroes of Soviet history, including Stalin. Although she stated that a member of her own family had been a victim of the purges of the Stalin era, she was critical of what she regarded as the present-day fixation on Stalin's victims, preferring that they remain buried in history the same way that Peter the Great's (Romanov tsar, 1681–1725) victims are largely forgotten in present-day Russia. She criticized Soviet youth for not being sufficiently nationalistic, and she singled out those whom she felt were too "cosmopolitan" rather than nationalistic. (This last reference relates to the Stalin era, when Bolsheviks of Jewish background were easy to single out for persecution for not adhering to Great Russian nationalism. This nationalism pertains to the non-Belarussian and non-Ukrainian core territory of Russia.)

Publication of Andreeva's letter caused a great controversy and propelled her into national prominence within the conservative faction of the party. In 1989 she was elected chairperson of the political executive committee of a pro-Communist society called Unity: For Leninism and Communist Ideals. She was in favor of the August 1991 coup attempt, and in the following November, as plans were being made to replace the USSR with the non-Communist CIS, she partipated in the founding of a new Communist organization called the All-Union Communist Party of Bolsheviks, which claimed it had 35,000 members and wanted to restore "Marxist-Leninist norms and principles" in Russia. She was elected general secretary of the organization. Since 1991 she has openly criticized the government of Boris Yeltsin and has called for a restoration of the USSR.

Yuri V. Andropov (1914–1984)

The fifth leader of the Soviet Union, Yuri Andropov was interested in reforming the Soviet economy and reducing the size of the government bureaucracy, but he died after only 15 months in office.

He was born on June 15, 1914, the son of a railway worker at Nagutskaya station in Stavropol krai. In 1930 Andropov left school to work at several short-term jobs, including telegraph boy, movie projectionist, and boatman on the Volga River transport system. He joined the Komsomol (Communist Youth League) in 1930 and entered a water transport technical school in Rybinsk in 1933. After his graduation in 1936, Andropov stayed on as the school's Komsomol secretary, and he also became the Komsomol organizer at the Volodarsky shipyard in Rybinsk.

His superiors were impressed by his work, and in 1938 Andropov was promoted to first secretary of the Yaroslavl oblast regional committee (*obkom*) of the Komsomol. He joined the CPSU in 1939 and received an important appointment in 1940 when he was made the Komsomol first secretary in the newly formed Karelo-Finnish republic. This republic consisted of territory ceded by Finland to the USSR after the Russo-Finnish War of 1939–1940. Andropov was charged with helping transform the new territory into a thoroughly Soviet republic. He also played a high-level organizational role in anti-Axis partisan activities in Karelia after German and Finnish troops invaded the USSR in 1941. The Axis alliance included Nazi Germany, Fascist Italy, and Imperial Japan.

When Soviet forces recaptured Karelia in 1944, Andropov became the second secretary of the party in Petrozavodsk, and within three years he was the second secretary of the party in the Karelo-Finnish republic. The first secretary of the Karelo-Finnish party apparatus, Otto Kuusinen, had supported Andropov's advancement in Karelia and would subsequently support his later promotions as well. In 1951 Andropov became a section head in a department within the CPSU's Central Committee dealing with timber. The springboard for higher levels of power, however, was his diplomatic work, which he began in 1953 as counsellor to the Soviet Embassy in Hungary.

Andropov learned Hungarian and got to know the intricacies of the Hungarian party. He was elevated to ambassador in 1954 and played an important role in the brutal Soviet suppression of the Hungarian revolt of October–November 1956. It has been suggested that Andropov developed an ulcer and other health problems from the stress of helping coordinate the KGB, the Soviet military, and the pro-Soviet faction of the Hungarian Communist Party in the destruction of the Hungarian resistance. Nevertheless, he performed his coordinating functions well, and he was called back to Moscow in March 1957 to become head of the new foreign relations department of the Central Committee (the Department for Relations with Communist and Workers' Parties of Socialist Countries).

He headed this department for 10 years and—perhaps as a result of his knowledge of reform efforts in other Communist nations—became interested in the idea of reform within the USSR. In 1965 he was the intermediary in a quarrel between Trofim Lysenko, the powerful head of the Lenin Academy of Agricultural Sciences who was opposed to the idea of genetics, and staff at the Czech Academy of Sciences, which wanted to celebrate the centenary of Gregor Mendel, the Czech pioneer of genetics. Andropov sided with the Czechs, and the event was eventually held, although the Soviet Academy of Sciences did not participate.

Andropov became a member of the 300-member Central Committee of the CPSU in 1961, and he soon joined the Central Committee's Secretariat, which ran the daily business of the party. Mikhail Suslov, a rigid Stalinist, came to regard Andropov as a rival in the mid-1960s and helped engineer Andropov's transferral from the Secretariat to the KGB. In 1967 Andropov was made head of the KGB (a post he held until his election as general secretary in 1982). Despite Suslov, General Secretary Leonid Brezhnev liked Andropov's record and promoted him to candidate membership of the all-powerful Politburo in 1967 as well. In the late 1970s, Andropov investigated cases of corruption within Brezhnev's inner circle, which convinced him of the need for reform.

What he was able to learn about party leaders may have served him well, for he was returned to the Secretariat of the Central Committee shortly after Suslov died in January 1982; and when Brezhnev died in November 1982, Andropov was elected general secretary of the party. He stated that the USSR should examine and perhaps even use methods used in other socialist countries. After he came to power, articles appeared in *Izvestia* and *Pravda* that discussed massive economic problems and the need for reform. *Izvestia* and *Pravda* were official Soviet newspapers, which represented the views of the Soviet government and the Communist party.

Andropov disappeared from public view in August 1983 due to a worsening diabetic condition, and his reform agenda was not carried out, although his deputy (and future general secretary) was the reform-minded Mikhail Gorbachev. In the month following his illness, a Soviet combat aircraft shot down a Korean passenger jet with Americans on board (KAL 007), which had flown into Soviet airspace. Then the U.S. invasion of Granada, a potential Soviet client in the Caribbean, occurred in October 1983. As a result of these incidents, reform took a back seat to Cold War considerations. When Andropov died from diabetic problems and kidney failure on February 9, 1984, the hope for reform was set back temporarily in the choice of Konstantin Chernenko to replace him. Nevertheless Andropov had introduced the possibility of reform, which would be attempted again just three years later by Mikhail Gorbachev.

Leonid I. Brezhnev (1906–1982)

Leonid Brezhnev was the fourth leader of the USSR. During his tenure the Soviet Union became a rival superpower of the United States through enormous expenditures on weapons systems and overseas client regimes. His policies gave rise to the term *Brezhnev Doctrine*, but his last foreign adventure—the Afghan War—ultimately undermined the security of the USSR by escalating the Cold War priorities of his rivals in the NATO countries.

Born in Dneprodzerzhinsk in Ukraine on December 19, 1906, Brezhnev was educated at the Dneprodzerzhinsk Metallurgical Institute. He became the deputy chief of the Urals Land Department and joined the CPSU in 1929. From 1933 to 1939 he served in the Red Army and in 1937 was chief of a department in the Dnepropetrovsk regional party committee. When Germany invaded the USSR in 1941, however, Brezhnev rejoined the military, serving as a political officer in the Red Army. In 1944 he was a major-general.

After World War II, Brezhnev went back to full-time political work. In 1950 he became first secretary of the CPSU Central Committee of the Moldavian Soviet Socialist Republic, an important promotion that provided him with many contacts who became useful to him later in his career. He joined the elite Central Committee of the CPSU in 1952 and was transferred to the Kazakh Soviet Socialist Republic in 1954, where he became the second secretary of the CPSU in that republic.

Brezhnev was charged with establishing General Secretary Nikita Khrushchev's Virgin Lands program of new collective farms in the Kazakh republic. He made other important contacts in Kazakhstan who served him well later in his career. He did his job so effectively in Kazakhstan that Khrushchev brought him to Moscow in 1956. Khrushchev became his mentor, and in 1956 Brezhnev became a secretary of the Central Committee and a member of the Politburo. In 1960 Brezhnev was also appointed chairman of the Presidium of the Supreme Soviet. When Khrushchev fell from power in 1964 (allegedly for fostering a "cult of personality," like Stalin), Brezhnev succeeded him as first secretary of the party. For a few years he shared power with Alexei Kosygin, chairman of the Council of Ministers, under the guise of "collective leadership." However, Brezhnev had a wider base of support than Kosygin, and he exerted control over the party apparatus. In 1966 he was granted the title of party general secretary and began shaping a more vigorous foreign policy. He relied heavily on his friend and USSR foreign secretary, Andrei Gromyko.

Under the Brezhnev Doctrine the Soviets exerted a great deal of influence abroad, including crushing the Czechoslovakian revolt in 1968 and the Solidarity labor movement in Poland in 1981, and supporting the spread of Communism to South Yemen, South Vietnam, Laos, Angola, Mozambique, Ethiopia, Congo, Benin, Nicaragua, and Afghanistan.

Brezhnev also outspent the United States on nuclear and conventional weapons, and during his tenure the Warsaw Pact surpassed NATO in both nuclear and conventional weapons capabilities. Brezhnev employed Cuban troops and Warsaw Pact technical operatives (especially East Germans) to do his bidding abroad because he believed that direct Soviet involvement would be more provocative to NATO. However, he also tried to foster détente with the United States and signed two Strategic Arms Limitation Treaties (in 1972 and 1979) to create a global balance of power between the USSR and the United States.

Under Brezhnev the USSR received a new constitution in 1977, in which the supreme political and social position of the party was guaranteed in writing for the first time in Soviet history, in Article 6. During Brezhnev's tenure, more high-ranking party functionaries enjoyed privileges of membership than in previous years. These apparatchiks numbered in the tens of thousands, and the perks granted to them helped drain the Soviet economy as surely as Brezhnev's overseas operations or his military buildup did. Dissidents (prominent opponents of the regime) were persecuted through incarceration in "psychoprisons" or exiled internally or abroad. Andrei Sakharov, a leading Soviet nuclear scientist and dissident who won the Nobel Peace Prize in 1975, was punished by internal exile to the city of Gorky in 1980. He was released by Gorbachev in 1986 and died in 1990.

Alexander Solzhenitsyn, a leading Russian writer and Soviet-era dissident who won the Nobel Prize in Literature in 1970, was deported from the Soviet Union for opposing the regime in 1974. As of 1997, he is still alive.

Corruption spread through the party hierarchy and government bureaucracy during Brezhnev's tenure. The KGB was aware of this but was unable to prosecute, because some of Brezhnev's inner circle were involved (even members of his own family—his daughter was involved in diamond smuggling and currency speculation schemes with members of the Moscow State Circus). As his health deteriorated after 1976, Brezhnev also developed senility and once read the wrong speech on national television without realizing his mistake until a subordinate handed him the proper text.

Brezhnev's last foreign operation, in 1979—the invasion of Afghanistan by Soviet troops to prop up a Communist client regime—resulted in a 10-year war with U.S.-backed Muslim resistance fighters called *mujahidin*. The war was politically disastrous for his successors. Brezhnev died on November 10, 1982, and was succeeded by KGB chief Yuri Andropov, a moderate reformer whose agenda included eliminating the corruption among Brezhnev's protégés and making the apparatchiks work for their privileges.

Konstantin U. Chernenko (1911–1985)

Sixth leader of the USSR, Konstantin Chernenko was a Brezhnev protégé whose 13-month tenure as general secretary was a step back from the tentative reform of Andropov.

Born on September 24, 1911, in the Siberian village of Bolshaya (later called Krasnoyarsk krai), he was the child of peasants. Chernenko served in the Border Guards in 1930–1933. He joined the CPSU in 1931 and began working for the propaganda and agitation departments of the district and regional party committees in 1933. He rose through party propaganda ranks in the 1930s to become secretary of the Krasnoyarsk regional party committee. He served in this capacity until 1945, when he became head of the Penza regional party committee.

In 1948 he was transferred to become head of the propaganda and agitation department of the party Central Committee in the Moldavia republic. There he was befriended by Leonid Brezhnev, the first secretary of the Moldavian branch of the CPSU. This contact would serve Chernenko well for the rest of his career, for Brezhnev brought his friend along with him on his own rise to the highest levels of power in the USSR. When Brezhnev went to work in Moscow in 1956, he got Chernenko the job of sector head in the department of propaganda and agitation of the CPSU's Central Committee. In 1960 Brezhnev became chairman of the elite 39-member Presidium of the Supreme Soviet (the top legislative body in the union), and Chernenko served as his chief of staff.

When Brezhnev became the CPSU's general secretary (and thus leader of the USSR) in 1964, Chernenko benefited from his friend's promotion as well. In 1965, he became head of the Central Committee's General Department, the branch that worked most closely with the general secretary. In the following year he became a candidate member of the Central Committee, and in 1971 he became a full member of the elite 300-member body. Chernenko gained valuable experience while accompanying his mentor on high-level diplomatic conferences—including the 1975 Helsinki Conference and the Vienna Summit with U.S. president Jimmy Carter in 1979, which produced the SALT II agreement.

In 1977 Chernenko was elevated to candidate membership in the most powerful body in the Soviet government, the 13-member Politburo. Just one year later he was a full member of the body and thus poised to succeed his mentor. However, being only five years younger than Brezhnev, he was at a disadvantage when Brezhnev died in November 1982. Chernenko lost the power struggle with KGB chief Yuri Andropov, who was only three years his junior but who represented a younger generation interested in ending the stagnation and corruption that seemed to characterize Brezhnev's later years. Although Chernenko was not implicated in the illegal activities of some of Brezhnev's other associates, he represented to many reformers the inefficiency and stagnation of the system, and many of his younger peers had a poor opinion of his educational background and his job performance.

When Andropov died unexpectedly in February 1984, the choice for succession was between the "old guard's" Chernenko and the reformers' choice, Mikhail Gorbachev (who had assumed many of Andropov's duties when the general secretary first became ill). In light of Chernenko's advanced age and health problems, the choice of Chernenko was not as much a setback for reform as it otherwise might have been. It was also an indication of the strategic insecurity felt in the USSR as a consequence of the international tension caused by the shooting down of KAL 007 by a Soviet military plane, and by the U.S. invasion of Grenada (two incidents that occurred while Andropov was ill and Gorbachev was handling affairs of state).

During Chernenko's 13-month tenure as general secretary, the Brezhnev status quo was temporarily restored. No moves were taken toward reform, and the Cold War received top priority on the Soviet government's agenda. His tenure was entirely uneventful, and only one high-level Politburo appointment was made while he was in power (after the death of Dmitri Ustinov). The Afghan War and Warsaw Pact commitments received the same attention as they had during Brezhnev's long tenure. However, when Chernenko died on March 10, 1985, the younger generation received its opportunity to select one of its own as general secretary—Mikhail Gorbachev.

Mikhail S. Gorbachev (1931–)

Mikhail S. Gorbachev was the originator of perestroika (restructuring), which inadvertently caused the collapse of Communism in the Soviet Union. He was the last general secretary of the CPSU and the last leader of the USSR.

Gorbachev was born in the village of Privolnoe in Stavropol krai, a technically autonomous region in southern Russia, on March 2, 1931. His father was a tractor driver, and in 1946 (at age 15) Gorbachev became an assistant to a combine operator. He joined the Komsomol (the Communist Youth League) and in 1949 received the Red Banner of Labor for his work in Komsomol as well as his model agricultural training. In 1950 he entered the law school of Moscow State University and joined the CPSU in 1952. After graduating from Moscow State University in 1955 he returned to Stavropol, where he became the secretary of the Stavropol krai Komsomol Committee. He transferred to the Stavropol branch of the CPSU in 1962 and began to study economics at the Stavropol Agricultural Institute, from which he graduated in 1967.

Gorbachev became secretary of the Stavropol City Committee of the CPSU in 1966, and first secretary of the Stavropol krai Committee of the CPSU in 1970. He made his first trip abroad when he visited Czechoslovakia in 1969, a year after Brezhnev crushed the Czechoslovakian revolt known as Prague Spring. He visited Belgium (1972), West Germany (1975), and Canada (1983) prior to becoming general secretary.

Gorbachev's ascent to the highest level of power began in 1970, when he was elected to the 1,500-member Supreme Soviet. In the following year, at the Twenty-Fourth Party Congress, he was elected a member of the elite 300-member Central Committee. This body governed the daily operation of the party between the party congresses. Over the next several years he made important contacts with senior party leaders such as Yuri Andropov, Alexei Kosygin, and Mikhail Suslov. In 1977 Gorbachev oversaw a massive agricultural project (the "Ipatovsky Experiment") in Stavropol, which caught the attention of the party leaders. He subsequently received the prestigious Order of the October Revolution.

Because of the excitement generated by his work in Stavropol, he became the head of the Central Committee agricultural department in 1978 and in the same year was made secretary of the Central Committee. He was then advancing so rapidly within the Soviet hierarchy that he moved to Moscow to be near the imperial nerve center. A candidate member of the elite and powerful Politburo in 1978, Gorbachev was made an alternate member in 1979 and a full member of the 13-man body in 1980.

When Brezhnev died in 1982, Gorbachev supported Andropov over Chernenko and became Andropov's close associate. Gorbachev was a supporter of Andropov's tentative moves toward reform, and in fact he represented the younger generation of party members who sought to change the system more than Andropov wanted or Khrushchev had done. When Andropov became ill from diabetic complications and was unable to peform his duties, Gorbachev worked in his place, along with Dmitri Ustinov and Andrei Gromyko. When Andropov died in February 1984, however, power passed to Konstantin Chernenko, an older conservative Brezhnev protégé who was regarded as having seniority over Gorbachev. The younger generation of party reformers whom Gorbachev represented had to bide their time, knowing that Chernenko's advanced age (he was 73 at the time) and poor health meant his tenure would probably be brief. When Chernenko died just over a year later, the younger reformers got their chance to promote one of their own, and Gorbachev was made general secretary on March 10, 1985.

Gorbachev fostered the program of perestroika to make Communism profitable and popular, making sweeping changes in the style of Soviet government. Under glasnost (political openness) his regime tolerated criticism of recent Soviet policies. His supporters reevaluated the Soviet past to explain the necessity of reform in the present. Gorbachev noticed a relationship between the poor domestic conditions in the USSR and the military and foreign policy expenditures of his predecessors.

Consequently, he sought to drastically reduce Soviet conventional and nuclear weapons expenditures, and slash the subsidies granted to the Warsaw Pact and overseas clients. Like Andropov, he wanted to make the economic infrastructures in industry and agriculture within the USSR more productive. He also wanted to reduce the size of the Soviet government bureaucracy and cut back the extra benefits granted to the apparatchiks.

But while his domestic reforms stalled, he made enormous strides in ending the Cold War (which was as costly to the USSR and Warsaw Pact as it was to the United States and NATO). In 1988 Gorbachev negotiated the Intermediate Nuclear Forces Treaty with the United States and announced in a speech at the United Nations that he intended to end Soviet involvement in Afghanistan and withdraw military units from the Warsaw Pact. Soviet forces pulled out of the costly 10-year Afghan War in February 1989, and the Warsaw Pact collapsed in the fall of 1989. Gorbachev allowed the demolition of the Berlin Wall, the reunification of Germany, and the termination of the Soviet-led Communist order that had dominated eastern and central Europe since the end of World War II.

The combination of (1) glasnost press coverage of resurgent ethnic-territorial conflicts within the USSR and (2) the Soviet withdrawal from eastern Europe led to disturbances in the USSR's national republics that Gorbachev was unable to control. His poor handling of the 1986 Chernobyl nuclear accident, including an obvious attempt at a coverup, harmed his credibility when the glasnost press fanned discontent in Ukraine and Belarus. Beginning with the 1986 anti-Russian riots in Kazakhstan and elsewhere in Central Asia, the union seemed to unravel as conflicts arose in the Caucasus (Armenia, Azerbaidjan, and Georgia) and the Baltics (Estonia, Latvia, and Lithuania). When Gorbachev approved of the use of force to restore order in Georgia (1989), Azerbaidjan (1990), and Lithuania (1991), his domestic image was irreparably damaged.

Following the advice of economists Abel Aganbegyan, Leonid Abalkin, and Stanislav Shatalin, Gorbachev tried to introduce market reform but was hindered by the entrenched command economy and the dissent of apparatchiks. The Reform Commission (appointed in 1989) and the "Shatalin Group" (formed in 1990) each failed to bring about genuine market reform. Gorbachev was consequently criticized by the public for the slow pace of economic change and by the apparatchiks for trying to terminate the subsidized system that benefited them most.

The hard-line apparatchiks were also fearful that the constitutional changes introduced by Gorbachev would undermine the previously guaranteed supremacy of the CPSU. His 1988 electoral law allowed for multicandidate elections and term limits for the first time in Soviet history.

The new legislature created in 1989, the Congress of Peoples' Deputies, became the first popularly elected body in Soviet history since the short-lived Constituent Assembly of 1918. However, the 1990 constitutional change made the party leaders even more fearful of losing their status. Article 6 of the USSR constitution, which had guaranteed the political monopoly of the CPSU, was now dropped. As the position of general secretary was consequently less powerful, Gorbachev made the USSR presidency an executive office. Many apparatchiks viewed Gorbachev as a traitor who had only used the party as a vehicle to personal power.

Gorbachev's wife, Raisa, also took on a prominent role, comparable to the first lady in the United States. She promoted an organization that she helped found in 1987, the Soviet Cultural Fund. Although Western observers were impressed by Raisa's abilities and intellect (she had earned a Ph.D. in sociology from Moscow State Pedagogical Institute), many Russians criticized her for allegedly influencing her husband's appointments.

Gorbachev felt that the best way to bring about economic reform was to decentralize the union, and he permitted popular elections within each of the republics, including Russia. This inadvertently led to a serious undermining of his authority within the union. The Congress of Peoples' Deputies became a political springboard for Boris Yeltsin, formerly Gorbachev's protégé and now his chief critic from the ranks of the reformers. Yeltsin was elected to the Russian republic's Congress of Peoples' Deputies and was made its speaker. He became a hero to many reformers in the Russian republic when he walked out of the Twenty-Eighth Party Congress and quit the CPSU in July 1990. In the March 1991 referendum that registered popular support for a new, decentralized, union treaty, the population of the Russian republic also indicated that it supported the creation of the post of president of the republic. When Yeltsin was elected to the Russian republic's presidency in June 1991, a dual government system had been created that (ironically) was similar to that of Russia in 1917 when the Provisional Government and the Soviet of Workers' and Soldiers' Deputies contended for supremacy. Yeltsin made it known that the Russian republic was going to embark on reforms at a more rapid pace than Gorbachev was undertaking within the USSR.

Gorbachev nevertheless was confident that he could hold the USSR together in a looser union and bring about the prosperity that had so far eluded the measures of perestroika. The details of the new union treaty were clarified by mid-August 1991, and Gorbachev planned for a formal signing to take place after his return from a vacation in Foros, Crimea. However, hard-line apparatchiks were planning to subvert his plans. A group of his subordinates staged a coup against him on August 19. They sent KGB general Yuri Plekhanov to place Gorbachev under arrest in Foros on August 18, and announced on August 19 that Gorbachev was ill and unable to perform his duties.

The conspirators formed an eight-man Emergency Committee consisting of Vice President Gennady Yanaev (who was proclaimed president), Prime Minister Valentin Pavlov, Interior Minister Boris Pugo, Defense Minister Dmitri Yazov, KGB chief Vladimir Kryuchkov, USSR Defense Council deputy chairman Oleg Baklanov, USSR Peasants' Union chairman Vasili Starodubtsev, and Association of State Enterprises president Alexander Tizyakov. An important figure behind the scenes was the speaker of the USSR Supreme Soviet, Anatoly Lukyanov, whom some later regarded as the mastermind of the conspiracy.

Gorbachev had promoted these individuals to please the hard-line faction within the party, but apparently he was unaware that they were so strongly opposed to the reform process that they would risk a coup. While Gorbachev was held captive along with his wife, Raisa, at Foros for three days, he could only listen helplessly on his radio to the events unfolding in Moscow. Yeltsin resisted the coup by gathering support for Gorbachev, but Gorbachev had become historically irrelevant by the time Yeltsin's vice president, Alexander Rutskoi, came to Foros to retrieve him on the night of August 21–22.

Returning to Moscow, Gorbachev still believed that he could salvage the union and his presidency. He stated at a press conference that he still believed in Communism and that the party as a whole was not to blame for the coup. He was stunned to learn from documents provided by Yeltsin that almost his entire government and the party leaders were in support of the conspiracy. He also lacked the power to stop Yeltsin and the other republic leaders from dismantling the USSR. Yeltsin suspended the activities of the CPSU within the Russian republic, making the old union an impossibility without the cohesive qualities of the party. The new union that had been planned by Gorbachev prior to the coup was also an impossibility, given his own political irrelevance.

After learning of the depth of party support for the coup, Gorbachev stepped down as leader of the party on August 24 and dissolved the party. He gave his assent to the December 8 Minsk Agreement, which replaced the USSR with a loose confederation, the Commonwealth of Independent States (CIS). On December 25, when the Soviet flag was brought down from over the Kremlin and replaced with Peter the Great's old Russian tricolor, Gorbachev officially relinquished power to Yeltsin as head of the Russian Federation (this included control of the Soviet nuclear arsenal).

Gorbachev presided over the decline and fall of the Soviet empire— first the external empire of the Warsaw Pact and overseas client states, then the internal empire of the union itself. Although giving up the external empire was a critical part of perestroika, Gorbachev did not intend for the internal empire to collapse. His goal had been to transform the totalitarian Soviet state into a democratically elected and partly capitalist regime, but the system and its supporters were unable to make the change.

Gorbachev was unable to judge the people's hatred of Communism, and their resurgent nationalisms were a mystery to him.

After his retirement from political power Gorbachev started his own foundation, wrote his memoirs, and addressed interested audiences around the world. His popularity within Russia, however, was measured by opinion polls at around 1 percent. Many citizens blamed him for making Russia a second-rate power. In June 1996, however, he attempted a political comeback in the presidential elections. He traveled throughout the country establishing contacts, but he never rose in the opinion polls. He received only 0.52 percent of the vote. Since his election loss, Gorbachev has pledged to work for global environmental issues.

Vladimir A. Kryuchkov (1923–   )

Chairman of the KGB, Vladimir Kryuchkov was opposed to perestroika and played an important role in organizing the August 1991 coup attempt.

He was born on February 29, 1924, in Tsaritsyn (later Stalingrad) and worked in factories there and in Gorky (Nizhny Novgorod) in the early 1940s. He became a Komsomol construction site organizer in Stalingrad in 1943 and joined the CPSU in 1944. He subsequently rose in the Komsomol ranks to become secretary for the Barrikadny raion committee in Stalingrad, and then second secretary for the Stalingrad city Komsomol committee. He changed professions in the mid-1940s, becoming an investigator for area procurators' offices in Stalingrad (serving in the Traktorozavodsky and Kirov raions).

Kryuchkov graduated from the All-Union Extra-Mural Institute of Law in 1949 and then from the Higher Diplomatic School of the Soviet Ministry of Internal Affairs. In that year he became third secretary of a department in the Ministry of Internal Affairs. In 1955 he became third secretary in the Soviet embassy in Budapest, Hungary, and may have been involved in espionage work there. Kryuchkov worked at the embassy when Yuri Andropov also worked there, and Kryuchkov's rise in the system depended in part on the career of Andropov (both men later became head of the KGB). Kryuchkov, however, was interested in preserving the status quo and did not advocate ideas of reform later, as would Andropov. Kryuchkov became a sector head in the Department for Relations with Communist and Workers' Parties of Socialist Countries of the CPSU's Central Committee in 1959. Andropov was then head of this department.

Kryuchkov next became an administrative assistant in the Central Committee in 1965, and then in 1967 he joined the KGB. He rose rapidly within the KGB ranks, becoming deputy chairman in 1978 (serving under Andropov) and chairman in 1988. Kryuchkov also reached the highest levels of power within the party and the government in the 1980s—he was elected to the Central Committee and the Supreme Soviet in 1986 and the Politburo in 1990. In 1988 he was also promoted to a generalship in the army. Gorbachev made him a member of his Presidential Council in March 1990 to appease the hard-line faction of the party.

However, Kryuchkov was uncomfortable with perestroika and was a crucial participant in the conspiracy to oust Gorbachev and Yeltsin in the summer of 1991. Many Russians consider him to have been the mastermind of the August coup attempt. It was KGB troops who arrested Gorbachev in the Crimea, but the coup failed in large part because the KGB Alpha Team, like the army, refused to shoot civilians outside Yeltsin's headquarters in Moscow. Kryuchkov was arrested on August 21 when the coup collapsed and was relieved of his duties officially on August 22. Along with other conspirators, he was held at the Matrosskaya Tishina Isolator, a prison, but was released when Yeltsin decided not to prosecute the coup plotters. He subsequently participated in several demonstrations against Yeltsin and has advocated restoration of the USSR.

Yegor K. Ligachev (1920–   )

Originally a supporter of moderate reform, Yegor Ligachev came to oppose perestroika and became Gorbachev's chief rival.

Ligachev was born on November 29, 1920, in Novosibirsk oblast. He graduated from the Moscow Aviation Institute in 1943 and became secretary (later, first secretary) of the Novosibirsk Komsomol Committee. Ligachev joined the CPSU in 1944. He became deputy chairman of the Novosibirsk oblast Soviet in 1949 (a post he held until 1961) and graduated from the Party Higher School in Moscow in 1951. He remained in a midlevel regional administrative position for ten years, however, until in 1961 he became deputy head of the propaganda and agitation department of the CPSU Central Committee for the Russian Soviet Federated Socialist Republic.

In 1963 Ligachev became deputy head of the department of party organizations of the Central Committee. Two years later he was transferred to become first secretary of the Tomsk oblast committee, and in 1966 he became a candidate member of the elite Central Committee and also a member of the USSR Committee for Industry, Transport, Post and Telecommunications. In 1968 Ligachev became a member of the Committee for Youth Affairs, and in 1974 he was appointed to the Planning and Budget Committee of the USSR Supreme Soviet.

Ligachev became a full member of the powerful, 300-member Central Committee in 1976 and began working with Mikhail Gorbachev in 1980, during the later period of Leonid Brezhnev's tenure. At the time, both men were interested in the ideas of reform held by the younger generation of party members. In 1983, during Andropov's tenure (and while Gorbachev was Andropov's deputy), Ligachev became secretary of cadres and ideology for the Central Committee. In 1985, when Gorbachev was general secretary, Ligachev reached the highest level of power in the Soviet system when he was made a member of the elite, 13-member Politburo (the arm of Soviet government that established domestic and foreign policy, and set economic policy as well). He was also made chairman of the Foreign Affairs Committee of the Soviet (Council) of the Union in the USSR Supreme Soviet. He became head of the Agricultural Commission of the Central Committee in 1988 and was elected to the USSR Chamber of Deputies in 1989.

Ligachev was interested in reforming the Soviet system, but he came to oppose perestroika on the grounds that too many changes were taking place too rapidly, to the detriment of the system. He feared that the re-writing of Soviet history by glasnost authors would cause a sweeping rejection of the Soviet legacy, and he stated that he did not approve of importing and applying capitalist principles in the Soviet Union.

Ligachev came to represent the hard-line faction of the party that was against further reform. Consequently he opposed Gorbachev's lessening of the constitutional guarantees granted to the CPSU, and he unsuccessfully challenged Gorbachev for the position of general secretary of the party at the Twenty-Eighth Party Congress in July 1990. He was not elected to the new Politburo, and he thereafter retired from politics.

Boris K. Pugo (1937–1991)

Interior minister under Gorbachev, Boris Pugo was one of the principal conspirators behind the August 1991 coup attempt.

Pugo was born in Kalinin in 1937, the son of a Latvian Communist who emigrated to the USSR. Pugo moved to Latvia following the Soviet annexation of the republic in World War II and began working for the Latvian Komsomol organization. He began to rise in the hierarchy in the early 1960s, and by 1969 he was first secretary of the Komsomol Committee of the Latvian Soviet Socialist Republic. In 1970 he became first secretary of the All-Union Komsomol.

He began to rise within the party apparatus in 1975 when he was appointed first secretary of the Riga city party committee. Two years later he transferred to the Latvian branch of the KGB. He was deputy chairman of the KGB of Latvia in 1977 and chairman in 1980. He received a major promotion in 1984 when he became first secretary of the CPSU in the Latvian republic. Pugo then became chairman of the All-Union Committee of Party Control (one of whose responsibilities was the "rehabilitation" of victims of Stalin's purges).

Gorbachev appointed Pugo a candidate member of the Politburo in 1989, although he was not a staunch supporter of perestroika. Pugo was thought to be a safe choice by Gorbachev because he was regarded as conservative enough to placate the hard-line faction of the party, but not a great threat to perestroika. This was Gorbachev's thinking in December 1990, when Pugo was chosen to succeed Vadim Bakatin as interior minister. Bakatin had been using subtle diplomacy rather than direct force to try to placate the rising nationalism in the republics, but this policy had earned him many enemies among the hard-liners and the ultra-nationalist Russians in Gorbachev's government. Pugo therefore was given authority to use force to curb the demands for independence within the republics. Pugo sent Interior Ministry OMON units (from the Russian acronym meaning "special purpose militia detachment") to use extraordinary means to crush independence protests in Lithuania and Latvia in January 1991.

Pugo and KGB chief Vladimir Kryuchkov accused the West—in particular, the American CIA—of trying to undermine Russia in the midst of its growing separatist crisis. They obtained permission to investigate and harass the new Russian companies that were doing business with the West. Pugo and Kryuchkov also played an important role in organizing the August 1991 coup attempt. Pugo ordered OMON units to attack the supporters of Yeltsin and Gorbachev in Moscow and Leningrad on August 19 and 20, but their efforts were half-hearted. After the coup attempt collapsed, police officers arrived at Pugo's home to arrest him, but he refused to surrender and committed suicide with a pistol.

Stanislav S. Shatalin (1934–)

One of the principal economists who influenced Mikhail Gorbachev's perestroika program, Stanislav Shatalin was the individual for whom the ambitious plan for market reform of the Soviet economy was named in the summer of 1990.

Shatalin was born on August 24, 1934, in Pushkino, Leningrad oblast. His father was a Bolshevik commissar and party secretary in Kalinin oblast. Shatalin studied economics and mathematical methods of economic analysis at Moscow State University. After graduating in 1958, he became an economist at the Scientific Research Institute of Finance in the USSR Ministry of Finance. In the following year he became a junior research assistant (later, chief economist) in the Scientific Research Institute of Gosplan.

Shatalin joined the CPSU in 1962 and in the same year was promoted to chief of the Sector of Inter-Branch Balances of the Scientific Research Institute of Gosplan. In 1965 he became deputy director of the main theoretical department of the Central Mathematical Economics Institute of the USSR Academy of Sciences. Five years later he became chairman of the Department of Mathematical Methods for Economic Analysis at Moscow State University. He lectured on the optimal functioning of the socialist economy. He completed his doctorate in economics in 1971 and was made full professor. Then Shatalin began advising the Soviet government on its annual and five-year plans.

Shatalin became a corresponding member of the USSR Academy of Sciences in 1974, and in 1976 he became deputy director of the All-Union Scientific Research Institute for Systems Research of the USSR State Committee on Science and Technology. Only two years later, however, he lost his job as deputy director because he was blamed personally for the emigration of some two dozen of his research assistants to Israel and the United States. At that time he began working on projects with Hungarian economists. A crucial opportunity occurred for Shatalin in 1983 when Andropov brought him in to work with a group of economists to improve the Soviet economy.

With the arrival of perestroika, Shatalin openly supported changes in the Soviet economy. In 1986 he became head of a laboratory at the Institute of Economics and Forecasting of Scientific Technical Progress in the USSR's Academy of Sciences (and in 1987 he was made a full member of the Academy). He met Mikhail Gorbachev in 1989 and joined the State Commission on Economic Reform under Leonid Abalkin. Shatalin positioned himself in the group of radical reformers when he criticized the CPSU's economic platform at the plenum of the Central Committee in 1990 (he later revised his speech to be published as an article in the party journal *Kommunist*). In the same year he was appointed to Gorbachev's Presidential Council and was elected to the elite CPSU Central Committee. In 1990 he also headed the group that prepared the 500-Day Program of economic reform, which was named the Shatalin Plan after him. The plan proposed radical market reform in the Soviet economy to boost production. Gorbachev's hope of making the Soviet system profitable now depended more on Shatalin's approach than the overly cautious approach of Abel Aganbegyan. However, when the 500-Day Program failed to bring about the immediate results that many hoped for, both dissatisfied citizens and party hard-liners criticized the reform group. Shatalin was as upset as Gorbachev. The reform group had hoped for the creation of NEP-like conditions in the Soviet Union, but party hard-liners were not eager to see Soviet socialism replaced by capitalism or proto-capitalism.

Shatalin resigned from the CPSU in January 1991 over the Vilnius Massacre, in which Soviet Interior Ministry forces killed Lithuanian independence demonstrators. He then began working on behalf of Boris Yeltsin's 1991 election campaign in the Russian republic, judging Yeltsin to be interested in the kind of sweeping economic reforms that he advocated. In July 1991, Shatalin became co-chairman of the Movement of Democratic Reforms, International. He supported Yeltsin during the August coup attempt, and in September became president of the Fund of Economic and Social Reform. He is currently chairman of the Movement of Democratic Reforms, International.

Eduard A. Shevardnadze (1928–)

Eduard Shevardnadze was Mikhail Gorbachev's foreign minister and played a critical role in negotiating the end of the Cold War. He proved to be one of the staunchest supporters of domestic reform within the Soviet Union.

Born on January 25, 1928, in the village of Mamati in Lanchkhutsky raion in the Georgian Soviet Socialist Republic, Shevardnadze studied at Tbilisi Medical College from 1946 to 1948. He began working in the Komsomol in 1946, joined the CPSU in 1948, and graduated from the Georgian Communist Party School in 1951. Serving as secretary of the Komsomol committee at the medical college, he subsequently became a Komsomol instructor and then Komsomol head in the Ordzhonikidze raion in Tbilisi. He next became an instructor in the Georgian republic Komsomol organization, then secretary and second secretary of the Kutaisi oblast Komsomol committee. Shevardnadze was elected second secretary of the Central Committee of the Komsomol of the Georgian republic in 1956, and one year later he was made first secretary.

During the 1960s he began ascending the Georgian party hierarchy. In the early 1960s he was first secretary of the Georgian branch of the CPSU in the Mtskhetsky and Pervomaisky raions of Tbilisi. He became first deputy minister of the Maintenance of Public Order in the Georgian republic in 1964, and minister in 1965. Rising to become minister of internal affairs in the Georgian republic in 1968, he also became first secretary of the Central Committee of the CPSU in the Georgian republic in 1972.

His regional party connections were his means of gaining power in the union-wide party hierarchy. He became a member of the CPSU Central Committee in 1976 and a candidate member of the Politburo in 1978. Supporting the reform position of Gorbachev, Shevardnadze was elevated to full membership in the Politburo in July 1985 and at the same time succeeded Andrei Gromyko as foreign minister of the USSR. He supported Gorbachev's initiatives to end Cold War tensions, and he participated in summit meetings between Gorbachev and the U.S. president. Although he sustained a great deal of criticism from party hard-liners when he gave his assent to the breakup of the Warsaw Pact and the reunification of Germany, he became a member of Gorbachev's Presidential Council in 1990. However, as the criticisms of the conservative faction of the party became stronger, Shevardnadze resigned as foreign minister in December 1990. He left the CPSU in 1991 to become one of the founders of the Movement for Democratic Reform. He warned of an impending coup in late 1990 and early 1991, and he became a vocal (and visible) opponent of the August 1991 coup attempt.

Following the breakup of the USSR, he returned to Georgia and became a member of the Georgian State Council in March 1992. He formally converted and became a member of the Georgian Orthodox Church in 1992. After the removal of Georgian president Zviad Gamsakurdia (who fostered civil war between Georgians and minority Ossetians and Abkhasians), Shevardnadze was elected president of Georgia (literally, "head of state") in 1992.

Gennady I. Yanaev (1937–   )

Gennady Yanaev, last vice president of the USSR, served under Mikhail Gorbachev but became a member of the Emergency Committee that tried to overthrow Gorbachev and restore hard-line Soviet rule in the August 1991 coup attempt.

He was born on August 27, 1937, into a peasant family in the village of Perevoz in Gorky (Nizhny Novgorod) oblast. He studied agronomy at the Gorky Agricultural Institute and graduated in 1959. He then began working for the Rabotinsky Repair Tractor Station in Gorky oblast in 1959 and ultimately became its chief engineer. He joined the CPSU in 1962 and was appointed second secretary of the Gorky Oblast Komsomol Committee the very next year. He was elevated to the position of first secretary of the Gorky Komsomol in 1966 and managed to graduate from the All-Union Extra-Mural Institute of Law in 1967.

He rose to the post of chairman of the USSR Committee of Youth Organizations in 1968. His rise in the national hierarchy was stalled in this position for 12 years, however, until in 1980 he was made deputy chairman of the presidium of the Union of Soviet Societies of Friendship and Cultural Ties with Foreign Countries. In 1986 he was made secretary for international questions of the All-Union Central Union of Trade Unions, and he rose through the ranks to become deputy chairman (1989) and then chairman (1990). He was elected to the Supreme Soviet in 1989 and worked on the Supreme Soviet Committee on International Problems. Twice during his career he won the Red Banner of Labor. Yanaev was a dutiful party functionary, and his career advancement after 1985 reflects the fact that he had paid his dues, not that he was a loyal follower of Gorbachev. In fact, Yanaev believed that the pace of perestroika reforms was eroding the system in which he had placed his confidence.

Yanaev received a major career boost in January 1991 when he became

Gorbachev's vice president. He was not chosen because of strong support for perestroika but because Gorbachev had been feeling pressure from party hard-liners, and the president believed Yanaev to be a safer choice than many other party conservatives. However, when the hard-liners within the government began plotting a coup against Gorbachev, Yanaev was a crucial participant in the conspiracy. In June 1991 several members of the government decided it was time to remove Gorbachev from power because of the worsening economy. This group consisted of Prime Minister Valentin Pavlov, Interior Minister Boris Pugo, Defense Minister Dmitri Yazov, and KGB chief Vladimir Kryuchkov—but not Yanaev. By August, however, Yanaev had been won over to the idea of removing Gorbachev by force and rolling back perestroika.

Although he may not have been the mastermind of the coup attempt, Yanaev was placed in charge of the self-proclaimed Emergency Committee as the new national president on August 19. Yanaev stated on television that due to Gorbachev's alleged illness and the national distress, the country would be placed under martial law. He appeared nervous during the committee's press conference, and his hands were shaking. It was later revealed that he and Prime Minister Pavlov were so tense over the plot that they consumed excessive amounts of vodka and were drunk during most of the attempted coup (August 19–21). Yanaev lacked both the charisma and the contacts of Yeltsin, and after the coup collapsed he was placed under arrest (August 22) in the Matrosskaya Tishina Isolator. He made the seemingly preposterous claim that Gorbachev actually supported the coup. Although originally they faced the death penalty, Yanaev and his co-conspirators were eventually released from prison because of Yeltsin's interest in putting the affair to rest. Thereafter, Yanaev has been involved in pro-Communist demonstrations against Boris Yeltsin's government.

Dmitri T. Yazov (1923–   )

Appointed minister of defense and marshal of the USSR by Mikhail Gorbachev, Yazov was supposed to foster perestroika in the armed forces; but he turned on his patron and helped organize the unsuccessful coup attempt of August 1991.

Born on November 8, 1923, in the village of Yazovo in Omsk oblast, Yazov came of age during World War II and served as an officer during the conflict known to Russians as the Great Patriotic War. He joined the Red Army in 1941, the year of the German invasion of the USSR, and graduated from the Infantry Technical School of the Russian Soviet Federated Socialist Republic in Moscow in 1942. He rose through the military ranks during the war as platoon commander and deputy company commander on the Volkhovisk and Leningrad fronts. After the war he continued to rise through the military hierarchy, becoming a commander on the company, battalion, and regimental levels by 1956. In that year Yazov graduated from the Frunze Military Academy, and in 1967 he graduated from the Military Academy of the General Staff of the USSR Armed Forces.

His promotions continued throughout the next decade—command on the divisional, army corps, and then army level by 1975. In 1976 he became deputy commander of one of the 14 Soviet theaters of military operations (TVDs). He served in the Far Eastern TVD, with some 50 divisions covering Siberia, the Soviet Far East, Mongolia, China, the Korean peninsula, Japan, and Alaska. Yazov was transferred in 1980 to become commander of the Southern TVD, with some 30 divisions under him covering Soviet Central Asia, the Caucasus, Afghanistan, and Iran. In 1984 he became commander of the Far Eastern TVD. Yazov also was made a candidate member of the CPSU Central Committee in 1981 (he became a full member in 1987).

He met Gorbachev when the general secretary was touring the Far East, and in January 1987 Yazov was promoted to deputy minister of defense. He was now in the Stavka (headquarters) of the Soviet Supreme High Command—the inner circle of the Soviet military—and was supposed to foster perestroika in the officer corps. In May 1987 he was promoted over other senior officers to become minister of defense, the highest military position in the USSR. Other officers had been tainted along with the previous defense minister, Marshal Sergei Sokolov, because they continued to follow the anti-reform position of party hard-liners, and because Soviet security had been penetrated by the low-level flight of a West German pilot named Mathias Rust who landed on Red Square in Moscow. Yazov gained increased political powers in June 1987 when he was made a candidate member of the elite Politburo. In March 1990 Yazov was appointed to Gorbachev's Presidential Council, and one month later he was made a marshal of the Soviet Union.

Yazov, like other party conservatives, believed that perestroika was weakening the system that had given him sustenance throughout his career. He was thus a leading member of the conspiracy that unfolded in the summer of 1991 to eliminate the reform process and the politicians who promoted it. Mistakenly believing that he had the support of low- and mid-level officers, he ordered military force to be used in the August coup attempt and was astounded when his orders were not obeyed. When the army refused to shoot the Muscovite citizens who had rallied around the headquarters of Boris Yeltsin's government, the coup was doomed. Along with the other conspirators, Yazov had inadvertently hastened the collapse of the system that he wanted to preserve. Yazov was arrested on August 21, 1991, and was charged with treason. He was dismissed as minister of defense on August 22 and held in the Matrosskaya Tishina Isolator prison, but he was eventually dismissed along with the other conspirators. Subsequently he has participated in anti-Yeltsin demonstrations and argued for the restoration of the USSR.

Boris N. Yeltsin (1931–   )

Boris N. Yeltsin is the first president of the post-Soviet Russian Federation, and he was an important figure in the collapse of Communism in the Soviet Union.

Yeltsin was born on February 1, 1931, in the village of Butka in Sverdlovsk oblast in the Ural Mountains area of northcentral Russia. His father was a peasant who turned to construction work to escape Stalin's collectivization. Growing up in an environment of construction work, Yeltsin decided to study civil engineering at Kirov Urals Polytechnical Institute, from which he graduated in 1955. Receiving practical experience through brief stints in a wide range of building trades, Yeltsin was hired by the Yuzhgorstroi trust, a governmental construction project, in 1955. He quickly rose through the ranks from foreman to head by 1963, and he joined the CPSU in 1961. From 1963 to 1968 he worked for the Sverdlovsk home construction combine, rising from chief engineer to head.

His party work began in 1968. In that year he began working for the regional branch of the CPSU in Sverdlovsk, and by 1974 he was elected a people's deputy to the USSR Supreme Soviet. In 1976 he became the regional first secretary in the Sverdlovsk party oblast committee. One of his responsibilities was the demolition (in 1977) of the state-owned site of the execution of Tsar Nicholas II and the imperial family, the Ipatiev house in Sverdlovsk. The site of the July 1918 execution was becoming a shrine for Russian nationalists and crypto-royalists (people who secretly sought to restore monarchy) and was therefore a national embarrassment to the Kremlin. Rewarded for his loyalty, Yeltsin was elevated to the elite, 300-member Central Committee in 1981. In 1984 he was also made a member of the 39-member Presidium of the Supreme Soviet, the USSR's highest parliamentary body.

When Mikhail Gorbachev was elected general secretary of the CPSU in 1985, Yeltsin became an early and unwavering supporter of perestroika. Sponsored by Yegor Ligachev, Yeltsin was called to Moscow by Gorbachev to help the reform process in March 1985. That June, Yeltsin became head of the construction department of the Central Committee's Secretariat. Gorbachev then appointed Yeltsin first secretary of the Moscow city Communist Party organization (the *gorkom*) in December and charged him with reforming the body. The Moscow party organization had become a focal point of corruption under Viktor Grishin, who commanded a following referred to as "Grishin's mafia" that stole money from city housing projects. Grishin had also challenged Gorbachev for overall leadership of the CPSU. Gorbachev forced Grishin's resignation under threat of prosecution.

Yeltsin began his new job enthusiastically, trying to end the corruption of the Moscow party machine and also trying to end the policy of providing excessive privileges to party apparatchiks. He gave up his own private car and dacha (summer cottage) and urged others to do the same. He preferred to take public transportation such as the subway or bus to emphasize that it was time for austerity measures within the party in order to improve the country's economy. Such behavior, in addition to his much-publicized hunt for corruption, was extremely popular with the citizens of Moscow. The slow pace of perestroika reforms, compared to Yeltsin's energetic local reforms in the national capital, helped his popularity and detracted from Gorbachev's base of support.

However, the party rank-and-file, as well as the apparatchiks, despised Yeltsin for his attempts to cut the privileges that they thought were their due. In March 1986 Yeltsin became a candidate member of the Politburo, the most powerful body in the Soviet system. The Politburo's 13 voting members determined the country's domestic and foreign policy, and Yeltsin was now poised to enter the highest level of Soviet leadership. However, his quarrels with the party became more bitter in 1987. Yeltsin and his one-time mentor, Ligachev, now disagreed and parted ways over reform issues. Ligachev set the stage for Yeltsin's removal from his positions of power in an October 1987 Politburo meeting in which he claimed that Yeltsin was dividing the party and opening it up to unnecessary and unfair criticisms from the nonparty public. This conflict brought on such stress that Yeltsin suffered a heart attack on November 9, 1987. Still weak from his heart attack, Yeltsin was brought before the Moscow party organization to explain himself on November 13. Soon thereafter the party stripped him of many of his powers, including his leadership of the Moscow party.

In February 1988 Yeltsin also was removed as a candidate member of the Politburo. However, he was so popular with the public that he could not be denied power altogether. In the era of glasnost, the party did not have the same options to crush dissent as it had in earlier years. Yeltsin was allowed to remain on the Central Committee, and he was granted a less illustrious position (but still an important one)—minister of the building industry. In June 1988 Yeltsin was elected as a delegate (from Karelia) to the nineteenth CPSU conference. Although some senior party leaders had tried to prevent his participation, they could not entirely stifle him in the glasnost era.

The nineteenth party conference was carried live on Soviet television, and Yeltsin was given the opportunity to present his position to the entire viewing public. His performance was masterful, as he requested that he be "rehabilitated"—and not posthumously—by the party and have his reputation restored. He received enormous public support as a result of his appearance at the conference. He also received positive foreign press coverage during the June 1988 visit to Moscow of U.S. president Ronald Reagan.

As a consequence of the national attention he received, Yeltsin had a larger following than most other politicians going into the March 1989 elections to the Congress of Peoples' Deputies. He ran in the Number One Constituency in Moscow, the nation's largest constituency, and won a staggering 89 percent of the vote (decisively beating the CPSU's official candidate). In the following July he became one of five co-chairmen of the "Inter-Regional Group" of the congress, which consisted of reform-minded deputies from throughout the union who wanted to decentralize the union government and transfer power to the various national republics. There were a number of economists who believed that political decentralization would be the most effective means of achieving the shift to a market economy (the goal of perestroika).

Yeltsin was thereafter elected to the Supreme Soviet, made chairman of the Committee for Construction and Architecture, and named a member of the Presidium of the Supreme Soviet. He had reascended the Soviet political hierarchy. In 1990, however, he began building a political base within the Russian Soviet Federated Socialist Republic. In March he was elected to the Russian republic's Congress of Peoples' Deputies for Sverdlovsk, and then he became speaker of the congress. He also became chairman of the Presidium of the Russian republic's Supreme Soviet (holding a position equivalent to a president).

Confident that these new positions reflected a new political reality—a kind of dual government—Yeltsin felt that the CPSU was now unnecessary. At the Twenty-Eighth Party Congress, Yeltsin walked out and publicly resigned from the party, along with other radicals (July 12, 1990). This earned Yeltsin even more public support in the Russian republic, because a good many citizens now regarded the corrupt and stagnant party apparatus as the biggest barrier to the success of market reform. In the fall of 1990 Yeltsin and the Russian republic's parliament declared a unilateral effort to enact market reforms within the borders of the Russian republic, claiming that Gorbachev had given up on substantive reform within the USSR.

A nationwide referendum was held within the USSR in March 1991 regarding the new union treaty that would decentralize the Soviet system. The referendum also contained specific questions in each of the republics that were of regional, rather than national, interest. In Russia, Yeltsin had a question inserted on the ballot concerning whether the Russian republic should have a directly elected presidency. The answer was overwhelmingly affirmative. Yeltsin was elected president of the Russian republic on June

12, 1991, with Alexander Rutskoi as his vice president. As the CPSU had its primary base of support in the Russian republic, and many members had followed Yeltsin's lead and resigned from the party in 1990–1991, the dissatisfied and fearful apparatchiks planning a coup against Gorbachev also decided to eliminate Yeltsin in August 1991.

Whereas the conspirators saw Gorbachev as a traitor and therefore their primary opponent, they viewed Yeltsin as an enormous threat to the party and the Soviet system of government. The Emergency Committee accordingly tried to seize control of the governments of both the USSR and the Russian republic. They gained the advantage over union president Gorbachev when they were able to place him under house arrest at his vacation home in Foros, Crimea, on August 18. The committee declared a state of emergency within the USSR, claiming that Gorbachev was ill and thus unable to carry out his duties as head of state.

The timing of the coup attempt relied on the the fact that Gorbachev was away on vacation and the new union treaty was not yet signed. However, Gorbachev's absence from Moscow placed a greater importance on neutralizing as quickly as possible Yeltsin's ability to resist. What the plotters did not realize, though, was the extent of Yeltsin's contacts with younger Russian military officers. During the crisis of August 19–20, Yeltsin urged soldiers and civilians to support Gorbachev, and tens of thousands of Yeltsin's supporters surrounded the headquarters of the Russian government, called the White House. At one point Yeltsin heroically climbed onto a tank and read his proclamations of resistance to the assembled crowd. Maintaining contact with the heads of the other republics, Yeltsin got assurances from them that they were in support of Gorbachev and opposed to the dictates of the Emergency Committee.

The critical moment came on the night of August 20 when the KGB Alpha Team refused orders to storm Yeltsin's headquarters. The coup fell apart at that point, and Rutskoi flew to the Crimea to bring Gorbachev back home. Following their return to Moscow, Rutskoi ordered the arrest of the coup plotters. While Gorbachev tried to salvage the union and the party, Yeltsin successfully dismantled both when he suspended the operations of the CPSU on Russian republic soil. Without the party, the USSR was doomed. Gorbachev stepped down as head of the party and dissolved it on August 24, after he realized the extent of popular support for the attempted coup within the ranks of the party. Yeltsin and Gorbachev negotiated the Minsk Agreement with the other republics of the union on December 8, and on December 25 the USSR officially gave way to a loose confederation of sovereign states, the Commonwealth of Independent States.

Yeltsin has been president of the Russian Federation since the collapse of the USSR. He has tried to implement market reforms despite a host of difficulties: lingering Soviet-era infrastructure problems in manufacturing and agriculture; the infiltration of businesses by organized crime syndicates; and an inability to collect tax revenues. He has maintained stable diplomatic relations with neighboring members of the CIS, and he has enjoyed the assistance of the United States and NATO in keeping watch over the dispersed former Soviet nuclear arsenal. His seemingly uncompromising stand in his quarrel with parliament (1992–1993) harmed his domestic image, as did Russian military intervention in the Caucasian autonomous republic of Chechniya (1994–1996). In his June 1996 reelection bid he won a narrow margin over a wide field of competitors, but the Communist Gennady Zyuganov was close enough (32 percent to Yeltsin's 35 percent) that a runoff election had to be held in July. Yeltsin managed to gain a decisive victory over Zyuganov in the runoff because of lingering fears of Communist government held by a majority of the Russian population. He remains unpopular, however, among a sizable percentage of the Russian population, who blame him personally for the country's economic hard times. His future success may well depend on the country's economy. He is challenged by the need to change the economic infrastructure and make use of the country's vast natural resources, many of which are in Siberia. He also must maintain stable relations with fellow members of the CIS and Russia's own minority national republics.

Gennady A. Zyuganov (1944–   )

Gennady Zyuganov is the leader of the Communist Party of the Russian Federation (CPRF) and was a major challenger to Boris Yeltsin in the 1996 presidential elections in Russia.

He was born in the village of Mymrino in Orel oblast on June 26, 1944, to parents who were schoolteachers, although neither belonged to the Communist Party. After completing high school Zyuganov coached youth sports teams and then entered Orel Pedagogical Institute, but he joined the military in 1963 before graduating. He joined the CPSU while in the military. Returning to study mathematics at the Pedagogical Institute in 1966, he became involved in Komsomol work. After graduating he became a mathematics instructor and also began working within the regional hierarchy of the CPSU in Orel oblast. He became head of the Department of Agitation and Propaganda in the regional branch of the party.

In 1983 Zyuganov was brought to Moscow to work as an instructor in the CPSU's Central Committee's ideological department. When the era of perestroika began, however, Zyuganov was so dissatisfied with the reform process that he joined a hard-line Communist splinter group—the Russian Communist Party. He was elected to the post of secretary of the Central Committee (one of only seven secretaries on the committee).

Zyuganov teamed up with ultra-nationalist writer and editor Alexander

Prokhanov and others to sign an open letter in July 1991 entitled "A Word to the People," which attacked Gorbachev and the reform process. However, he was not important enough within the Communist hierarchy at that time to be involved in the coup preparations during the following month. When Gorbachev was placed under house arrest in Foros, Crimea, Zyuganov happened to be on vacation also at a nearby party-owned home. He was thus removed from the events unfolding in Moscow, although he was in sympathy with the attempted coup.

After the collapse of the coup attempt, Zyuganov was involved in the grassroots effort to revive the party. Yeltsin outlawed the CPSU and any Communist organization on Russian soil, but the Russian courts reinstated the legality of a Communist party within the Russian republic. Soon thereafter the Communist Party of the Russian Federation (CPRF) was created, and Zyuganov became its head. When Yeltsin's quarrels with the hard-liners in the Russian parliament became violent in October 1993, Zyuganov appealed for peace and subsequently received more attention on the national level. His CPRF won 181 seats in the December 1995 parliamentary elections, which was by far the largest single bloc of seats (some 32 percent). He became the CPRF candidate for the June 1996 Russian presidential elections and scored far ahead of Yeltsin in the February tally of Russian public opinion (14 percent for Zyuganov, only 4 percent for Yeltsin). At that time CPRF membership was realistically estimated to be some 500,000, but many members were elderly former CPSU members who resented the loss of their former privileges and the pensions to which they felt entitled. Yeltsin's campaign operatives, however, had much greater resources at their disposal than Zyuganov and the CPRF had, and Yeltsin managed to win the June primary by a narrow margin (35 percent to 32 percent). In the runoff election in July, however, Yeltsin's campaign linked Zyuganov with Russia's terrible Communist past and easily won the election. Zyuganov still hopes that Communism will be restored in Russia and that the USSR will be reconstructed, but as his constituents continue to age, that scenario becomes increasingly unlikely.

Primary Documents of the Collapse of Communism

One
GORBACHEV ON PERESTROIKA

In *Perestroika* (1987), Mikhail Gorbachev explained his reform program to Soviet citizens and the world at large. The passages excerpted here discuss the need for reform of the Soviet system, the manner in which Gorbachev expected such reform to occur, and the role of the Communist Party of the Soviet Union (CPSU).

Perestroika is an urgent necessity arising from the profound processes of development in our society. This society is ripe for change. It has long been yearning for it. Any delay in beginning perestroika could have led to an exacerbated internal situation in the near future, which, to put it bluntly, would have been fraught with serious social, economic and political crises. . . .

Accustomed to giving priority to quantitative growth in production, we tried to check the falling rates of growth, but did so mainly by continually increasing expenditures: we built up the fuel and energy industries and increased the use of natural resources in production.

As time went on, material resources became harder to get and more expensive. On the other hand, the extensive methods of fixed capital expansion resulted in an artificial shortage of manpower. In an attempt to rectify the situation somehow, large, unjustified, i.e. in fact unearned, bonuses began to be paid and all kinds of undeserved incentives introduced under the pressure of this shortage, and that led, at a later stage, to the practice of padding reports merely for gain. Parasitical attitudes were on the rise, the prestige of conscientious and high-quality labor began to diminish and a "wage-leveling" mentality was becoming widespread. The imbalance between the measure of work and the measure of consumption, which had become something like the linchpin of the braking mechanism, not only obstructed the growth of labor productivity, but led to the distortion of the principle of social justice.

So the inertia of extensive economic development was leading to an economic deadlock and stagnation.

The economy was increasingly squeezed financially. The sale of large quantities of oil and other fuel and energy resources and raw materials on the world market did not help. It only aggravated the situation. Currency earnings thus made were predominantly used for tackling problems of the moment rather than on economic modernization or on catching up technologically.

Declining rates of growth and economic stagnation were bound to affect other aspects of the life of Soviet society. Negative trends seriously affected the social sphere. This led to the appearance of the so-called "residual principle" in accordance with which social and cultural programs received what remained in the budget after allocations to production. A "deaf ear" sometimes seemed to be turned to social problems. The social sphere began to lag behind other spheres in terms of technological development, personnel, know-how and, most importantly, quality of work....

The CPSU congresses hold a special place in our history, making as it were, milestones on our way. For many reasons the 27th Congress had to give answers to the most urgent issues of the life of Soviet society. The time for holding it was determined by the Party Rules. The preparation of a new edition of the Party Program was under way, and the plans for the Twelfth Five-Year-Plan period and for the period ending in the year 2000 were being drawn up. The difficulty was that the political directives for the Congress began to be shaped in conditions which changed dramatically after the 1985 March and April Plenary Meetings of the CPSU Central Committee. New processes had begun both within the Party itself and in society as a whole....

The 27th Congress adopted major resolutions which are of tremendous importance for the future of the USSR. It formulated the guidelines for the Party's work to implement the concept of acceleration of social and economic development advanced by the April Plenary Meeting of the Central Committee. Yes, it was a congress to which its delegates brought not only their concerns and truth but also their thoughts, plans and determination to give a fresh and powerful impetus to the development of socialism.

It was a courageous congress. We spoke openly about the shortcomings, errors and difficulties. We emphasized the untapped potential of socialism, and the Congress adopted a detailed long-term plan of action. It became a congress of strategic decisions.

But at the time we failed or were just unable to fully realize the dramatic character and scope of the processes under way. Now we can see better, and it is clear that we have to resolutely continue the work started in the pre-Congress period and at the Congress itself, and simultaneously to study more deeply the society we live in. To do this, we had to return to the sources, to the roots, to better assess the past, and to decide on our priorities and on ways to accomplish them. Without understanding this we could lose our way.

Even nearly a year after the 27th Congress some people in various strata of society and in the Party itself continued to think that perestroika was not a long-term policy but just another campaign. Many local officials kept the active supporters of perestroika in check, warning those of them who were too demanding: wait, comrades, don't make a fuss, and everything will blow over in a year or two. They sincerely believed that everything would go full circle, as had been the case more than once before. There were also self-styled skeptics who would chuckle in the office corridors: we've been through different periods, and we'll live through this one as well. . . .

In preparing the Plenary Meeting, the Politburo spent several months examining the results of a comprehensive and strictly objective analysis of the activities of the Council of Ministers of the USSR, Gosplan[1], Gossnab[2], Minfin[3], Gosbank[4], economic ministries and departments and industrial management bodies. Ordinances were drafted to govern the operation of central agencies so as to make it (and their official functions) strictly consistent with the Law on the State Enterprise, not contradict it in any way. They were discussed at the Plenary Meeting, finalized, adopted and implemented.

The June Plenary Meeting of the CPSU Central Committee, its decisions, and the "Basic Provisions for Radical Restructuring of Economic Management" it adopted, are, in effect, completing the construction of a modern *model* of socialist economy to meet the challenge of the present stage of national development.

The Plenary Meeting and the session of the Supreme Soviet of the USSR that followed it developed and consolidated the policy of promoting the people's active involvement in economic and production processes, closely

[1]*Gosplan (USSR State Planning Committee)*—a government agency in charge of long-term and current planning of the country's economic and social development and control over the fulfillment of those plans.

[2]*Gossnab*—USSR State Committee for Material and Technical Supply, a government agency.

[3]*Minfin*—USSR Ministry of Finance.

[4]*Gosbank*—State Bank of the USSR, the country's main bank.

combining the interests of the state with those of the individual and the work collective, and of making the Soviet working people the true master.

Of course, we will still have things to complete or, perhaps, re-do. No society can ever have any system of economic management replaced overnight by a different, even a more advanced one, as if it were a kind of mechanical contrivance. We will have to adjust a dynamic and flexible mechanism sensitive to changes in production and capable of being constantly modernized, accepting what is advanced and rejecting what has outlined itself. The main danger here is stopping the belief that since decisions have been taken they will always be relevant in their present form. . . .

In the course of perestroika a new concept of democratic centralism is taking shape. It is important to have its two sides correctly balanced, bearing in mind that at different stages different aspects will be highlighted.

The situation now stands as follows: there are many people who are calling for stronger centralism. Balance sheets, proportions, the need for incomes to correspond to the mass of commodities and volume of services, structural policies, state finances, defense—all these require a firm centralized principle. All our republics and all our peoples should feel that they are placed in equal conditions and have equal opportunities for development. In this lies the guarantee of Soviet society's stability. That is why we do not want to weaken the role of the center, because otherwise we would lose the advantages of the planned economy. . . .

We started perestroika in a situation of growing international tension. The *détente* of the 1970s was, in effect, curtailed. Our calls for peace found no response in the ruling quarters of the West. Soviet foreign policy was skidding. The arms race was spiraling anew. The war threat was increasing.

In ascertaining how to achieve a turn for the better, one had to ask the following questions. Why is this happening? What juncture has the world approached in its development? To do this we had to cast a sober and realistic glance at the world panorama, to get rid of the force of habit in our thinking. As we say in Russia, to look at things "with a fresh eye."

What is the world we all live in like, this world of the present generations of humankind? It is diverse, variegated, dynamic and permeated with opposing trends and acute contradictions. It is a world of fundamental social shifts, of an all-embracing scientific and technological revolution, of worsening global problems—problems concerning ecology, natural resources, etc.—and of radical changes in information technology. It is a world in which unheard-of possibilities for development and progress lie side by side with abject poverty, backwardness and medievalism. It is a world in which there are vast "fields of tension."

Everything was a great deal simpler many years ago. There existed several powers which determined their interests and balanced them if they so managed, and warred if they failed. International relations were built on the balance of the interests of these several powers. This is one domain, that is another, and that one is still another. But have a look at what has happened over the forty postwar years to the present.

The political tableau of the world includes the sizable group of socialist countries which have gone a long way in their progressive development over not so long a history; the vast tract of developed capitalist states with their own interests, with their own history, concerns and problems; and the ocean of Third World countries which emerged in the past thirty to forty years when scores of Asian, African and Latin American countries gained independence.

It seems obvious that every group of states and every country has interests of its own. From the viewpoint of elementary logic, all these interests should find a reasonable reflection in world politics. But this is not so. I have more than once told my interlocutors from the capitalist countries: let us see and take into account the realities—there is the world of capitalism and the world of socialism, and there is also a huge world of developing countries. The latter is the home of millions of people. All countries have their problems. But the developing countries have a hundred times more than other states and this should be taken into consideration. These countries have their own national interests. For decades they were colonies, stubbornly fighting for their liberation. Having gained independence, they want to improve their peoples' lives, to use their resources as they like, and to build an independent economy and culture.

Is there a hope for normal and just international relations, proceeding exclusively from the interests of, say, the Soviet Union or the United States, Britain or Japan? No! A balance of interests is needed. For the time being, no such balance exists. For now the rich get richer and the poor get poorer. Processes which could shake the entire system of international relations are, however, taking place in the Third World.

No one can close down the world of socialism, the developing world or the world of developed capitalism. But there exists the view that socialism is an accident of history and one long overdue for the ash-heap. Then the Third World would become tame and everything would return full cycle, and prosperity would again be possible at the expense of others. An escape into the past is no reply to the challenges of the future, being merely adventurism based on fear and diffidence.

Two
THE AFGHAN CLUBS: OVERCOMING OFFICIAL
SILENCE ON THE AFGHAN WAR

Brezhnev-era dissident and historian Roy Medvedev coauthored *Time of Change* with Giulietto Chiesa in 1989, calling the book an "insider's view on Russia's transformation." Medvedev was expelled from the Communist Party in the 1960s, and his writings were suppressed within the USSR. He was readmitted to the Communist Party during Gorbachev's tenure, and his writings were finally published in the USSR. In the following passage Medvedev answers a question posed by Chiesa about the unsuccessful attempt by Soviet leaders prior to Gorbachev to keep the Soviet public uninformed about the war in Afghanistan.

In Brezhnev's time no one in the USSR wrote about Afghanistan. From the Soviet press you might even get the idea that our troops were not engaged in combat. How much of the territory was controlled by government troops and how much by the enemy was unknown. The relatives of the soldiers who died there received the news with the words "died in fulfilling international duty." But this could have been anywhere, in Africa or on the border with China. Official figures on the dead and wounded were not known; it was easier to make a list of what you didn't know. Western observers were equally uninformed, including those who risked their lives by entering into Afghanistan as part of a guerrilla incursion. The country's domestic politics were also difficult to analyze because of the lack of information. In recent years the amount of news in the mass media began to increase, but so did the number of young men—hundreds of thousands—who did their military service in Afghanistan, came back, and got together in Afghan clubs where they told other people about their experiences there.

Excerpted from Roy A. Medvedev and Giulietto Chiesa, *Time of Change*, trans. Michael Moore (New York: Pantheon, 1989), p. 275.

Three
THE ECONOMIC CHALLENGE OF PERESTROIKA

Abel Aganbegyan, Gorbachev's economic advisor, was one of the principal figures behind perestroika. His book entitled *The Economic Challenge of Perestroika* (1988) explained the need for economic reform and the mechanisms for change in the Soviet system. However, his argument for reform was put forth tentatively, to prevent alarm among the party hard-liners. The following passage from the book is entitled "Efficiency as the Driving Force of *Perestroika*" (Chapter 3).

One of the hardest problems to solve in the acceleration of the socio-economic development of the country, is that this must be achieved in circumstances of a falling growth of natural productive resources. This process started in the 1971–75 plan period. Let us consider the tendencies of Soviet economic development since the 1970s (see Table 4 below).

This shows that the 1971–75 period was the last in which there was a significant growth in productive resources. In this respect it was a five-year period that was typical of the whole post-war period of Soviet economic development. In the three five-year periods between 1956 and 1970, productive resources increased in roughly the same degree as in the 1971–75 period. Projections for the future show that 1971–75 was the last period in our generation with high growth in productive resources. More recently growth rate of productive resources has greatly decreased. Above all, beginning in the 1981–85 period the growth of labour resources was falling and thereby the number of workers in the branches of production. Normally over a five-year period the population of working age (in the Soviet Union this is from 16–55 years for women and up to 60 for men) increased by ten and eleven million. In the past five-year period the growth in the

Table Four
Development of the USSR economy, resources and efficiency, 1971–85:
percentage change over five-year periods (official figures)

| | Five-year plan periods | | |
| | IX | X | XI |
Indicators	1971–75	1976–80	1981–85
Global indicators			
National income	28	21	16.5
Real per capita income	24	18	11
Productive resources			
Basic productive funds	52	43	37
Productive capital investment	44	23	17
Production of mining industry	25	10	8
Number of workers in all branches of production	6	6	2
Efficiency of national production[1]			
Capital output ratio	−16	−15	−15
Efficiency of capital investment	−11	−2	−0.5
Efficiency of use of industrial material inputs[1]	2	10	8
Productivity of labour	21	14	14

Note: [1]Index of efficiency calculated in relation to index of national income according to official statistics.

labour force even exceeded this figure, because of higher participation rates in the labour market. (While in the 1960s for every 100 people of working age roughly 18 were not employed, the proportion is now 8 to 9 per 100.) Out of the additional labour force in the 1961–70 period four and a half million workers went into manufacturing industry, approximately one million into construction, one million into transport, up to two million into trade and supply, two million into state farms (there was actual decline in the membership of collective farms), roughly two to three million into the health service, education, culture and science, and up to one million into housing and services.

From 1981 to 1985 the Soviet Union entered a demographic slump directly reflecting the consequences of World War Two. In the 1980s the children of parents born during the war are coming of working age. The birth rate fell during the war and the number of adult parents, and thus their children, is consequently smaller than for other generations. Also from the mid-1980s the numbers of persons reaching pensionable age was rising sharply. Up to now the proportion of men who fought in the war and had become pensioners was relatively small as many of this generation perished. The post-war generations—correspondingly two, three and even five times larger—are now reaching pensionable age. These two trends are coinciding. Therefore the growth in numbers of persons of working age in the population is falling sharply. Instead of the former normal increase of ten to eleven million workers, in the 1981–85 period it was three and a half million only and in the current period, 1986–90—the demographically most acute years—it was about two and a half million.

It should also be noted that the rates of growth of the working population in the periods 1981–90 are mainly occurring because of an increase in the size of populations in Central Asia and Azerbaidzhan. These are regions far from the territories occupied during the war and where the traditionally high birth rate was maintained. In Russia, the Ukraine, Belorussia and the Baltic republics the size of the working population in the 1980s will not increase at all and in certain regions it will fall.

All this is leading to a decline in the number of workers employed in branches of production. This fall is occurring at an even greater pace because of the redeployment of the population into the service sectors. Therefore in the 1981–85 period the number of workers employed in industry rose overall by one million and in agriculture by less than half a million. In construction the figure hardly grew, in transport it rose by only half a million, in commerce by half a million but in health and education by more than a million. The falling growth in the number of workers requires increases in labour productivity. If earlier 20%–25% of all growth in social production was achieved through increased numbers of workers, and 75%–80% through higher productivity than in the 1981–85 period the element of productivity growth was 90% and the impact of the number of workers fell to 10%.

Simultaneously growth in productive capital investment has declined more than two and a half times and growth of overall productive resources has slowed down. This is connected with the reduction in the proportion of capital accumulation in the national income as a consequence of the increased share of resources going to consumption. This share has increased from 71% in 1970 to 75% in 1985; the accumulation fund declined correspondingly from 29% to 25%. This redistribution within the national income was connected with the wish to find additional resources for raising the standard of living. It was necessary to raise the efficiency of productive capital investment and therefore to improve the capital output ratio since only this would sustain the required rate of growth of the national income in conditions of declining productive resources. But it is obvious from the indicators shown that this has only been partially achieved, through stabilising the efficiency of capital investment. At the same time the capital output ratio continued to worsen against the slow growth of resource inputs.

The growth in the extraction of fuel and raw materials has fallen even more, by three times. This fall is mainly the result of worsening geological and economic conditions in the mining industries. The quantities of fuel and raw materials extracted in the USSR are immense. In 1985 for example, 615 million tonnes of oil, 686 billion cubic metres of gas, 751 million tonnes of coal, 112 million tonnes of iron ore were extracted in the USSR and 295 million cubic metres of timber prepared. With such rates of extraction, good deposits and favourable fields are rapidly becoming exhausted, and to maintain these rates of extraction it is necessary to transfer to new more difficult deposits, deeper fields and worse conditions. Thus the yield of oil and the extraction of iron ore are falling and mining for coal and precious metals has to be done at greater and greater depths.

In the Soviet Union the centres of production are not evenly distributed. More than 70% of production and the corresponding population are situated in the European part of the USSR and in the Urals. It is here that most resources are consumed. Yet these regions make up less than a quarter of the territory of the USSR with only one tenth of the reserves of fuel, only one quarter of the forests, a fifth of water resources etc. A large proportion of resources are concentrated in Siberia and the Soviet Far East—more than four fifths of the fuel reserves, three quarters of the timber and, if one takes into account the flow of rivers, three quarters of all fresh water. (This excludes Lake Baikal which represents 80% of Soviet resources and 20% of the world's supply of fresh water.) At the same time Siberia and the Far East account for only one tenth of production and population. Kazakhstan and Central Asia occupy as much as one third of the land area of the country. They are rich in mineral resources, have large populations (one sixth of the total USSR population), and a high proportion of Soviet agricultural production. But these regions have only 5% of the river waters and practically no timber.

When the level of development of the economy was still relatively low, the intensive processing of fuel and raw materials in the inhabited European part of the country ensured the development of the economy in these regions. Coal came mostly from the Don region, oil from the Volga and Baku, timber from the northern regions of the European part of the country and the Urals, precious minerals were mined in the Kola Peninsula, the Urals and the Caucasus etc. But the needs of the growing economy increased the demand for fuel and raw materials. By the mid-1970s the flow of fuel and raw materials extracted in the European part of the USSR could not grow any further. Additional requirements were met primarily by the rapid development of the extraction industry in Siberia. In the 1976–85 period, despite the fact that capital investment increased, oil extraction in the Volga region began to fall, coal from the Don coal fields fell, as did the preparation of timber in the northern regions and the Urals. Nickel extraction on the Kola Peninsula stopped completely, nickel being brought to the Kola enterprises from Norilsk by the northern sea route.

All this required the transfer of mining to the uninhabited regions of the east and north. In Western Siberia, mainly the Tyumen Region, in the mid-1960s an oil and gas complex was created as the main fuel and energy base of the USSR. Timber production increasingly moved to Eastern Siberia and the Far East. The extraction of precious metal ores was significantly expanded there also; for example in Norilsk, situated further north than the Arctic circle in Krasnoyarsk Province. The establishment of new fuel and mineral bases necessitated the development of these regions, the construction of transport and communication systems, the creation of towns and the transfer of hundreds of thousands of people. Suffice it to say that more than one and a half million people moved to West Siberia from other parts of the country. In the 1981–85 period on average about ten billion roubles of capital investment was made there each year, as much as the whole costs of the 3,000km Baikal-Amur link. With such resources three enormous Volga-type car factories could be built, with an annual production of more than 700,000 vehicles.

All this led to serious increases in the prices of fuel and raw materials, particularly as the result of the high capital investment incurred. While 20–25 years ago one rouble of production in the extraction industry required two roubles of capital investment, by 10 years ago this figure had grown to three to four roubles of capital investment and in the 1981–85 period it exceeded seven roubles. Production costs grew for many types of raw materials as did the labour intensity needed for their extraction. A further price increase occurred through the tightening up of ecological and safety requirements in mining. In these conditions it is more advantageous to concentrate on measures designed to economise in the use of raw materials than on additional extraction. It requires two to two and a half times less resources to save one tonne of fuel in the USSR by economising than it does to mine an extra tonne.

Here it should be noted that the previous low prices of fuel and raw materials and their abundance in the USSR led on many occasions to the most extravagant use. This is still the case now because of the low prices for fuel and raw materials, which are usually two to three times lower than the world price. Therefore the Soviet Union has a large potential for economies in the use of fuel and raw materials as a part of a resource conservation policy.

As is evident major *perestroika* was necessary in many directions, and especially a change from extensive to intensive development. This has not yet occurred, although there have been some successes in this area. If one compares the three recent five-year periods then it is obvious that in the 1971–75 period efficiency of production was increased mainly through higher productivity. However, this result suffered to a considerable extent by the worsening of the capital output ratio and the efficiency of capital investment, the more so since the rates of consumption of materials in production hardly fell.

In the 1976–80 and 1981–85 periods better use of industrial raw materials was achieved and a slight decline occurred in the consumption of materials in production. At the same time the indicator of efficiency of capital investment was static. The rates of growth of productivity in the past could not be maintained, indeed they fell substantially. Thus the rate of growth of productivity in industry fell from 34% in the 1971–75 period to 17% in the 1976–80 period and the same low rate was repeated in 1981–85. Over the same period, there was a decline in the growth of productivity in all other sectors—construction, transport and agriculture.

We will try to present in a general way the ongoing tendencies of development. For this let us recall that labour lies at the base of all productive resources. At any time the basic fund of capital investment which is created by labour is being used up in the extraction of fuel and raw materials and the production of equipment, in construction and assembly work. Since at the basis of any productive resource there is in the end only labour, it is possible to conflate indicators of these various resources into one measure, which we can call an index of efficiency in the use of resources (see Table 5).

A small advance was achieved in the 1976–85 periods with a larger contribution to growth through intensive factors. However these could not compensate for a still larger decline in the use of productive resources, leading to a consequent fall in the speed of economic development.

In the 1986–90 period and in the following years the growth of productive resources will fall further and the average index will hardly grow more

Table Five
Indices of efficiency in the USSR economy, 1971–85: percentage growth per five-year period (official figures except where indicated)

| Indicators | Five-year periods | | |
	IX 1971–75	X 1976–80	XI 1981–85 (forecast)
National income	28	21	16.5
Productive resources*	21	13	9
Efficiency of productions*	6	7	7
Contribution of factors of economic growth in the rise in national income			
extensive %	75	67	60
intensive %	25	33	40

*Our estimate

than 7% in the period 1986–1990 (compared with 10% in 1981–85, 13% in 1976–80 and 21% in 1971–75). In the following five-year period after 1990 growth will fall to 5%–6% for the following reasons:

1) The 1986–90 period coincides with the least favourable post-war demographic period mentioned above and no growth is expected in the number of workers in production. For the first time in the history of the Soviet Union all growth in production must be realised through increased labour productivity.

As early as 1986, the first year of the current five year period, the number of workers in all branches of production has only increased by a total of 0.3%. In manufacturing it also increased by 0.3%. At the same time in agriculture and railway transport the growth in productivity has outstripped growth of production and the number of workers has substantially fallen.

In the first few months of 1987 growth in the number of workers in production came to an end and all growth of production in industry and in other branches is occurring through increased productivity. In the future, considering the need to redeploy large numbers of people into health, education, housing and other branches of the service sector, the number of workers in industry, agriculture, construction and transport will have to fall; and this can only come about as a result of more rapid growth of productivity than in the volume of production in these branches.

2) Because of the existing structure of the economy and the shortfall in investment in certain branches (machine building, construction, metallurgy) capital investment will barely grow beyond 25% in the five years. This planned growth of capital investment in the 1986–90 period seems greater than it was in the 1981–85 period (17%), although it is less than

in all the preceding five-year periods (28% in 1976–80, 43% in 1971–75). A slight increase in the growth of capital investment in the 1986–90 period compared with the 1981–85 period derives primarily from the necessity for considerable investment in the reconstruction of existing enterprises to create conditions for the acceleration of scientific technological progress.

At the same time capital investment is increasing in fuel and energy where there was a shortfall in the past and in branches of the production infrastructure. As has been mentioned, the proportion for the social sector is also rising in the total volume of capital investment in the economy.

How will this accelerated increase of capital investment be ensured? One of the main sources is the higher growth of final output in the 1986–90 period compared with the 1981–85 period resulting from the acceleration of the country's socio-economic development. On the other hand in the 1986–90 period, no decline is envisaged in the proportion of accumulation in the national income. It is possible that it will even grow slightly.

3) With the worsening of geological and economic conditions the tendency towards limited growth in the extraction of fuel and raw materials will persist, although in the 1986–90 period the mobilisation of reserves will mean an improvement in the rate of growth in some branches of the mining industry. We have managed to overcome a decline in the development of the oil industry. Having achieved a maximum extraction in 1983 of 616 million tonnes, extraction then fell to 595 million tonnes in 1985. The growth rate of extraction fell even in Western Siberia, where it was until recently rising rapidly, making up for the shortfall from older deposits. After the 1985 Party Management Conference, serious measures were taken in the city of Tyumen to open up new deposits, to intensify oil extraction, to mechanise the industry and to increase drilling etc. In the intervening two years an additional thirty-six oil wells were sunk in Western Siberia, more than in the whole previous period. All this made it possible to overcome the unfavourable tendencies in Western Siberia. In one year, 1986, the increase in the extraction of oil in the Soviet Union was 20 million tonnes and in 1987 growth in oil extraction was continuing.

The same negative tendency in the coal industry has been overcome. While in the whole of the 1981–85 period the volume of coal extracted grew by only 10 million tonnes, in 1986 alone it rose by 25 million. Natural gas extraction is being stepped up. The volume of extraction is growing at an unprecedented rate. Gas is replacing fuel oil and in large towns also replacing coal with a view to improving the environment. This is helping to intensify technological progress in industry, to improve the environment and to switch to gas for a large part of the fuel and energy balance of the Soviet Union. Thanks to the enormous gas pipeline construction a nation-wide gas network is gradually being laid down.

It has also been possible to overcome the decline in the timber industry. In the preceding five-year period the volume of output was static, but has

Table Six
National income and resources of the USSR: 11th five-year period (1981–85) and future projections for the 12th, 13th and 14th periods up to the year 2000: percentage growth per five-year period (official figures except where indicated)

Indicator	XI 1981–85	XII 1986–90 (forecast)	XIII & XIV 1991–2000 (average 5-year projection)
National income	16.5	22	28
Productive resources*	9	7	5–6
Efficiency of production*	7	14	10
Impact of categories of economic growth on the rise in the national income			
extensive%	60	33	25
intensive%	40	67	75

*Our estimate

been rising since 1986. But these successes in additional extraction of certain raw materials do not make it possible to stave off the general tendency to falling growth rates in the extractive industries. This tendency will appear even more clearly in the 1990s.

The limited increases in extensive factors in economic growth cannot be relied upon to achieve acceleration of the socio-economic development of the country. The economy must move decisively and rapidly to intensive development and to the acceleration of efficiency through better use of resources. The situation which has arisen during the 1981–85 period and projections for the future are shown in Table 6 above.

To accelerate the annual rate of growth of the national income from 3% to 4% the rate of growth in efficiency needs to be doubled, ensuring that the five-year growth rate rises from 7% to 14%. Such an increase in efficiency can only be achieved if the rate of growth of productivity is increased one and a half times, if the rate of use of material resources in production is halved and the capital output ratio is improved two and a half times compared with the indicators of the 1981–85 period.

In the last 15 years the efficiency indicator of the economy in each five-year period rose by roughly 7%. The economy continued, through inertia, to develop extensively. In the new conditions, these tendencies in economic development are to be overcome and the whole of the economy is to be steered onto the path of intensive methods so as to achieve a marked acceleration in socio-economic development. The most important reserve for increasing economic and social efficiency in the whole economy and the means also to accelerate socio-economic development lies in improving the quality of production. At the XXVII Party Congress the importance was clearly recognised of placing the improvement of quality in production at the centre of all economic policy. "Quality and again quality" is our slogan for today. Only having solved the problem of quality, can the problem of quantity be resolved? Although questions of raising the quality of production were repeatedly posed earlier, it is especially important now to turn attention to this key problem for our economic management. It should be noted that quality is a good general index of efficiency. Material resources and social labour which are used up in low quality production and even in defective production are resources wasted as the products fail to meet social needs. Improving the quality is therefore the only possible way to end the shortages in the economy.

The problem of quality is particularly obvious if one considers a product's life cycle. Take for example machines and tools. The matter does not end with the investment of energy, material and labour in the making of the machine. After this, during the use of the machine further expenditure is needed. In the case of a tractor or a car, the investment during the production process may make up 3%–4% of the aggregate cost borne by society during its working life. The rest consists of maintenance costs, running costs, spare parts and many other things. Cost depends directly on the quality of production. Spending an extra 50 roubles on a new tractor model to improve its reliability can mean an annual saving of about 500 roubles. This is a fairly typical example. High quality is a decisive factor in increasing efficiency in production.

Indivisibly linked to the problem of quality is the question of the breadth of re-equipment, especially in relation to machinery and tools. Machines cannot be operated without tools and jigs and if, having bought the machine itself, a factory does not obtain the equipment to go with it the machine will stand idle. To an even greater extent this is true in the case of computer technology, when it is set up without all the necessary additional hardware and full software. Machinery can produce high quality results only if it is set up properly and is put immediately to work. There is a great potential in the country for improvement of quality, but to make a radical improvement, it is necessary to work hard in perfecting production and the related technology, to increase the qualifications of the personnel, and to adapt the planning, management and incentive systems to achieve all this.

To achieve high efficiency and quality there lies ahead for us the implementation of a whole system of crucial economic management measures, aimed at the acceleration of socio-economic development. These measures can be divided into two groups.

Firstly, there are measures for mobilising organisational, economic and social reserves and the potential for better use of available resources. To have an impact, these measures, as a rule, do not require capital investment and can be achieved in the short term. But such reserves and their potential are limited.

Secondly, the more significant and more profound potential lies in scientific and technological progress and therefore this represents a major
strategic element in the acceleration of socio-economic development.

The resolution of both requirements depends to a certain extent on the
creation of new economic and organisational conditions during a major
perestroika of the planning and management of the whole economic system.

The hardest period will be that running from 1986 to 1990, when we
face two tasks. The first is to accelerate the current rate of socio-economic
development. The second is to prepare conditions for large scale acceleration in the following five-year periods (1991–2000). Thus in the 1986–
90 period we will not yet be able to use scientific and technological factors
to the full in order to raise efficiency because time is needed to renew
capital and to change the structure of production for introducing new machinery and new technology.

Here is an example. For about 20 years petrol-driven goods vans with
not very powerful engines have been produced at the Gorky Car Factory.
A new model, the GAZ-6308, has been prepared: with a more powerful
diesel engine and a fuel consumption of 14 litres per 100km (compared
with 19 litres for the current model) as well as a trailer of 8.5mt (instead
of 4.5mt). Expected mileage was raised from 250 to 350 thousand km
before capital repairs are needed, and maintenance costs reduced by one
and a half times. The productivity of drivers is set to rise on average 1.7
times. The state commission, when approving the new model, noted that
the new vehicles represent an annual saving to the national economy of
393 million roubles, i.e. a colossal saving. When can this be expected?
Mass production lines have to be converted, i.e. a diesel factory costing
800 million roubles built and a further 500 million roubles spent on refit-
ting and reconstruction. Recovering this outlay will take only about three
years. From 1988 production of these machines should begin (the first
stage of reconstruction) but the real effect will be felt only when old vehicles are replaced on a large scale by the new, i.e. in the 1991–95 period,
and the greatest effect will be felt in the period up to the year 2000 (the
second stage of reconstruction).

Are there sufficient reserves to increase the efficiency of the existing
productive base through better attitudes to work and higher productivity,
through higher quality production, economies in use of materials and resources etc.? That is the question. There are numerous examples testifying
to the enormous potential offered in the short term by raising productivity,
economising in fuel and raw materials, improving the indicators of the
capital-output ratio and efficiency of capital investment. Every economic
organisation has such reserves, and significant progress can be made if
each can be involved and the interests of working collectives harnessed.

According to economists' estimates it is possible to raise the rate of growth of the national income by these means in the order of 1.3 to 1.5 times and to accelerate the growth of productivity and other indices of efficiency one and a half to two times. This is shown by the current experience of the other socialist countries where a decision to use existing resources better by perfecting the economic system has been consistently pursued. The Soviet experience of economic reform in 1965 showed the same.

Let us recall that in the 1966–70 period the rate of socio-economic growth fell substantially and negative tendencies arose because of errors that were made. Thus the official rate of growth of national income fell: in 1960 it was 8%, in 1961 7%, in 1962 6% and in 1963 4%. The capital-output ratio, and efficiency of capital investment also worsened. Use of fuel and raw materials increased. The rate of growth of productivity sharply declined. In consequence the rate of growth of real income slowed down and the supply of foodstuffs and industrial products deteriorated.

The October 1964 Plenary of the Central Committee renewed the leadership and made major changes to the system of planning, management and incentives. The ministries and related management structures were reestablished, and the role of centralised planning and of the Central Planning Office was increased. The March 1965 meeting of the Central Committee introduced a new form of planning and a new economic system for agriculture, upgrading this crucially important sector of the economy. The September 1965 meeting of the Central Committee took steps to implement reforms in industry, oriented towards its transition from administrative to economic methods of management, and increased independence for enterprises. All these measures were reinforced by Party work to provide for the well-being of the people and the expansion of opportunities for working people's initiatives. As a result the rate of socio-economic development rose sharply in the period 1966–70 compared with the previous period, as is shown in the data in Table 7.

It should be noted that in fact the turn in 1966–70 was sharper than is evident from the indicators above, because the table compares five-year periods and the upgrading of the economy had already begun in 1965. Moreover, the conditions for the upgrading in 1963 and the beginning of 1964 were much worse than the average indicators for the whole 1961–65 period. Nevertheless it is quite clear that the rate of socio-economic development rose sharply. This was mostly the result of the doubling of the rate of growth in agriculture, the total growth of which in the 1966–70 period was 21% compared with 11% in the preceding five-year period.

Because the growth of productive resources in the 1966–70 period was even lower than in the 1961–65 period, all the acceleration of socio-economic development was achieved through the rise in efficiency of production, the growth rate of which more than doubled. The capital output ratio trebled and the efficiency of capital investment grew one and a half

Table Seven
*Basic socio-economic indicators for the USSR for the five-year periods 1961–65
and 1966–70: percentage growth* (official figures)

	1961–65	1966–70
Overall indicators		
National income	32	41
Per capita income	19	33
Productive resources (total)	22	20
Basic productive funds	59	48
Mining industry production	32	28
Number of workers employed in branches of industry	6.5	6
*Efficiency of social production (total)**	8	18
Capital output ratio	-17	-5
Efficiency of capital investment	-16	-10
Efficiency of use of industrial raw materials	0	10
Productivity of social labour	24	33

*Indices of efficiency are calculated in relation to indices of national income.

times, while significant economies were made in fuel and raw materials (in the previous period there had been none). The rate of growth of the national income rose almost one and a half times.

We have dwelt in some detail on this interesting experience of significant acceleration of the country's socio-economic development since similar tasks face us now—both to overcome existing negative tendencies, and to achieve a major breakthrough in the 1986–90 period, by doubling the rate of growth of efficiency of social production. Of course the circumstances now are different. Scientific, technological and economic potential have greatly increased and there are opportunities to activate not only new organisational and economic reserves but also the potential of science and technology in upgrading the economy.

Excerpt from Abel G. Aganbegyan, *The Economic Challenge of Perestroika*, ed. Michael B. Brown (Bloomington: Indiana University Press), pp. 67–81. Copyright © 1988 by Abel Gezevich Aganbegyan. Reprinted by permission of Indiana University Press. World rights granted by Hutchinson Publishers.

Four
"I CAN'T FORGO MY PRINCIPLES"

The publication of a letter written by Nina Andreeva, a Leningrad chemistry teacher, in *Sovetskaya Rossiya* (March 13, 1988) caused a sensation in the USSR because it was a scathing and systematic attack on perestroika. Yegor Ligachev, a conservative Communist theorist and opposer of Gorbachev's perestroika policies, was suspected of having had a hand in its publication. In the following excerpts, Andreeva identified supporters of perestroika as unpatriotic and subversive to good order in Soviet society.

I decided to write this letter after a great deal of thought. I am a chemist, and I teach at the Leningrad Soviet Technological Institute in Leningrad. Like many others, I am an adviser for a group of students. In our days, after a period of social apathy and intellectual dependence, students are gradually beginning to be charged with the energy of revolutionary changes. Naturally, debates arise—about the paths of restructuring and its economic and ideological aspects. Openness, candor and the disappearance of zones closed to criticism, as well as emotional fervor in the mass consciousness, especially among young people, are frequently manifested in the posing of problems that, to one extent or another, have been "prompted" by Western radio voices or by those of our compatriots who are not firm in their notions about the essence of socialism. What a wide range of topics is being discussed! A multiparty system, freedom of religious propaganda, leaving the country to live abroad, the right to a broad discussion of sexual problems in the press, the need for the decentralization of the management of culture, the abolition of compulsory military service—Among students, a particularly large number of arguments are about the country's past. . . .

The constant harping on "terrorism," "the people's political servility," "uninspired social vegetating," "our spiritual slavery," "universal fear," "the entrenched rule of louts"—It is from these mere threads that the history of the period of the transition to socialism in our country is often woven. Therefore, it comes as no surprise, for example, that in some students nihilistic views are intensifying, and ideological confusion, a dislocation of political reference points and even ideological omnivorousness are appearing. Sometimes one hears assertions that it is time to call to account the Communists who supposedly "dehumanized" the country's life after 1917. . . .

In talking with students and pondering crucial problems with them, I automatically come to the conclusion that a good many distortions and one-sided views have piled up in our country, notions that obviously need to be corrected. I want to devote special attention to some of these things.

Take the question of the place of J. V. Stalin in our country's history. It is with his name that the entire obsession with critical attacks is associated, an obsession that, in my opinion, has to do not so much with the historical personality itself as with the whole extremely complex transitional era—an era linked with the unparalleled exploit of an entire generation of Soviet people who today are gradually retiring from active labor, political and public activity. Industrialization, collectivization and the cultural revolution, which brought our country into the ranks of the great world powers, are being forcibly squeezed into the "personality cult" formula. All these things are being questioned. Things have reached a point at which insistent demands for "repentance" are being made on "Stalinists" (and one can assign to their number whomever one wishes). Praise is being lavished on novels and films that lynch the era of tempestuous changes, which is presented as a "tragedy of peoples."

Let me note at the outset that neither I nor the members of my family have any relationship to Stalin or his entourage, retainers or extollers. My father was a worker in the Leningrad port, and my mother was a mechanic at the Kirov Plant. My older brother worked there, too. He, my father and my sister were killed in battles against the Hitlerites. One of my relatives was repressed and was rehabilitated after the 20th Party Congress. Together with all Soviet people, I share the anger and indignation over the large-scale repressions that took place in the 1930s and 1940s through the fault of the Party and state leadership of that time. But common sense resolutely protests the mono-chromatic coloring of contradictory events that has now begun to prevail in certain press organs.

I support the Party's call to uphold the honor and dignity of the trailblazers of socialism. I think that it is from these Party and class positions that we should assess the historical role of all Party and state leaders, including Stalin. In this case, one must not reduce the matter to the "court" aspect or to abstract moralizing by people far removed from that stormy time and from the people who lived and worked then. Indeed, they worked in such a way that what they did is an inspirational example for us even today....

Recently, one of my students startled me with the revelation that the class struggle is supposedly an obsolete concept, as is the leading role of the proletariat. It would be all right if she were the only one maintaining such a thing. But, for example, a furious argument broke out recently over a respected academician's assertion that the present relations between states of the two different social and economic systems are devoid of class content. I admit that the academician did not deem it necessary to explain why for several decades he had written the exact opposite—that peaceful coexistence is nothing other than a form of class struggle in the international arena. It turns out that the philosopher has now repudiated that notion. Well, views do change. However, it seems to me that the duty of a leading philosopher does enjoin him to explain, at least to those who have learned and are learning from his books: What—does the international working class today, in the form of its state and political organs, really no longer act as a countervailing force to world capital? ...

The first, and deepest, ideological current that has already revealed itself in the course of restructuring claims to be a model of some kind of left-liberal dilettantish socialism, to be the exponent of a humanism that is very true and "clean" from class incrustations. Against proletarian collectivism, the adherents of this current put up "the intrinsic worth of the individual"—with modernistic quests in the field of culture, God-seeking tendencies, technocratic idols, the preaching of the "democratic" charms of present-day capitalism and fawning over its achievements, real and imagined. Its representatives assert that we have built the wrong kind of socialism and that only today, "for the first time in history, has an alliance come about between the political leadership and the progressive intelligentsia." At a time when millions of people on our planet are dying from hunger, epidemics and imperialism's military adventures, they demand the immediate drafting of a "legal code for the protection of animal rights," ascribe a singular, supernatural intelligence to nature, and claim that cultivation is not a social but a biological quality, transmitted genetically from parents to children. Tell me: What does all this mean?

It is the champions of "left-liberal socialism" who are shaping the tendency to falsify the history of socialism. They suggest to us that in the country's past only the mistakes and crimes are real, in doing so keeping quiet about the supreme achievements of the past and the present. Laying claim to complete historical truth, they substitute scholastic ethical categories for social and political criteria of the development of society. I would very much like to understand: Who needs, and why, to have every prominent leader of the Party Central Committee and the Soviet government compromised after he leaves office and discredited in connection with his actual or supposed mistakes and miscalculations, made while solving some very complex problems on roads uncharted by history? Where did we get this passion for squandering the prestige and dignity of the leaders of the world's first socialist country?

Another special feature of the views of the "left-liberals" is an obvious or camouflaged cosmopolitan tendency, a sort of nationality-less "internationalism." I have read somewhere that when, after the Revolution, a delegation of merchants and factory owners came to the Petrograd Soviet to see Trotsky "as a Jew," complaining of oppression by Red Guards, he declared that he was "not a Jew but an internationalist," which thoroughly bewildered the supplicants.

For Trotsky, the concept of the "national" meant a kind of inferiority and narrowness in comparison to the "international." That's why he emphasized the "national tradition" of October, wrote about "the national element in Lenin," maintained that the Russian people "had received no cultural legacy," etc. For some reason, we are ashamed to say that it was the Russian proletariat, which the Trotskyists slighted as "backward and uncultured," that carried out, in Lenin's words, "the three Russian Revolutions," or that the Slavic peoples were in the vanguard of mankind's battle against fascism. . . .

Here is something else that alarms me: Militant cosmopolitanism is now linked with the practice of "refusenikism"—of "refusing" socialism. Unfortunately, we suddenly think of this only when its neophytes plague us with their outrages in front of Smolny or under the Kremlin's walls. More-over, we are somehow gradually being trained to see this phenomenon as an almost inoffensive change of "place of residence," not as class and nationality betrayal by persons most of whom have been graduated from higher schools and graduate schools at public expense. In general, some people are inclined to look at "refusenikism" as some kind of manifes-tation of "democracy" and "human rights," feeling that the talents of those involved have been prevented from blossoming by "stagnant so-cialism." Well, if over there, in the "free world," their tireless enterprise and "genius" aren't appreciated and selling their conscience doesn't in-terest the special services, they can come back— . . .

Whereas the "neoliberals" are oriented toward the West, the other "al-ternative tower" (to use Prokhanov's expression), the "guardians and tra-ditionalists," seeks to "overcome socialism by moving backward"—in other words, to return to the social forms of presocialist Russia. The spokesmen for this unique "peasant socialism" are fascinated with this image. In their opinion, a loss of the moral values that the peasant com-munity had accumulated through the dim haze of centuries took place 100 years ago. The "traditionalists" have rendered undoubted services in ex-posing corruption, in fairly solving ecological problems, in combating al-coholism, in protecting historical monuments and in countering the dominance of mass culture, which they rightly assess as a psychosis of consumerism.

At the same time, the views of the ideologists of "peasant socialism" contain a misunderstanding of the historical significance of October for the fatherland's fate, a one-sided appraisal of collectivization as "frightful arbitrary treatment of the peasantry," uncritical views on religious-mystical Russian philosophy, old tsarist concepts in scholarship relating to our country's history, and an unwillingness to see the postrevolutionary stratification of the peasantry and the revolutionary role of the working class.

In the class struggle in the countryside, for example, there is frequently an overemphasis on "village" commissars who "shot middle peasants in the back." There were, of course, all kinds of commissars in our enormous country, which had been stirred to new life by the Revolution. But the basic tenor of our life was determined by those commissars who were themselves shot. It was they who had stars cut into their backs or were burned alive. The "attacking class" had to pay not only with the lives of commissars, Chekists [state security personnel], village Bolsheviks, mem-bers of poor peasants' committees and "twenty-thousanders" [industrial workers who helped in the collectivization of agriculture in the early 1930s—**Trans.**], but also those of the first tractor drivers, rural correspon-dents, girl-teachers and rural Young Communists, with the lives of tens of thousands of other unknown fighters for socialism.

The difficulties in the upbringing of young people are deepened still more by the fact that unofficial [*neformalny*] organizations and associations are being created in the pattern of the ideas of the "neoliberals" and "neo-Slavophiles." In some cases, extremist elements are capable of provocations are gaining the upper hand in the leadership of these groups. Recently, the politicization of these grass-roots [*samodeyatelny*] organizations on the basis of a pluralism that is far from socialist has been noted. Frequently the leaders of these organizations talk about "power-sharing" on the basis of a "parliamentary regime," "free trade unions," "autonomous publishing houses," etc. In my opinion, all this makes it possible to draw the conclusion that the main and cardinal question in the debates now under way in the country is the question of recognizing or not recognizing the leading role of the Party and the working class in socialist construction, and hence in restructuring—needless to say, with all the theoretical and practical conclusions for politics, the economy and ideology that stem therefrom. . . .

Today, the question of the role and place of socialist ideology has taken on a very acute form. Under the aegis of a moral and spiritual "cleansing," the authors of opportunistic constructs are eroding the boundaries and criteria of scientific ideology, manipulating openness, and propagating an extrasocialist pluralism, which objectively impedes restructuring in social consciousness. This is having an especially detrimental effect on young people, something that, I repeat, we higher-school instructors, schoolteachers and all those who deal with young people's problems are distinctly aware of. As M. S. Gorbachev said at the February plenary session of the CPSU Central Committee: "In the spiritual sphere as well, and perhaps in this sphere first of all, we must be guided by our Marxist-Leninist principles. Comrades, we must not forgo these principles under any pretexts."

We stand on this, and we will continue to do so. We have not received these principles as a gift: We have gained them through suffering at decisive turning points in the history of the fatherland.

English translation from *The Current Digest of the Soviet Press*, vol. 40, no. 13. Translation copyright © 1988 by *The Current Digest of the Soviet Press*, published weekly at Columbus, Ohio. Reprinted by permission of the Digest.

Five
YELTSIN ON THE END OF EMPIRE

Boris Yeltsin was in agreement with Mikhail Gorbachev that the Soviet external empire in eastern Europe could be abandoned in the fall of 1989. The following excerpt from Yeltsin's book *The Struggle for Russia* (1994) describes his thoughts on Russia's changing role in the world at the time of the collapse of the Warsaw Pact.

The Soviet Union could not exist without the image of the empire. The image of the empire could not exist without the image of force. The USSR ended the moment the first hammer pounded the Berlin Wall. Everything that was Soviet in people's heads—not all of them, but the most active and thinking parts of society—had by then receded. It was from this fresh perspective that the country approached the election of a new leader.

I came to the presidency with the idea of making a clean break with our Soviet heritage, not merely through various reforms but geopolitically, through an alteration of Russia's role as a powerful, enduring, long-suffering nation.

Excerpt from Boris Yeltsin, *The Struggle for Russia*, trans. Catherine A. Fitzpatrick (New York: Random House, 1994), pp. 35–36.

Six
THE AUGUST COUP: YANAEV TAKES CHARGE

The Soviet public became aware of the attempted coup by hard-liners in Gorbachev's government when Gennady Yanaev made the following statement that Gorbachev was ill and that he (Yanaev), as vice president, had the authority to assume power as acting president. Following is the text of Yanaev's brief statement made on August 18, 1991.

DECREE OF THE VICE-PRESIDENT OF THE USSR. (Pravda and Izvestia [No. 197], Aug. 20, p. 1. Complete text:) In connection with the inability of Mikhail Sergeyevich Gorbachev to perform his duties as President of the USSR due to the state of his health, I have, on the basis of Art. 127.7 of the USSR Constitution, assumed the duties of acting President of the USSR as of Aug. 19, 1991.

G. I. YANAYEV,
Vice-President of the USSR.

Aug. 18, 1991.

English translation from *The Current Digest of the Soviet Press*, vol. 43, no. 33. Translation copyright © 1991 by *The Current Digest of the Soviet Press*, published weekly at Columbus, Ohio. Reprinted by permission of the Digest.

Seven
ESTABLISHMENT OF THE EMERGENCY COMMITTEE

Gennady Yanaev, along with Prime Minister Valentin Pavlov and Oleg Baklanov, first vice-chairman of the USSR Defense Council, informed the Soviet public on August 18, 1991, of the creation of an eight-man Emergency Committee charged with the preservation of law and order. All who read the following statement, however, knew that the committee's goal was to eliminate perestroika and the supporters of reform.

In connection with the inability of Mikhail Sergeyevich Gorbachev to perform the duties of President of the USSR due to the state of his health, and the transfer of the powers of President of the USSR to Gennady Ivanovich Yanayev, Vice-President of the USSR, in accordance with Art. 127.7 of the USSR Constitution;

with the aim of overcoming the profound and comprehensive crisis, the political and civil confrontation, the confrontation between nationalities, and the chaos and anarchy that are threatening the lives and security of the citizens of the Soviet Union and the sovereignty, territorial integrity, freedom and independence of our fatherland;

proceeding from the results of the nationwide referendum on the preservation of the Union of Soviet Socialist Republics;

guided by the vitally important interests of the peoples of our homeland and of all Soviet people,

WE STATE:

1. That, in accordance with Art. 127.3 of the USSR Constitution and Art. 2 of the USSR law "On the Legal Conditions Applying in a State of Emergency," and moving to accommodate the demands of broad strata of the population concerning the need to take very decisive measures to prevent society from sliding toward a nationwide catastrophe and to safeguard legality and order, a state of emergency is introduced in certain localities of the USSR for a period of six months, beginning at 4 A.M. Moscow time on Aug. 19, 1991.

2. That it is established that the USSR Constitution and USSR laws have unconditional supremacy throughout the USSR.

3. That, to administer the country and provide effective implementation of the conditions applying in a state of emergency, a State Committee for the State of Emergency in the USSR (USSR SCSE) is formed, with the following members: O. D. Baklanov, First Vice-Chairman of the USSR Defense Council; V. A. Kryuchkov, Chairman of the USSR State Security Committee (KGB); V. S. Pavlov, Prime Minister of the USSR; B. K. Pugo, USSR Minister of Internal Affairs; V. A. Starodubtsev, Chairman of the USSR Peasants' Union; A. I. Tizyakov, President of the Association of State Enterprises and Industrial, Construction, Transportation and Communications Facilities; D. T. Yazov, USSR Minister of Defense; and G. I. Yanayev, acting President of the USSR.

4. That unswerving fulfillment of the decisions of the USSR State Committee for the State of Emergency is mandatory for all bodies of power

and administration, officials and citizens throughout the USSR.—[signed] G. YANAYEV, V. PAVLOV and O. BAKLANOV.

Aug. 18, 1991.

English translation from *The Current Digest of the Soviet Press*, vol. 43, no. 33. Translation copyright © 1991 by *The Current Digest of the Soviet Press*, published weekly in Columbus, Ohio. Reprinted by permission of the Digest.

Eight
RESOLUTION NUMBER ONE OF THE EMERGENCY COMMITTEE

The Emergency Committee assumed sweeping powers and outlined its program to return to pre-perestroika domestic policies in the following document, issued on August 20, 1991.

RESOLUTION NO. 1 OF THE STATE COMMITTEE FOR THE STATE OF EMERGENCY IN THE USSR. (Pravda and Izvestia [No. 197], Aug. 20, p. 1. Complete text:) For the purpose of protecting the vitally important interests of the peoples and citizens of the USSR and the independence and territorial integrity of the country, restoring legality and law and order, stabilizing the situation, overcoming the grave crisis and preventing chaos, anarchy and a fratricidal civil war, the State Committee for the State of Emergency in the USSR resolves that:

1. All bodies of power and administration of the USSR, the Union and autonomous republics, territories, provinces, cities, districts, settlements and villages are to ensure unswerving observance of the conditions applying in a state of emergency, in accordance with the USSR law "On the Legal Conditions Applying in a State of Emergency" and the resolutions of the USSR State Committee for the State of Emergency. In cases of inability to ensure fulfillment of these conditions, the powers of the relevant bodies of power and administration are to be suspended, and the performance of their functions is to be assigned to individuals specially empowered by the USSR State Committee for the State of Emergency.

2. Structures of power and administration and paramilitary formations acting in defiance of the USSR Constitution and USSR laws are to be immediately disbanded.

3. Laws and decisions of bodies of power and administration that are at variance with the USSR Constitution and USSR laws are henceforth to be considered invalid.

4. Activity by political parties, public organizations and mass movements that impedes the normalization of the situation is to be suspended.

5. In connection with the fact that the State Committee for the State of Emergency in the USSR is temporarily assuming the functions of the USSR Security Council, the activity of the latter is suspended.

6. Citizens, institutions and organizations are to immediately surrender all types of firearms, ammunition, explosives and military equipment that are in their possession illegally. The USSR Ministry of Internal Affairs, the State Security Committee and the Ministry of Defense are to ensure the strict fulfillment of this requirement. In cases of refusal, the firearms, etc., are to be taken by force and strict criminal and administrative charges are to be brought against the violators.

7. The USSR Prosecutor's Office, the Ministry of Internal Affairs, the State Security Committee and the Ministry of Defense are to organize effective interaction among law-enforcement agencies and the Armed Forces to ensure the safeguarding of public order and the security of the state, society and citizens in accordance with the USSR law "On the Legal Conditions Applying in a State of Emergency" and the resolutions of the USSR State Committee for the State of Emergency.

The holding of rallies, street processions and demonstrations, as well as strikes, is not permitted.

When necessary, a curfew may be introduced, patrolling may be instituted, inspections may be conducted, and measures may be taken to reinforce border and customs regulations.

The most important state and economic facilities, as well as systems providing vital services, are to be taken under control, and, when necessary, put under guard.

The dissemination of inflammatory rumors, actions that provoke violations of law and order and the stirring up of discord between nationalities, and failure to obey officials who are ensuring the observance of the conditions applying in the state of emergency are to be resolutely curbed.

8. Control is to be established over the news media, with the implementation of this control assigned to a specially created agency under the USSR State Committee for the State of Emergency.

9. Bodies of power and administration and executives of institutions and enterprises are to take measures to enhance the level of organization and to establish order and discipline in all spheres of the life of society. The normal functioning of enterprises in all branches of the national economy, the strict fulfillment of measures to preserve and restore—during a period of stabilization—vertical and horizontal ties among economic-management entities throughout the USSR, and the unswerving fulfillment of established volumes of production and of deliveries of raw and other materials and components are to be ensured.

A policy of strict economizing with respect to materials, equipment and currency is to be established and maintained, and concrete measures are to be worked out and implemented to combat the mismanagement and squandering of public property.

A decisive struggle is to be waged against the shadow economy, and inescapable measures of criminal and administrative liability are to be ap-

plied in instances of corruption, embezzlement, speculation, the conceal-
ment of goods from sale, mismanagement and other law violations in the
sphere of the economy.

Favorable conditions are to be created for increasing the real contribution of all types of entrepreneurial activity, carried out in accordance
with USSR laws, to the country's economic potential and for providing
for the urgent requirements of the population.

10. The holding of a permanent position in the structures of power and
administration is to be considered incompatible with participation in entrepreneurial activity.

11. Within one week, the USSR Cabinet of Ministers is to conduct an
inventory of all available resources of prime-necessity foodstuffs and industrial commodities, report to the people on what the country has at its
disposal, and put the safekeeping and distribution of these resources under
the strictest possible control.

All restrictions impeding the shifting of food and consumer goods from
one place to another in the USSR, as well as of material resources for
their production, are to be lifted, and observance of this directive is to be
strictly monitored.

Special attention is to be given to the top-priority supplying of children's
preschool institutions, children's homes, schools, specialized secondary and
higher educational institutions and hospitals, as well as of pensioners and
disabled persons.

Within one week, proposals are to be submitted on putting in order,
freezing and reducing prices for certain types of manufactured goods
and foodstuffs, first of all goods for children, services to the population
and public catering, and also on increasing wages, pensions, allowances
and compensation payments for various categories of citizens.

Within two weeks, measures are to be worked out to put in order the
size of salaries for executives at all levels of state, public, cooperative and
other institutions, organizations and enterprises.

12. In view of the critical situation regarding harvest operations and the
threat of hunger, emergency measures are to be taken to organize the
procurement, storage and processing of agricultural output. Rural toilers
are to be provided with the greatest possible assistance in the form of
equipment, spare parts, fuel and lubricants, etc. The sending of workers
and office employees from enterprises and organizations, students and
servicemen to the countryside in the numbers needed to save the harvest
is to be organized immediately.

13. Within one week, the USSR Cabinet of Ministers is to work out a
resolution stipulating the provision, in 1991–1992, of plots of land up to
0.15 hectares in size to all urban residents who wish to use this land to
grow fruit and vegetables.

14. Within two weeks, the USSR Cabinet of Ministers is to complete

the planning of urgent measures to bring the country's fuel and energy complex out of crisis and to prepare for winter.

15. Within one month, real measures for 1992 aimed at fundamentally improving housing construction and providing housing to the population are to be prepared and reported to the people.

During a six-month period, a concrete five-year program for the accelerated development of state, cooperative and individual housing construction is to be worked out.

16. Central and local bodies of power and administration must devote top-priority attention to the social needs of the population. Possibilities for a substantial improvement in free medical services and public education are to be sought out.

Nine
YELTSIN'S RESISTANCE TO THE COUP ATTEMPT

From his headquarters in the Russian parliament building, Boris Yeltsin began a popular resistance movement against the attempted coup. In the following statement, issued on August 19, 1991, Yeltsin declared the Emergency Committee's actions to be illegal and warned of a return to totalitarianism and Cold War if the people did not show their support for Gorbachev. Yeltsin called for a general strike by workers as a sign of support for Gorbachev, and a show of defiance against the Emergency Committee.

TO THE CITIZENS OF RUSSIA. (Megapolis-Express, special edition, Aug. 19, p. 1. Complete text:) On the night of Aug. 18–19, 1991, the legally elected President of the country was removed from power.

Whatever reasons are used to justify this removal, what we are dealing with is a right-wing, reactionary, unconstitutional coup.

Despite all the difficulties and very grave trials that the people are experiencing, the democratic process in the country is assuming ever deeper dimensions and is becoming irreversible. The peoples of Russia are becoming the masters of their fate. The uncontrolled rights of unconstitutional bodies, including Party bodies, have been substantially restricted. The leadership of Russia has taken a resolute position on the Union Treaty, striving for the unity of the Soviet Union and the unity of Russia. Our position on this question made it possible to significantly accelerate the drafting of this treaty, clear it with all the republics, and set a date for signing it—Aug. 20, 1991.

This development of events aroused the animosity of reactionary forces and drove them into irresponsible, adventurist attempts to solve very complicated political and economic problems by methods of force. There were earlier attempts to stage a coup.

We have believed and continue to believe that these methods of force are unacceptable. They discredit the USSR before the whole world, undermine our prestige in the world community, and return us to the era of the cold war and the Soviet Union's isolation from the world community.

All this compels us to declare the so-called committee that has come to power illegal. Accordingly, we declare all the decisions and orders of this committee illegal.

We are confident that bodies of local power will unswervingly follow constitutional laws and the decrees of the President of the Russian SFSR. We call on the citizens of Russia to give the putschists the response they deserve and to demand that the country be returned to normal constitutional development.

Certainly Gorbachev, the country's President, must be given an opportunity to speak to the people. We demand the immediate convening of an Extraordinary Congress of USSR People's Deputies.

We are absolutely certain that our fellow countrymen will not allow the high-handedness and lawlessness of the putschists, who have lost all shame and conscience, to become firmly established. We appeal to servicemen to display lofty civic spirit and not to take part in the reactionary coup.

Until these demands are fulfilled, we call for a general strike of unlimited duration. We have no doubt that the world community will make an objective assessment of this cynical attempt at a right-wing coup.—[signed] Yeltsin, President of Russia; Silayev, Chairman of the RSFSR Council of Ministers; and Khasbulatov, acting Chairman of the RSFSR Supreme Soviet.

Aug. 19, 1991, 9. A.M.

Ten
YELTSIN TAKES CHARGE IN RUSSIA

In a bold move, Yeltsin declared the actions of the Emergency Committee illegal on Russian soil on August 19, 1991, and used the powers conferred on him as president of the Russian republic to supersede the powers assumed by the members of the committee.

DECREE OF THE PRESIDENT OF THE RUSSIAN SOVIET FEDERATED SOCIALIST REPUBLIC. (Kuranty [Chimes], Aug. 19, special edition No. 1, p. 1. Complete text:) In connection with the actions of a group of individuals who have declared themselves the State Committee for the State of Emergency, I decree that:

1. The declaration forming the committee is unconstitutional, and the actions of its organizers constitute a coup d'etat, which is nothing less than a crime against the state.

2. All decisions made in the name of the so-called Committee for the State of Emergency are to be considered illegal and invalid on the territory of the RSFSR. A legally elected government is in operation in the Russian Federation, consisting of the President, the Supreme Soviet and the Chairman of the Council of Ministers, and all state and local bodies of power and administration of the RSFSR.

3. Actions by officials to carry out the decisions of the aforesaid committee fall under the purview of the RSFSR Criminal Code and are subject to prosecution under the law.

This decree takes effect as of the moment it is signed.

B. YELTSIN,
President of the RSFSR.

English translation from *The Current Digest of the Soviet Press*, vol. 43, no. 33. Translation copyright © 1991 by *The Current Digest of the Soviet Press*, published weekly at Columbus, Ohio. Reprinted by permission of the Digest.

Eleven
RUSSIA VERSUS THE USSR

Yeltsin attempted to ensure the support of government functionaries in the Russian Soviet Federated Socialist Republic in the struggle against the Emergency Committee by ordering the transfer of power from union agencies to republic agencies within the Russian republic on August 19, 1991.

DECREE NO. 61 OF THE PRESIDENT OF THE RUSSIAN SFSR. (Kuranty [Chimes], Aug. 19, special edition No. 1, p. 2. Complete text:) An attempt has been made to carry out a coup d'etat. The President of the USSR, who is the Supreme Commander in Chief of the USSR Armed Forces, has been removed from his position. The Vice-President of the USSR, the Prime Minister of the USSR, the Chairman of the USSR State Security Committee [KGB] and the USSR Ministers of Defense and of Internal Affairs have become members of an unconstitutional body, thereby committing a crime against the state. As a result of these actions, the activity of the legally elected executive authorities of the USSR has been paralyzed. In view of the current emergency situation, I decree that:

1. Until an extraordinary Congress of USSR People's Deputies is convened, all USSR bodies of executive power, including the USSR State

Security Committee, the USSR Ministry of Internal Affairs and the USSR Ministry of Defense, that operate on RSFSR territory are to be shifted to direct subordination to the popularly elected President of the RSFSR.

2. The RSFSR State Security Committee, the RSFSR Ministry of Internal Affairs and the RSFSR State Committee on Defense Questions are to temporarily exercise the functions of the corresponding USSR bodies on the territory of the RSFSR. All territorial and other agencies of the Ministry of Internal Affairs, the State Security Committee and the Ministry of Defense on the territory of the RSFSR must immediately comply with the decrees and orders of the President of the RSFSR and the RSFSR Council of Ministers and the orders of the RSFSR State Security Committee, the RSFSR Ministry of Internal Affairs and the RSFSR State Committee on Defense Questions.

3. All RSFSR agencies, officials and citizens are to take immediate measures to rule out the implementation of all decisions and orders of the unconstitutional Committee for the State of Emergency. Officials who carry out the decisions of the aforesaid committee are to be relieved of their duties, in accordance with the RSFSR Constitution. Agencies of the RSFSR Prosecutor's Office are ordered to take immediate measures to bring criminal charges against these individuals.

B. YELTSIN,
President of the Russian SFSR.

Aug. 19, 1991.

English translation from *The Current Digest of the Soviet Press*, vol. 43, no. 33. Translation copyright © 1991 by *The Current Digest of the Soviet Press*, published weekly in Columbus, Ohio. Reprinted by permission of the Digest.

Twelve
THE VIEW ON THE STREET

British journalist Martin Sixsmith was caught up in the resistance to the coup attempt on the streets in Moscow. The following passage relates the events of Tuesday, August 19, 1991, as recorded by Sixsmith in his book *Moscow Coup* (1991).

The drama of Monday had left us alarmed, but relieved that a full-scale assault had not materialized. There were those who said we were foolish to reduce the numbers around the parliament, because day-time was no guarantee that the army would not attack. Experience in the Baltics, though, suggested that the military did prefer night-time to do its dirty business, so the daylight hours of Tuesday were widely considered to be a moment of reprieve, an opportunity to strengthen defences and prepare for the battle which everyone now expected once the sun went down.

But before that could happen, the people of Moscow had a final chance to show what they thought of the Yanayev regime, to demonstrate to the men in the Kremlin, and to the world, that if they were doomed once again to be subjugated to an oppressive Communist junta, they would not go meekly. In response to calls from Boris Yeltsin and radicals in the Russian parliament, and from the liberal Moscow City Council (Mossoviet), the people were to turn out on Manezhnaya Square at eleven in the morning. The declared aim of the rally's organizers was a peaceful demonstration under the walls of the Kremlin to demand the reinstatement of Mikhail Gorbachov. But Moscow's rumour mill was working overtime that morning, and the talk of the city was that there would be some attempt to enter the Kremlin, possibly to bring about the forceful ejection of the usurpers of power.

In such an atmosphere, and with all demonstrations officially banned since the previous day, there was a mood of trepidation as the time for the rally drew near. It appeared certain that the army would not allow its authority to be flaunted in the centre of Moscow; it was equally certain that the thousands of would-be demonstrators were not going to flinch from a clash, and the prospect of bloodshed seemed to come a step nearer.

In front of the Bolshoi Theatre, next to Manezh, we found units of riot troops drawn up the full length of Neglinnaya Street—more than I had ever encountered for a city centre demonstration in the past. The mood was different too. During the Gorbachov years, with a few exceptions, the troops deployed to control demonstrations adopted a low-profile approach, not seeking confrontation and usually prepared for a certain amount of good-natured banter with the crowd. But when we tried to speak to the men deployed at the Bolshoi, we were met with curses and threats from narrow-eyed Central Asians. Marshal Yazov was clearly not prepared to risk using Slav troops to combat a largely Slav demonstration, and the importation of units from the far corners of the Union was, it seemed, another signal that he was serious about the use of force. Later, when we tried to film a unit deployed on Gorky Street, their commander gave the order to rough us up—something which riot troops in previous times had been reluctant to do (presumably under orders from Gorbachov not to offend the foreign press and, through them, foreign public opinion).

The biggest surprise, though, was still to come. As we turned the corner into Manezhnaya Square, we were faced with an astounding sight. From the Lenin Museum, past the Moskva Hotel and across the vast square as far as the Nationalnaya Hotel, an unbroken line of tanks had been formed, with their crews standing in front of them cradling automatic weapons. In the background the Kremlin towers were visible, and behind those towers were the men who had ordered this extraordinary show of strength. Further inquires revealed that every approach to the Kremlin had been sealed off in a similar manner, making certain that no crowds could come within three hundred yards. For a regime which claimed to have the confidence of the people, the new men in power were making very serious efforts to keep that people at bay. It was, in effect, a return to the Stalinist ethic of complete separation between rulers and ruled, an approach which had been progressively broken down by the more open style of government adopted under Gorbachov.

Grim soldiers stared impassively as Yeltsin's supporters arrived in the square, having already run the gauntlet of closed roads and saturation policing of an area that stretched from one to two miles on all sides of the Kremlin. Even the most stubborn of the rally's organizers realized that there was no prospect of breaching such a cordon of steel, and stewards with megaphones were deployed to redirect demonstrators up the hill onto Gorky Street. The crowds thus began to move away from the Kremlin and towards the Moscow City Council building, where a large open square opposite had been designated as an alternative site. This change of direction involved opening a line of tanks which had been deployed across Gorky Street to stop crowds approaching the Kremlin from the other direction. The unit's commander was reluctant to do so (lack of orders seemingly outweighing the presence of common sense), but was eventually prevailed on to comply when it became clear that the crowd had no other way to leave if he did not step back.

Several thousand people eventually gathered in the square under a constant drizzle, carrying banners condemning the coup and chanting 'Yanayev—Judas, Fascism—out.' They heard speeches from the balcony of the City Council building. Eduard Shevardnadze and Aleksandr Yakovlev—the two men who had warned in advance that a military putsch was being planned—drew the greatest applause for their support of Yeltsin's stand, and for their demands that the coup leaders be removed and brought to trial. Shevardnadze repeated his gloomy assessment that the new regime was on the point of destroying all the foreign policy successes of the Gorbachov years and plunging the whole world back into cold war. But the speech which struck me in particular came from Sergei Stankevich, the young, articulate and clean-cut former Deputy Mayor of Moscow who had just been appointed a Senior Counsellor in the leadership of Boris Yeltsin's Russian Federation.

Stankevich started by asking the crowd what they thought of the coup—were they angry about it? did they regret it had taken place? 'Well,' said Stankevich, 'I am glad the coup happened.' Silence from the crowd. 'I'm glad,' he said, 'because now we know who is who. We've seen who those bastards are who want to overthrow democracy: this putsch has flushed them all out into the open; and when we get back to power, we're going to have them all put away.' The tumultuous applause was natural. Stankevich's certainty that things would turn out for the best was probably intended only to boost morale; but it was one of a number of statements which were later cited by journalists seeking to suggest that the whole coup had been stage-managed by the liberals and by Gorbachov—or at least carried out with their tacit blessing—to rid them of their hardline enemies in one fell swoop.

At the time, though, the crowd was less concerned with conspiracy theories than with the reaction of the troops sent by the conspirators in the Kremlin. Perhaps because of the weather, perhaps because of a fear of clashes with the army or because of army harassment on the way, or perhaps because a substantial percentage of the population secretly supported the coup and did not want to speak against it, the turn-out at the rally had been disappointingly small: several thousands, instead of the hundreds of thousands who had come to similar pro-Yeltsin demonstrations in peacetime. As a result, there was never any real threat of a storming of the Kremlin and the security forces presumably decided not to risk unnecessary bloodshed, eventually allowing the meeting to go ahead unhindered.

But in the eyes of many present, the lack of army intervention was another psychological victory for the democrats: the crowds had defied the Kremlin simply by demonstrating and had got away with it. The regime was made to look weak because it had banned demonstrations but then had not had the courage or the consistency to enforce its own decree. It was the second example of disarray by the junta (the first was over the Yeltsin speech on the back of the tank outside the Russian parliament), and it was not to be the last.

Buoyed by their success, the demonstrators unfurled a massive tricoloured Russian flag—almost one hundred yards long—as a symbol of their support for Yeltsin and his Russian democrats. The flag was then carried triumphantly on the heads of the crowd as they marched up Gorky Street, onto the inner ring-road and down to the Russian parliament itself. They arrived to a joyous reception from the defenders who had remained in place there during the morning, the flag being lifted onto the balcony at the rear of the parliament and fixed in place to mark the organizational centre of the operation to defend the building.

As stragglers and new arrivals from other parts of the city began to roll in, the numbers outside the parliament reached a high point of about fifty thousand—at last, the display of solidarity that the Yeltsin campaign so desperately needed. Their almost continuous chants of 'Yeltsin, Yeltsin!' must eventually have reached the ears of the man who had now been inside the parliament for more than twenty-four hours, and to storms of applause Boris himself emerged onto the balcony.

The speech that Yeltsin made that Tuesday afternoon was a rhetorical masterpiece, restoring the flagging morale of those who had been at the parliament since the previous day, on their feet virtually the whole time, with no sleep and little rest, and who were, not surprisingly, beginning to wonder whether they would ever see their homes again. At his bombastic best, Yeltsin began his address with a gloomy assessment of what would happen if the plotters were allowed to get away with their seizure of power. 'The shadows of darkness,' he said, to apprehensive silence from the crowd, 'have descended on our country, on Europe and on the world.' The apprehension of the defenders was aroused; the enormous import of their task made crystal clear. And then Yeltsin went on to raise our spirits, our pride and our belief that we could ultimately triumph. 'I have resolved,' he said, 'to resist these men, these usurpers in the Kremlin.' (He used the word *samozvansty*, redolent with historical overtones of imposters or pretenders who had dared to seize the God-given power of legitimate rulers and who suffered the bloody consequences of their temerity.) 'I have resolved this, and I call on you to do the same!' (Applause and cries of 'We are with you, Boris!') 'Without your help, I can do nothing' (murmurs from the crowd) ' . . . but together with you, and with the Russian people, we are capable of the greatest feats of heroism: we are capable of defeating these putschists and ensuring the triumph of democracy!'

The emotional catharsis of the moment was completed by a deafening roar of approval from the crowd. From being a disoriented and slightly uncertain mob, those present were transformed into dedicated, fearless enthusiasts, determined now to stay at their posts, full of personal loyalty to Boris Yeltsin and fired with the belief that they could change the course of history.

On the parliament's balcony, Yeltsin was flanked by men who had proved their commitment to the cause of democracy and who were about to prove the courage of their convictions by remaining with him throughout the denouement of the coup. They were Eduard Shevardnadze and Aleksandr Yakovlev; Stanislav Shatalin, the elderly and frail economist; Gavriil Popov, the radical mayor of Moscow; Sergei Stankevich; and Yeltsin's team of close advisers led by his Vice-President Aleksandr Rutskoi. These and others who rallied to the Russian parliament secured their reputations and their political future: presence on the barricades later became a litmus test of who could be trusted and who could not, in the same way that those who took part in, supported or did not oppose the coup were to become political pariahs. Only Mikhail Gorbachov, who was off the scene during the crucial hours of the coup, was to be left in an ambiguous position. Apart from the mysteries surrounding his role, the coup was to polarize Soviet politics with seemingly irreversible effect.

The role of the Soviet people was also under scrutiny that afternoon: those who came to the parliament or demonstrated on the streets had made their own decisive choice in favour of democracy. But there were, in truth, not that many of them: fifty thousand people from a city of ten million is not an overwhelming percentage. Many more may have opposed the coup in their hearts, but they did little or nothing to put that emotion to practical effect. Strikes did occur sporadically, but most enterprises kept going and there were enough transport workers willing to work to keep the buses and the metro in action. At this stage of the coup, Yeltsin was facing not only the Kremlin's tanks, but also the apathy of large sections of the population.

Even more challenging was the sentiment expressed by a considerable number of ordinary Soviets that the coup leaders should be given a chance, that they could hardly do worse than the previous lot in power, and that they might at least bring back law and order. Especially attractive to many people were the plotters' promises of ending the rise in crime, the spiralling ethnic conflicts which were dogging the country, and the attempts of independence-minded republics to break up the Union. The latter appealed to Soviet patriotism, as did Yanayev's talk of restoring the USSR's position and pride in the eyes of the world; but few who parroted Yanayev's words had thought for how these results would be achieved, for the inevitable bloodshed and suffering which would attend a campaign to repress the demands of ethnic minorities or republics, or for the international tensions which would flow from a reassertion of Moscow's old aggressive image in world politics. There had been serious problems under perestroika: material living conditions had worsened dramatically, discipline had fallen and crime had become a real issue; so it was understandable that some people would look to the junta as Italians did to Mussolini to 'make the trains run on time.' But in the final analysis, most of those who did not oppose the coup were probably, quite simply, scared.

Boris Yeltsin and his allies that Tuesday afternoon might well have hoped to arouse a much wider spectrum of public support. For the parliament's defenders, the laurels of triumph still looked a long way off as dusk began to fall, and with it all the fears of a night which most of us expected to be decisive. Rumours of an imminent storming of the building by Soviet forces had been growing since late afternoon. Announcements over the parliament's public address system had become more breathless, and general alerts among the defenders more frequent.

The tanks which had defected to Yeltsin's cause were still in place around the parliament, but they were lightly armoured vehicles and there were relatively few of them. What had looked and sounded immensely impressive as they roared into our midst in darkness the previous night had turned out in daylight to be a little less imposing. The paratroopers who had come over were—we assumed—inside the building preparing for the sort of hand-to-hand combat which had happened in January at the Vilnius TV tower, but the crowds outside could not see them so drew little comfort from their presence. The forces which had joined Yeltsin were not large, and they did not constitute proof of any major divisions within the army command—certainly not a split of the magnitude which would be needed to make a battle on the streets anything other than a one-sided walkover. Only a few hundred yards away, on the Kutuzovsky bridge over the Moskva river, the Kremlin's own tanks were in position, watching the goings-on at the parliament and ready to strike if ordered to do so. No one doubted that Marshal Yazov had at his command the endless supply of tank reinforcements which we so plainly lacked.

With the odds stacked against him, Yeltsin started to play the propaganda game. After dark on Tuesday evening his staff invited foreign journalists into the central part of the parliament building to see the inner offices which had been fortified against attack. Yeltsin did not appear, except as a fleeting presence moving between one corridor and another: we were told that he and his closest aides had a special inner sanctum which was the most heavily guarded and could be best defended if the building was stormed. We were not invited to visit Yeltsin's bunker, but the internal defences we were allowed to see were not impressive. In some offices sand bags had been piled against doors and windows, but in most cases it was simply a question of stacking filing cabinets and tables in the way of an onrushing enemy.

The paratroopers were there, though, and they looked confident and well prepared. They had spread their sleeping rolls on the floor of one of the committee rooms and—unlike us—they were not too nervous to get some rest, their weapons laid beside them on the floor ready for an urgent call to action. Several well-known deputies from the Russian and Soviet legislatures were also present, some of them carrying machine guns. Most of them looked as though they would probably have difficulty making the things work, and might well turn out to be a bigger danger to their own side than to the enemy. But it was clearly important for them to be there, and carrying a gun was the most potent symbol of their dedication and readiness for self-sacrifice that they could create.

Also carrying a gun, but looking rather more professional about it, was the Russian Vice-President Aleksandr Rutskoi. An intriguing character, Rutskoi was a former Soviet air force lieutenant; he had served longer in Afghanistan than nearly any other officer, been twice captured by the Mujehadin rebels and—according to all reports—horrifically tortured before escaping. When the war was over, he came back to Moscow and went into political life, first as a hardline Communist, spouting all the orthodox slogans but campaigning for servicemen's rights. His disillusionment at the system's failure to look after former soldiers was said to have prompted a radical rethinking of his political values and he swerved to the radical wing of the Communist party, eventually participating in a liberal 'Communists for Democracy' faction which supported Yeltsin in parliament. Rutskoi's reward was the offer to run with Yeltsin on the winning ticket for the Russian presidency, and his presence in the besieged parliament was now proving remarkably useful. With his personal hand-gun slung in its leather holster across his chest, Rutskoi explained in a matter-of-fact way that he was not intending to surrender if the troops came in to get him. 'I know the sort of bastards we're up against,' he said, 'and I know we have to fight to the end.'

Other members of Yeltsin's staff told us they knew of plans by the KGB and Special Forces to storm into the building and shoot out every person on the first and second floors. They said they knew that orders had been given for Yeltsin and his closest aides to be shot, with the troops specifically instructed not to take any prisoners. This was the story which Yeltsin himself was to repeat after the coup was over, and it was difficult even at that stage to determine whether he was speaking the truth or merely dramatizing the predicament he found himself in, to stress the inhumanity of his opponents and the bravery of his allies. But on that dark Tuesday night, inside a besieged parliament where all lights had been extinguished in a total black-out for security purposes, the atmosphere was tense enough for the suggestions of a ruthless enemy waiting to burst in firing to unnerve all of us present.

Yeltsin's aides seemed uncertain about what response would be offered in the event of an all out attack. Some suggested Yeltsin himself would attempt to escape via a helicopter from a friendly air force unit, which would land on the roof of the building. Others said there were plans for an evacuation through tunnels under the building.

There was confusion, too, about how the unarmed civilian defenders outside the parliament were meant to react in the event of an assault. The uncompromising Rutskoi seemed to be in favour of all out resistance to keep the tanks at bay, and messages to that effect were initially broadcast to the crowd. But later in the night, when an attack was looking almost certain, Yeltsin finally adopted a radically different approach. In repeated announcements over the public tannoy [public address system], it was stressed that civilians should offer no resistance to the army and should step back to let them through. This was, we were informed, on instructions from the President himself.

It is hard to say whether these divergences were the result of disagreements among the Russian leadership, or whether the uncertainty was deliberately sown to leave the army uncertain of the reception it was likely to face. But from the crowd's point of view it was confusing, and even at three o'clock in the morning, when the announcements were consistently advocating no resistance, many of those around me were still determined to fight the tanks come what may.

Inside the parliament that night, though, there was one voice of calm which did much to keep the situation under control. That was the voice of Colonel-General Konstantin Kobets, the Chairman of the Defence and Security Committee of the Russian Council of Ministers. He was the man Yeltsin appointed to oversee the defence of the parliament, and who must take most of the credit for the efficiency of the operation. Kobets directed the construction of the two rings of barricades around the parliament, advising on how best to thwart advancing tanks; and he was the central figure in organizing the thousands of civilian volunteers into a disciplined and responsive defence force. But most of all, Kobets personally directed the collection of intelligence about the movements of Soviet army units in the city, allowing at least some early warning of a potential attack. It was he who tried to negotiate with army commanders in the enemy camp, and who sent envoys to try to persuade Red Army units to defect: it was thus due to Kobet's activities that the elements of the Taman Guards, the Kantemirovskii Regiment and the Ryazan paratroopers under Colonel-General Grachov came to the parliament's defence.

A year earlier Kobets had been sacked from his post in the Soviet army command when he took a job on Yeltsin's staff, but at the height of the coup during the Tuesday night, Yeltsin was reported to have told Kobets, 'You know, I never trusted you until today'; and, in recognition of his loyalty, Yeltsin promoted him on the spot to the post of Russian Defence Minister.

Events were now moving rapidly towards what looked like being an unpleasant and dangerous battle for the parliament. On Tuesday evening Yeltsin's Foreign Ministry called diplomats from all Western embassies in Moscow to tell them the Russian leadership had firm information that the parliament was about to be stormed, and that they expected this to have bloody consequences. Personal telephone calls from Yeltsin to George Bush and other Western leaders carried the same message, with—it must be assumed—an appeal for the West to intervene with the Yanayev regime to try to avert the carnage.

While the diplomatic activity was continuing, though, the regime had ordered its military forces to stage an unprecedented show of strength on the streets of Moscow. Columns of tanks which had previously been held in reserve in the suburbs were called in to take part in a concerted operation to remove the makeshift road-blocks erected by demonstrators on all the approaches to the Russian parliament. These consisted of buses and lorries, either parked with their wheels removed, or overturned, on roads in concentric circles around the parliament, some of them up to a mile or so away from the building. In many locations the tanks were able to push aside the barricades with little difficulty, but some were not easily removed and clashes with demonstrators took place several times during the night. The most serious was outside the American Embassy on the city's inner ring road.

The reasons behind what happened on the Garden Ring between midnight and 6 A.M. are open to dispute, but the facts are clear and deeply disturbing. At around midnight light army tanks moved in to clear barricades on the ironically named Uprising Square (Ploschad' Vosstaniya) to the right of the US Embassy. These were light barriers and easily pushed aside, but the tank crews for some reason began firing off streams of bullets into the air.

This attracted several hundred demonstrators who had been manning heavier barricades on the far side of the Embassy. When they realized the ammunition being fired was live, the demonstrators ran away from the tanks, past the Embassy and into an underpass on the Garden Ring where it goes under Kalinin Prospekt, about five hundred yards up the hill from the Russian parliament.

Eight armoured personnel carriers followed the demonstrators down the slip road, where the APCs were set upon by crowds leaning over the underpass from the parapets on its side and the bridge above it. Two demonstrators managed to throw a large tarpaulin over the turret of the third APC in the column (number 536), and its crew—unable to see where they were going—panicked, revved up to full speed and ran into the side of the tunnel. The crowd who were in the tunnel ran for cover as the APC reversed and careered towards them, but thirty-seven-year old Volodya Usov was just too slow. He was caught in the tank tracks and crushed, his body dragged along by the APC for about twenty yards. There was later some debate about whether the vehicle's commander had run into the demonstrators while blinded by the tarpaulin, or whether it was a deliberate attempt to scatter the crowd. There was no doubt, though, that the troops on board the APCs fired live rounds into the air at this point, and one demonstrator who tried to pull Volodya Usov's body from under the tank tracks was hit and wounded.

The panic among the troops increased when it became clear that they were now trapped in the tunnel. Some of the APCs had already cleared the underpass, but those behind the crippled number 536 found their exit had been cut off by a line of buses. Their attempts to reverse out of the tunnel were also blocked, by a row of street-cleaning vehicles hastily put in place behind them. As the trapped APCs began rushing backwards and forwards, several demonstrators ran up with pieces of wood or metal spars, trying to thrust them into the tank tracks and disable them. Then the crowd began to attack, using Molotov cocktails which they had fetched from a nearby car, first throwing the home-made bombs from the parapet above, but then surrounding the APCs and pouring petrol over the lead vehicle as it tried to ram the buses blocking its way. This APC was set on fire with the crew still trapped inside (they were later rescued, and the threat of exploding ammunition averted thanks to water brought by the demonstrators themselves to extinguish the blaze).

By now the army's patience had been exhausted and firing broke out from all the trapped vehicles. A bullet fired by one of the soldiers ricocheted off the wall of the tunnel and flew into the crowd on the parapet above. Ilya Krichevsky, a twenty-six year old student who had taken no direct part in the attack on the armoured column, was hit and fatally wounded.

With the APCs repeatedly ramming the line of trolley-buses but unable to break through, the demonstrators were again emboldened to move closer, and that is when the third death occurred. Twenty-three-year-old Dmitri Komar was reported to have been trying to rescue a woman from the path of one of the charging vehicles when he slipped and was drawn under its tracks. He was crushed to death, but a companion who also fell under the APC emerged unscathed, having passed between the tank tracks.

With three demonstrators dead and one vehicle in flames, the army commanders gave the order to switch off the vehicles' engines, batten down the hatches and await help. The stand-off lasted for about half an hour, until the arrival of a delegation from the Moscow District Military command. Led by Lieutenant-General Nikolai Smirnov, the delegation managed to reach a compromise with the crowd to win the APCs' release: the terrified soldiers inside the vehicles would be guaranteed safe passage (the demonstrators had earlier been threatening to lynch them), in return for agreeing to hoist the colours of the Russian republic and renounce their allegiance to the Yanayev regime. The major who had been commanding the APCs reportedly ran away, presumably fearing retribution, but the soldiers themselves agreed to the deal and at six o'clock in the morning the remaining vehicles were driven away in triumph by the demonstrators.

Back at the Russian parliament, the sound of gunfire and revving engines from the incident outside the US Embassy had been clearly audible, and rumours of escalating military action were threatening to spark panic among the crowds of defenders. The public address system periodically broadcast news of tank movements heading in the direction of the parliament, and calls for a general alert were made on three separate occasions, quoting intelligence gathered by the parliamentary defence committee that an attack was imminent. Around two o'clock in the morning it was announced that units of the feared and hated OMON—the special Interior Ministry troops which had carried out the massacres in Latvia and Lithuania—had taken over the former Comecon building on the other side of the street (the building had been unoccupied since Comecon itself collapsed several months earlier), and were preparing to fire on the parliament's defenders. Whether or not this information was true, the threat of death from a sniper's bullet then seemed very real, and it is testimony to the defenders' courage that more of them did not leave at that stage.

Within an hour, the news that three young demonstrators had been killed outside the American Embassy was relayed to the crowd, and everyone present was convinced that we were to be the army's next target. The loudspeakers announced that all women should leave the area. The rest of us who remained behind prepared to meet the tanks. It was the darkest hour of the night, the coup looked about to succeed and democracy in the Soviet Union was all but extinguished.

Excerpt from Martin Sixsmith, *Moscow Coup* (London: Simon & Schuster Ltd., 1991), pp. 32–44. Reprinted by permission of Martin Sixsmith and A. M. Heath and Company, LTD. The author wishes to express his gratitude to Martin Sixsmith and A. M. Heath and Company, LTD.

Thirteen
YELTSIN'S APPEAL TO THE ARMY

The night of August 20, 1991, was the turning point of coup attempt, when soldiers ordered to attack Yeltsin's supporters refused to do so. Yeltsin, who had many contacts among junior officers, made the following stirring appeal to the army on August 20, in the hope that the army would not obey orders issued by the Emergency Committee.

APPEAL BY BORIS YELTSIN, PRESIDENT OF THE RUSSIAN SFSR, TO THE SOLDIERS AND OFFICERS OF THE USSR ARMED FORCES, THE USSR STATE SECURITY COMMITTEE AND THE USSR MINISTRY OF INTERNAL AFFAIRS. (Kuranty [Chimes], special edition No. 3, Aug. 20, p. 1. Complete text:) Servicemen! Fellow countrymen! A coup d'etat has been attempted. The President of the USSR, who is the Supreme Commander in Chief of the USSR Armed Forces, has been removed from his post. The Vice-President of the USSR, the Prime Minister of the USSR, the Chairman of the USSR State Security Committee and the USSR Ministers of Defense and of Internal Affairs have become members of an unconstitutional body, thereby committing high treason—a very grave crime against the state.

The country is threatened with terror. The "order" that the latter-day saviors of the fatherland are promising us will end in tragedy—the suppression of dissent, concentration camps, nighttime arrests. "A better life" will remain a propaganda fraud.

Soldiers and officers of Russia! I appeal to you at this tragic moment for Russia and the whole country. Do not let yourselves be caught in a web of false promises and demagogic talk about your military duty! Do not become a blind instrument of the criminal will of a group of adventurists who have flouted the Constitution and laws of the USSR.

Soldiers! I appeal to you. Think about your loved ones, your friends, your people. At the difficult moment of choice, do not forget that you have taken an oath of loyalty to the people. The people against whom they are trying to turn your weapons.

You can build a throne out of bayonets, but you cannot sit on it for long. There is no return to the past, nor will there be. The conspirators' days are numbered.

Soldiers, officers and generals! An hour ago (4 P.M.) I appointed a Chairman of the RSFSR Committee on Defense Questions. He is your comrade-in-arms, Col. Gen. Konstantin Kobets. A decree has been issued according to which all territorial and other agencies of the Ministry of Internal Affairs, the State Security Committee and the Ministry of Defense on RSFSR territory are ordered to immediately carry out all orders of the President of the RSFSR, the RSFSR State Security Committee, the RSFSR Ministry of Internal Affairs and the RSFSR State Committee on Defense Questions.

Dark clouds of terror and dictatorship have gathered over Russia and over the whole country, but they cannot become an eternal night. The law will triumph on our soil, and our long-suffering people will regain their freedom, this time once and for all.

Soldiers! I believe that in this tragic hour you will make the right choice, and that the honor and glory of Russian arms will not be stained with the blood of the people.

English translation from *The Current Digest of the Soviet Press*, vol. 43, no. 33. Translation copyright © 1991 by *The Current Digest of the Soviet Press*, published weekly at Columbus, Ohio. Reprinted by permission of the Digest.

Fourteen
GORBACHEV RETURNS TO MOSCOW

Yeltsin's vice president, Alexander Rutskoi, retrieved Mikhail Gorbachev from his Crimean incarceration and brought him back to Moscow on August 22, 1991. The following document is the text of Gorbachev's televised address to the Soviet people upon his return.

STATEMENT BY M. S. GORBACHEV ON SOVIET TELEVISION ON AUG. 22, 1991. (Pravda, Aug. 23, p. 1; Izvestia, pp. 1–2. 1,300 words. Condensed text:) Dear fellow citizens. I speak to you at a moment when I can already say with full justification that the coup d'etat has failed. The conspirators miscalculated. They underestimated the most important thing—the fact that during these years, difficult though they have been, the people have changed. They have breathed the air of freedom, and no one can take that away from them.

The outburst of popular indignation was provoked by criminals against the state, who encroached on democracy and attempted to restore the totalitarian regime. They tried to do the most terrible thing possible—to turn the Army against the people. But they failed at that, as well. Many commanders and officers and the majority of soldiers, whole units and large formations, refused to follow their orders. They remained loyal to their oath and stood side by side with the courageous defenders of democracy.

When, on Aug. 18, four of the conspirators came to me in the Crimea and presented an ultimatum—that I either give up my post, or voluntarily hand over my powers to them, or sign a decree on a state of emergency—I told them then: You are adventurists and criminals; you will ruin yourselves and do terrible harm to the people, and nothing will come of your plans anyway. The people are not going to resign themselves to your dictatorship and the loss of everything that has been gained in these past few years.

Come to your senses—the whole affair will end in civil war and great bloodshed, and you will have to answer for it. I rejected all their demands. Then they placed troops all around the house where I was spending my vacation, on both sea and land, put psychological pressure on me and watched my every move, totally isolating me from the outside world.

Evidently their objective was this—to break the President psychologically.

I realized this with particular clarity when I learned what had been said at the press conference given by this so-called State Committee for the State of Emergency, when they announced that I was incapable of performing the functions of President and, moreover, promised to produce a medical finding to that effect very soon.

So their objective stemmed from the idea that, if the facts did not correspond to their statements—i.e., if the President was not in the condition they claimed—any means available must be used to reduce him to a condition in which he was truly broken, physically and psychologically. For 72 hours I did not know what was happening in the country.

The conspiracy has been foiled, and the adventurists have been arrested and will be severely punished. But blood has been spilled. Defenders of freedom lost their lives. I want to convey my deepest condolences to their families, relatives and loved ones, and to their friends and colleagues. Their names should be engraved on commemorative plaques at the places where they died.

I want to thank all those who, risking not only their positions and their personal freedom but often their lives as well, stood in the front ranks of defenders of the constitutional system, defenders of the law and of human rights. Above all I must note the outstanding role played by Russian President Boris Nikolayevich Yeltsin, who stood at the center of the resistance to the conspiracy and dictatorship; by Ivan Stepanovich Silayev, Chairman of the Russian government; by Aleksandr Vladimirovich Rutskoi, Vice-President of Russia; and by many political and public figures, the whole Supreme Soviet of the Russian Federation, and the Muscovites and Leningraders who also rose to the defense of democracy. I cannot omit mention of the selfless devotion to their democratic professional duty that was shown by the vast majority of journalists and all the news media. At that difficult hour they unerringly decided where and with whom they should stand, did not take fright, did not lose their courage and did not kowtow to the usurpers.

The principled position taken by the Presidents and parliaments of most of the republics and by the majority of Russia's provinces and of local Soviets was very important in thwarting the conspiracy. They succeeded in firmly rising to the defense of legality and their sovereign rights.

I want to express my gratitude to the peoples and governments of foreign countries who, at this critical time for us, spoke out in defense of democracy in the Soviet Union and supported the country's legitimate leadership. . . .

What were the conspirators counting on? On the fact that the people are tired of waiting for their lives to improve, that the crisis continues, production is still declining, the situation in the market is grave, finances are in a state of disorder, and crime is on the rise. People don't want to put up with this. And they are right. But the conspirators did not take into account the fact that people want all these problems to be dealt with legally, within the framework of democracy, and not at the expense of freedom to exercise human rights, not through dictatorship and violence. . . .

In addition to punishment for the conspiracy's leaders, a sense of justice also demands an assessment of the actions of those officials who could have offered resistance to the coup but did not, took a wait-and-see position, or were even prepared to go hat in hand to the criminal Committee for the State of Emergency.

Of course, I don't mean that these people should be prosecuted if their actions were not of an illegal nature. But the public should know what caliber of people they are—who reacted how at this crucial moment, and what each one's true face is. I would consider it proper if those individuals who did not find the courage in themselves to rise to the defense of the law voluntarily resigned from their state posts.

I have already talked with the leaders of the republics about further plans of action, and it appears that a new date for the signing of the [Union] Treaty will be set very soon. This will be followed by the adoption of a new Union Constitution and a new election law and by elections to the Union parliament and the presidency. This work must be done within the established deadlines, without delay, since any prolonging of the transition period, as we can see, endangers democratic transformations.

We must draw the proper conclusions from the fact that there turned out not to be a sufficiently dependable system of state security. These matters require the most careful study, and they too must be addressed in the very near future.

I, as President, am deeply upset by everything that has happened. And

I feel a sense of responsibility to all of you—for the fact that I did not do everything possible to keep it from happening. I should say, what we all lived through in these past few days. It is a hard lesson, especially for me. A lesson with respect to my approach to the advancement of leadership cadres, among other things. It is now clear, for example, that the Congress of People's Deputies, which refused to elect the Vice-President in the first round of voting, was right, but the President, using his powers, insisted on having his way. And he was wrong. And you could say that it wasn't the only mistake.

Now the first priority is to bring the country out of shock. It would be unjustified to think that all the danger has passed. In this connection, right now the most essential thing is for all political forces that adhere to the principles of democracy to act responsibly. All of us who shattered this conspiracy, who stood firmly in the way of these criminal schemes, must by all means avoid following the methods they—the conspirators—resorted to. We must strictly adhere to the Constitution and the law and act in a concerted and responsible manner. The events of these past few days have shown that society has already reached a new level of development. That there will be no return to the past, no matter how much the reactionary forces want it, and that in principle we have chosen the correct path for the country's progress. . . .

English translation from *The Current Digest of the Soviet Press*, vol. 43, no. 34. Translation copyright © 1991 by *The Current Digest of the Soviet Press*, published weekly at Columbus, Ohio. Reprinted by permission of the Digest.

Fifteen
GORBACHEV'S PRESS CONFERENCE

In the following excerpts from an August 23, 1991, press conference, Gorbachev answered questions regarding his initial response to the coup attempt, his post-coup political relationship with Yeltsin, and his fears of an anti-Communist backlash in the USSR.

PRESS CONFERENCE BY THE USSR PRESIDENT. (Pravda, Aug. 23, p. 2. 5,400 words. Condensed text:) On Aug. 22 USSR President M. S. Gorbachev held a press conference in Moscow. Addressing reporters, he said: . . .

We have been through . . . the most difficult ordeal in all the years of the reformation of our society since 1985. We were faced with a genuine— without exaggeration—unconstitutional coup, organized by reactionary forces who turned out to be at the very center of the leadership, right next to the President. These people, whom I appointed, believed and trusted, turned out to be not only participants in but the organizers of a plot

against the President, against the constitutional system, against perestroika, against the people, against democracy.

At 4:50 P.M. on Aug. 18, the chief of my security guards informed me
that a group of people had arrived who were demanding to meet with me.
I said that I was not expecting anyone, I had not invited anyone, and no
one had notified me about this. The chief security guard said that he didn't
know anything, either. Why did you let them in, then? Because Plekhanov,
director of the State Security Committee's protection administration, was
with them, he said. Otherwise the guards would not have let them in to
see the President. Those are the rules. They are strict, but necessary.

I decided to find out who had sent them, since I had all my communications channels there—government, regular, strategic, satellite, and so on.
I picked up the receiver of one of the telephones—I was working in my
office just then—and it was dead. I picked up another phone, a third, a
fourth, a fifth—they were all dead. I picked up the internal telephone—
disconnected. That was it. I was isolated.

I realized that this mission was not going to be the sort of mission we
ordinarily deal with. I called together my wife, daughter and son-in-law
and told them what had happened. I didn't need any more information: I
could see that something very serious was going on. Evidently they were
about to try to blackmail me, or there would be an attempt to arrest me
or take me away or something. Indeed, anything at all might happen. I
told Raisa Maksimovna, Irina and Anatoly that if it was a question of the
key thing, of my policies, my course, I would stand my ground to the very
end. I would not give in to any blackmail, any threats or any pressure,
and I would not make any other decisions.

I considered it necessary to say this; you understand why: Anything at
all could happen next. Especially for the members of my family. We know
that, too.

The whole family said that the decision was up to me; they were ready
to share whatever might happen, right to the end. That was the end of
our consultation. . . .

One of the foreign reporters asked: Who has more power now, the
President of the USSR or the President of Russia?

I would not put the question that way, M. S. Gorbachev explained. In
recent months Boris Nikolayevich and I have been doing all we can to
ensure that concord and cooperation between us become a permanent
factor in the unification of all democratic forces, along with all the republics. The past few days have further demonstrated this. Let's think about
it. Some people are trying to undermine this position, but we have been
strengthened by the situation, and we know who is really who. . . .

One of the reporters was anxious: Do any roots of the unsuccessful plot
still remain in society? They have to be combated vigorously.

I do not think, M. S. Gorbachev answered, that after everything that has happened we ought to organize a "witch-hunt" and act as they did in the past. No. We need to deal with everything on the basis of the law, within the framework of democracy and glasnost and movement toward a law-governed state. Therefore, when I was told today that after the rally columns were moving toward Staraya Square, toward the KGB building, combined efforts were made to ensure that everything was done to prevent the occurrence of any dangerous incidents: That would have been a big present to the reactionary forces. Everything must be solely within the limits of law and legality.

Sixteen
COMMUNIST PARTY ACTIVITIES ARE BANNED IN RUSSIA

Yeltsin banned the activities of the Communist Party in Russia after the collapse of the attempted coup. Following is the text of his August 23, 1991, decree banning the Russian republic's branch of the CPSU. This act ended the viability of the CPSU, because Russia had always been the primary source of support for the Communist Party within the union.

Decree of the Russian SFSR President: ON SUSPENDING THE AC-TIVITY OF THE RSFSR COMMUNIST PARTY. (Rossiiskaya gazeta, Aug. 27, p. 3. Complete text:) The RSFSR Communist Party, which is operating on RSFSR territory and has not registered in accordance with the established procedure, supported the so-called State Committee for the State of Emergency in the USSR, which staged a coup d'etat and forcibly removed the President of the USSR from his position. Emergency committees (commissions) were created in a number of regions of the RSFSR with the direct participation of republic, territory and province agencies of the RSFSR Communist Party, which is a flagrant violation of the USSR law "On Public Associations."

In defiance of the RSFSR Constitution, agencies of the RSFSR Communist Party in republics, territories and provinces have repeatedly interfered in judicial activity and are hindering the implementation of the RSFSR President's July 20, 1991, decree "On Terminating the Activity of the Organizational Structures of Political Parties and Mass Public Movements in State Agencies, Institutions and Organizations of the RSFSR."

On the basis of the above, I decree that:

1. The RSFSR Ministry of Internal Affairs and the RSFSR Prosecutor's Office are to conduct an investigation into instances of unconstitutional

activity by agencies of the RSFSR Communist Party. The relevant materials are to be forwarded to judicial agencies for examination.

2. The activity of agencies and organizations of the RSFSR Communist Party is to be suspended pending final judicial resolution of the question of the unconstitutionality of the RSFSR Communist Party's actions.

3. The RSFSR Ministry of Internal Affairs is to ensure the safekeeping of the property and monetary resources of agencies and organizations of the RSFSR Communist Party pending the adoption of a final decision by judicial agencies.

4. The RSFSR Central Bank is to ensure the suspension, pending a special order, of operations involving the spending of money from the accounts of agencies and organizations of the RSFSR Communist Party.

5. The RSFSR Prosecutor's Office is ordered to ensure supervision over the implementation of this decree.

6. This decree goes into effect the moment it is signed.

B. YELTSIN,
President of the RSFSR.

The Kremlin, Moscow, Aug. 23, 1991.
No. 79.

Seventeen
CONFISCATION OF COMMUNIST PARTY PROPERTY IN RUSSIA

On August 25, 1991, Yeltsin confiscated the property held by the CPSU in the Russian republic, and by the Russian republic's branch of the party. Following is the text of Yeltsin's decree ordering that all party property now be considered the property of the Russian republic.

Decree of the Russian SFSR President: ON THE PROPERTY OF THE CPSU AND THE RSFSR COMMUNIST PARTY. (Rossiiskaya gazeta, Aug. 30, p. 2. Complete text:) In connection with the dissolution of the CPSU Central Committee and the suspension of the activity of the RSFSR Communist Party, I decree that:

1. All the real estate and other property belonging to the CPSU and the RSFSR Communist Party, including cash in rubles and foreign currency in banks, insurance and joint-stock companies, joint enterprises and other institutions and organizations situated in the RSFSR and abroad, is to be declared RSFSR state property.

CPSU funds abroad are to be distributed on the basis of an agreement among the republics after they sign the Union Treaty.

2. Within 24 hours, the RSFSR Central Bank, the RSFSR Bank for Foreign Trade and the RSFSR Ministry of Finance are to conduct a strict accounting of all cash, both in rubles and in foreign currency, of the CPSU and the RSFSR Communist Party in the USSR State Bank, the USSR Bank for Foreign Economic Activity, the USSR Ministry of Finance and other USSR organizations and institutions in the RSFSR, and to suspend the use of this money pending a special order from the President of the RSFSR or the Chairman of the RSFSR Council of Ministers.

3. The right to use, in the RSFSR, real estate and other property of the CPSU and the RSFSR Communist Party that belonged to the CPSU Central Committee and the RSFSR Communist Party Central Committee is to be transferred to the RSFSR Council of Ministers, and the right to use property that belonged to republic, territory, province, regional, city and district committees of the CPSU and the RSFSR Communist Party is to be transferred to the corresponding bodies of executive power in the RSFSR on whose territory these organizations are located.

The RSFSR Council of Ministers is to transfer some of the buildings of the CPSU Central Committee located in the city of Moscow to the Union republics that are part of the USSR.

4. The Public-Political Center of the Moscow City and Moscow Province Party Committees, located at 2 Tsvetnoi Boulevard, is to be turned over to the Presidium of the RSFSR Supreme Soviet.

5. All bodies of executive power in the RSFSR, the RSFSR Council of Ministers, the RSFSR Ministry of Internal Affairs and the RSFSR State Security Committee are instructed to prevent any attempts to damage or steal real estate or other property of the CPSU and the RSFSR Communist Party, as well as attempts by individuals or organizations to use this property for selfish purposes.

Bodies of executive power are required to provide extensive information to the population concerning their decisions on the use of the aforesaid property.

6. The RSFSR Ministry of Foreign Affairs is to urgently request that the governments of all countries freeze CPSU funds in banks and other organizations and institutions in those countries, and it is also to report data on the amounts of these funds and bank holdings to the RSFSR Council of Ministers.

7. This decree goes into effect the moment it is signed.

B. YELTSIN,
President of the RSFSR.

The Kremlin, Moscow, Aug. 25, 1991.
No. 90.

Eighteen
GORBACHEV'S RESIGNATION FROM THE PARTY

After he learned of the party's involvement in the attempted coup,
Mikhail Gorbachev resigned as general secretary of the CPSU on August 26, 1991, and dissolved the party's Central Committee. Following
is the text of Gorbachev's resignation statement.

THE PARTY HAS PLAYED ITSELF OUT.—A Statement That Is Not
Shaking the World. (Izvestia, Aug. 26, p. 2. 1,600 words. Condensed text:)
The Secretariat and Politburo of the CPSU Central Committee did not
speak out against the coup d'etat, and the Central Committee did not
manage to take a decisive position of condemnation and opposition, nor
did it stir Communists to combat the flouting of constitutional legality.
The conspirators turned out to include members of the Party leadership,
and a number of Party committees and media outlets supported the actions of the state criminals. This put millions of Communists in an awkward position.

Many Party members refused to cooperate with the conspirators, condemned the coup and joined the struggle against it. No one has the moral
right to make sweeping accusations against all Communists, and I, as President, consider myself obliged to defend them, as citizens, against unfounded accusations.

In this situation, the CPSU Central Committee must make the difficult
but honorable decision to dissolve itself. The republic Communist Parties
and local Party organizations will determine their own fates.

I do not consider it possible to continue performing the functions of
General Secretary of the CPSU Central Committee, and I resign from that
position. I believe that the democratically minded Communists who remained true to constitutional legality and the course aimed at the renewal
of society will call for the creation, on a new basis, of a Party that will be
capable of actively joining, together with all progressive forces, in the continuation of fundamental democratic transformations in the interests of
the working people.—[signed] M. GORBACHEV.

Nineteen
THE DISBANDING OF THE COMMUNIST PARTY

> Yeltsin had ordered the suspension of CPSU activities in in the days
> following the attempted coup. In November 1991 he banned the party
> completely within the Russian republic, claiming that its continued
> existence would imperil the Russian republic. Following is the text of
> his ban on "the gigantic mechanism of the Communist Party ma-
> chine."

Official Department: DECREE OF THE PRESIDENT OF THE RUS-
SIAN SOVIET FEDERATED SOCIALIST REPUBLIC ON THE AC-
TIVITY OF THE CPSU AND THE RSFSR COMMUNIST PARTY.
(Rossiiskaya gazeta, Nov. 9, p. 2. 1,100 words. Condensed text:) The events
of Aug. 19–21 made it glaringly obvious that the CPSU was never a party.
It was a special mechanism for shaping and exercising political power by
fusing with state structures or making them directly subordinate to the
CPSU. The CPSU's leadership structures exercised their own dictatorship
and created, at state expense, the property basis for unlimited power.

This was confirmed during the open hearings in the RSFSR Supreme
Soviet on the role of the CPSU in the coup d'etat of Aug. 19–21.

It is the CPSU's leadership structures, which to all intents and purposes
swallowed up the state and used it as their tool, that bear responsibility
for the historical impasse into which the peoples of the Soviet Union have
been driven and the state of disintegration we have reached.

The activity of these structures was clearly antipopular and unconstitutional in nature and was directly linked to the incitement of religious,
social and nationality-based strife among the country's peoples and to the
infringement of basic human and civil rights and liberties that are recognized by the entire international community.

The logical finale of its [the Party's] political activity was the unconstitutional coup of Aug. 19–21, 1991, which was supported by the CPSU's
leadership.

Despite the measures taken with respect to these structures, they have
not ceased their unlawful activity aimed at an even greater exacerbation
of the crisis and the creation of conditions for a new antipopular coup.

It has become obvious that as long as the CPSU structures continue to
exist there can be no guarantees against another putsch or coup.

Attempts to defame millions of rank-and-file Party members who had
nothing to do with the high-handedness and violence committed in their
name or to ban them from certain occupations are impermissible. But
attempts to resuscitate the gigantic mechanism of the Communist Party

machine and to give it an opportunity to crush the young shoots of Russian democracy are just as impermissible.

In view of the fact that the RSFSR Communist Party has not been registered according to established procedure and that the CPSU's registration by USSR state structures that used to be directly controlled by the CPSU Central Committee was carried out with flagrant violations of the law and has no pre-judicial force for the RSFSR, and on the basis of and in fulfillment of Arts. 7 and 121.4 of the RSFSR Constitution, I decree:

1. That the activity of the CPSU and the RSFSR Communist Party is to cease on the territory of the RSFSR and that their organizational structures are to be disbanded.

2. That state bodies of executive power of the RSFSR, its territories, provinces, autonomous province[s] and autonomous regions and the cities of Moscow and St. Petersburg, as well as agencies of the prosecutor's office, are to rule out the prosecution of RSFSR citizens for the fact of having belonged to the CPSU or the RSFSR Communist Party.

3. That the property of the CPSU and the RSFSR Communist Party on the territory of the RSFSR is to be transferred to the ownership of the state. The RSFSR Council of Ministers is to handle the transfer of CPSU and RSFSR Communist Party property on RSFSR territory and the process of placing it under the jurisdiction of bodies of state administration of the RSFSR and the republics that are part of the RSFSR.

4. That the RSFSR Council of Ministers, RSFSR ministries and departments and the corresponding state bodies of executive power in the republics that are part of the RSFSR, the territories, provinces, autonomous province[s] and autonomous regions and the cities of Moscow and St. Petersburg are to take the necessary measures for the immediate and comprehensive implementation of this decree.

B. YELTSIN,
President of the RSFSR.

English translation from *The Current Digest of the Soviet Press*, vol. 43, no. 45. Translation copyright © 1991 by *The Current Digest of the Soviet Press*, published weekly at Columbus, Ohio. Reprinted by permission of the Digest.

Twenty
THE MINSK AGREEMENT

Following is the text of the document signed on December 8, 1991, by Belarus, Russia, and Ukraine that terminated the existence of the USSR and created the Commonwealth of Independent States, or CIS. Member states pledged cooperation on economic, military, and environmental matters. Membership was open to the other former republics of the USSR. Only the Baltic states (Estonia, Latvia, and Lithuania) and Georgia declined the offer to join. Eight other republics—Armenia, Azerbaidjan, Kazakhstan, Kirghizstan, Moldavia (soon to be called Moldova), Tadjikistan, Turkmenistan, and Uzbekistan—joined the CIS at the Alma Ata (Kazakhstan) Agreement on December 21, 1991.

AGREEMENT ON THE CREATION OF A COMMONWEALTH OF INDEPENDENT STATES. (Rossiiskaya gazeta, Dec. 10, pp. 1–2. Complete text:) We, the Republic of Belarus, the Russian Federation (RSFSR) and Ukraine, as founder-states of the USSR and signatories to the Union Treaty of 1922, hereinafter called the High Contracting Parties, state that the USSR as a subject of international law and geopolitical reality is terminating its existence.

Based on the historic community of our peoples and the ties that have developed among them, and considering the bilateral treaties concluded between the High Contracting Parties,

seeking to build democratic states based on the rule of law,

intending to develop our relations on the basis of mutual recognition of and respect for state sovereignty, the inalienable right of self-determination, the principles of equality and noninterference in internal affairs, the renunciation of the use of force and economic or any other means of pressure, the settlement of disputed problems through conciliation, and other generally recognized principles and norms of international law,

considering that the further development and strengthening of relations of friendship, good-neighborliness and mutually advantageous cooperation among our states corresponds to the fundamental national interests of their peoples and serves the cause of peace and security,

confirming our commitment to the goals and principles of the United Nations Charter, the Helsinki Final Act and other documents of the Conference on Security and Cooperation in Europe,

pledging to observe generally recognized international norms on human rights and the rights of peoples,

have agreed on the following:

Art. 1.—The High Contracting Parties are founding a Commonwealth of Independent States.

Art. 2.—The High Contracting Parties guarantee equal rights and liberties to their citizens, regardless of nationality or other differences. Each of the High Contracting Parties guarantees to the citizens of other Parties, as well as to stateless individuals living on its territory, regardless of nationality or other differences, civil, political, social, economic and cultural rights and liberties in accordance with generally recognized norms of human rights.

Art. 3.—The High Contracting Parties, wishing to promote the expression, preservation and development of the distinctive ethnic, cultural, linguistic and religious features of the national minorities living on their territories and of existing unique ethno-cultural regions, take them under their protection.

Art. 4.—The High Contracting Parties will develop equal and mutually advantageous cooperation among their peoples and states in the fields of politics, economics, culture, education, public health, environmental protection, science and trade and in humanitarian and other fields, will further the broad exchange of information, and will observe mutual obligations conscientiously and unswervingly.

The Parties consider it necessary to conclude agreements on cooperation in the indicated fields.

Art. 5.—The High Contracting Parties recognize and respect one another's territorial integrity and the inviolability of existing borders in the framework of the Commonwealth.

They guarantee open borders and freedom of movement for citizens and freedom for the transfer of information within the framework of the Commonwealth.

Art. 6.—The member-states of the Commonwealth will cooperate in ensuring international peace and security and in implementing effective measures for reducing weapons and military spending. They are striving for the elimination of all nuclear weapons and general and complete disarmament under strict international control.

The Parties will respect one another's endeavors to achieve the status of nuclear-weapon–free zones and neutral states.

The member-states of the Commonwealth will preserve and support a common military-strategic space under a joint command, including unified control over nuclear weapons, the procedure for which will be regulated by a special agreement.

They also jointly guarantee the necessary conditions for the stationing, functioning, and material and social support of the strategic armed forces. The Parties pledge to conduct a coordinated policy on questions of the social protection of and pensions for servicemen and their families.

Art. 7.—The High Contracting Parties recognize that the sphere of their joint activity, conducted on an equal basis through the common coordinating institutions of the Commonwealth, includes:

—the coordination of foreign-policy activity;

—cooperation in the formation and development of a common economic space and of all-European and Eurasian markets, and in the field of customs policy;

—cooperation in the development of transportation and communications systems;

—cooperation in the field of environmental protection, and participation in the creation of an all-encompassing international system of ecological security;

—questions of migration policy;

—the struggle against organized crime.

Art. 8.—The Parties recognize the planetary nature of the Chernobyl catastrophe and pledge to unite and coordinate their efforts to minimize and overcome its consequences.

They have agreed to conclude a special agreement for this purpose, one that takes into consideration the gravity of the consequences of the catastrophe.

Art. 9.—Disputes concerning the interpretation and application of the norms of this Agreement are to be resolved through negotiations between the appropriate agencies, and if necessary at the level of heads of state and government.

Art. 10.—Each of the High Contracting Parties reserves the right to suspend this Agreement or individual articles of it after notifying the signatories to the Agreement one year in advance.

The provisions of this Agreement may be added to or changed by mutual agreement of the High Contracting Parties.

Art. 11.—From the moment this Agreement is signed, the norms of third states, including the former USSR, may not be applied on the territory of the states signing the Agreement.

Art. 12.—The High Contracting Parties guarantee the fulfillment of their international obligations stemming from the treaties and agreements of the former USSR.

Art. 13.—This Agreement does not affect the obligations of the High Contracting Parties with respect to third states.

This Agreement is open for accession by all member-states of the former USSR, as well as for other states that share the goals and principles of this Agreement.

Art. 14.—The official location of the Commonwealth coordinating agencies is the city of Minsk.

The activity of agencies of the former USSR on the territory of the member-states of the Commonwealth is terminated.

Done in the city of Minsk on Dec. 8, 1991, in three copies each in the Belorussian, Russian and Ukrainian languages, all three texts having equal force.—[signed] For the Republic of Belarus, S. SHUSHKEVICH and V. KEBICH; for the RSFSR, B. YELTSIN and G. BURBULIS; for Ukraine, L. KRAVCHUK and V. FOKIN.

English translation from *The Current Digest of the Soviet Press*, vol. 43, no. 49. Translation copyright © 1991 by *The Current Digest of the Soviet Press*, published weekly at Columbus, Ohio. Reprinted by permission of the Digest.

Twenty-one
CIS STATEMENT ON ECONOMIC POLICY

> The signatories of the Minsk Agreement agreed on a common eco-
> nomic policy on December 9, 1991. The following statement noted that
> they would work toward the creation of a market economy and co-
> ordinate monetary, banking, and tax policies.

STATEMENT BY THE GOVERNMENTS OF THE REPUBLIC OF
BELARUS, THE RUSSIAN FEDERATION AND UKRAINE ON
THE COORDINATION OF ECONOMIC POLICY. (Izvestia, Dec. 9,
p. 1. Complete text:) The preservation and development of the close economic ties that have developed among our states is vitally necessary in
order to stabilize the situation in the national economy and to create the
preconditions for an economic revival.

The sides have agreed on the following:

—to conduct coordinated, radical economic reforms aimed at creating
full-fledged market mechanisms, transforming property relations and ensuring free enterprise;

—to refrain from any actions that cause economic damage to one
another;

—to construct economic relations and settlements on the basis of the
existing monetary unit—the ruble. To introduce national currencies on the
basis of special agreements guaranteeing observance of the sides' economic interests;

—to conclude an interbank agreement aimed at restricting monetary
emission, ensuring effective control of the money supply and forming a
system for mutual settlements;

—to conduct a coordinated policy of reducing deficits in the republics'
budgets;

—to conduct a coordinated policy of freeing up prices and providing
social protection for citizens;

—to undertake joint efforts aimed at ensuring a single economic space;

—to coordinate current foreign-economic activity and customs policy
and ensure freedom of transit;

—to settle, by special agreement, the question of the debts of former
Union enterprises;

—in 10 days' time, to agree upon the amounts and procedures for fi-
nancing expenditures in 1992 on defense and on eliminating the
consequences of the accident at the Chernobyl Atomic Power Station;

—to ask the republic Supreme Soviets, when forming tax policy, to take
into consideration the need to coordinate value-added tax rates;

—to promote the creation of joint enterprises (joint-stock companies);

—during December, to work out a mechanism for implementing interrepublic economic agreements.—[signed] For the Republic of Belarus, V. KEBICH; for the Russian Federation, G. BURBULIS; and for Ukraine, V. FOKIN.

English translation from *The Current Digest of the Soviet Press*, vol. 43, no. 49. Translation copyright © 1991 by *The Current Digest of the Soviet Press*, published weekly at Columbus, Ohio. Reprinted by permission of the Digest.

Twenty-two
WHAT IS SOVIET AND WHAT IS RUSSIAN?

Historian G. R. Urban published an interesting conversation with Soviet specialist Adam B. Ulam in 1993 regarding the history and legacy of the Soviet empire. Following is an excerpt from the conversation about the "key to tyranny" in the Soviet system.

URBAN Much confusion and considerable resentment have been caused in Sovietological discussion by the cavalier use of the words "Soviet" and "Russian" as interchangeable adjectives. Those who believe with Alexander Solzhenitsyn that the Communist system is of Western provenance and has been imposed on the Russian people are profoundly offended. Others say that Russian traditions and political culture are so strongly woven into the fabric of Soviet Communism that it is nonsensical to search for a clear distinction. Far from being a matter of mere semantics, the quarrel touches upon the very nature—the durability and changeability—of the Soviet system.

If "Soviet" did correctly apply to all things Russian, then we in the West would be inclined to take a harsher view of Russian society than we would if we were persuaded that "Soviet" and "Russian" were not only *not* coterminous, but were clearly antithetical. In other words, we could either say that the Soviet system was as alien to the Russian nation as it has shown itself to be to Poles, Czechs and Hungarians, and shape our policies accordingly. Or we could say that the Soviet system was what the Russian people have sustained and defended for seven decades, and shape our policies to fit *that* view.

Where do you stand in this conflict?

ULAM In everyday parlance the two are used interchangeably. This may be wrong but it is done, and I feel that not to do so would be pedantic. I prefer to make a distinction whenever clarity demands that we should; but it would be pretentious not to say "Soviet" for "Russian" and vice versa, occasionally. In most cases it is perfectly clear what we are talking about—whether we say "Russian" or "Soviet."

URBAN I would have thought communism would have resulted in a very different system if Marx's ideas had been put into effect in Italy or Holland rather than Russia—

ULAM Yes, it would . . .

URBAN And it is, therefore, difficult to deny that the Soviet system carries the birthmarks of Russian traditions and culture. Wouldn't this argue for a very thin distinction between "Soviet" and "Russian"?

ULAM It's difficult to deny the strength of the Russian component. Let us, however, also remember that the Russian origins of the Soviet system have been used—by sympathisers and apologists on the Left—to underline the grave imperfections of the Russian realisation of Marxism, and to argue that, but for those origins, Marxism would have had a better chance to produce an acceptable model with appeal throughout the world. In either case, the conjunction between the corruptions of the Soviet system and the backwardness of Tsarist Russia from which it arose is broadly recognised—whether to condemn the system because it is "Russian," or to rescue Marxism from "the Russian connection."

On balance, however, I am not inclined to stress the link between Sovietism and the Russian heritage. It is striking that in several countries communism has assumed almost the same characteristics as define the Soviet system. The French Communists, for example, were for a long time just as obedient to Moscow as any oblast chief under Stalin in the USSR. They followed Soviet propaganda in every detail. No feat of mismanagement was too outrageous for the French party not to present it as "an economic victory," and no lie too transparent not to embrace it as a triumph of the truth. If *national* environment is the decisive influence on political behaviour, why did the French Party behave as it did?

No, communism has the notions of autocracy and imperialism deeply embedded in its dogmatic scheme, and wherever communism triumphs it tends to produce a tyrannical system. The Russian background certainly added to the depredations of Soviet Communism, but it is insufficient to explain it. It is *communism* that accounts for Soviet despotism, not the history of the Russian people.

URBAN Wouldn't you say that the French Communists obeyed Moscow because it was the world's anti-capitalist power centre, and thus the ultimate guarantor and paymaster of their existence—and not because they were propelled into submissive behaviour by Communist doctrine? "Polycentrism" notwithstanding, we have little experience of Communist parties that are not, in one way or another, beholden to Moscow.

ULAM Moscow as the ultimate anchor did, of course, have a powerful impact on the French Party's behaviour. But the source of French dogmatism was not just the power of Moscow, but the whole body of Communist thought.

The Chinese Party offers another good example. Quite early in their political life, the Chinese Communists diverged from Moscow. Yet, in their model of communism today, autocratic "Stalinist" features are as firmly established as before they came to power, and later under Mao's stewardship as leader of the ruling Party. I am also convinced that in Germany, had the local Communist rebellions turned into a nationwide revolution in the early 1920s, as Lenin hoped, that nation would have ended up as a dictatorship very similar to the one Lenin founded and Stalin perfected in Russia. The key to the tyranny of communism is communism, not the country in which it is enacted.

URBAN Richard Pipes thinks otherwise. He seems to believe that the Soviet system is a product of Russian history and political culture at least as much as of Bolshevism.

ULAM Pipes thinks the system is a logical continuation of tsarist autocracy. This is unjust to prerevolutionary Russia, which was opening up in different directions, including liberal and Westernising ones. I would not deny the impact of the Russian milieu—how could one? But it is greatly exaggerated to say that Bolshevism is specifically and exclusively *Russian*, and to single out Russian political culture for special condemnation.

URBAN But wasn't there fertile ground for collectivism and egalitarianism in the Russian *artel* and *mir*—as many late 19th-century Social Democrats argued?

These men and women were in a hurry. They were worried that if they went by the book of Marxist theory, Russian society could not undergo a final Communist revolution before it had gone through "capitalism" and "a bourgeois revolution"—and that would take time. . . . Hence, they said, the existing collectivist *mir* system in the Russian villages should be used as a shortcut to Communism—there was no need to wait for a bourgeois revolution.

Wouldn't you say that the spirit of egalitarianism in the Russian countryside predisposed Russia to accepting first Leninism and then the full egalitarian rigours of Stalinism? Even under Gorbachev, seven decades on, egalitarianism is a massive stumbling block to economic reform and private enterprise. The peasants are reluctant to accept the land they are offered under Gorbachev's leasehold arrangements, and many of the newly formed cooperatives have had to be closed down in response to public anger. Don't these signs rather confirm the view that in some respects "the spirit of Bolshevism" isn't fundamentally at odds with "the spirit of Russia"?

ULAM No, I don't think they do. It's true that Marx himself, in an incautious moment a few years before his death, said that Russia might (as an exception to the rule) "skip" the stage of bourgeois revolution and capitalism, and advance, through the *mir* system, straight to a Communist revolution. But most historians would disagree with the view that the *mir* background automatically predisposed the Russian Muzhiks to embracing collectivisation.

The best proof that this was not so was the bloody resistance they offered to Stalin's collectivisation campaigns in the 1929–32 period and the passive resistance they have offered ever since—ultimately compelling the régime to start reexamining, under Gorbachev, the whole concept of collectivisation. That the Russian farmer is now hesitating to accept land is not due to his innate reluctance to take charge of his destiny, but to the haunting memory of what happened to his father and grandfather under Stalin's terror—and how "the *NEP*-men" were treated when Stalin decreed that the New Economic Policy had come to an end.

URBAN You have said that wherever communism takes hold, a tyrannical system is bound to emerge because of the inherently totalitarian character of Bolshevism. Aren't there other explanations? I would have thought reasons could be found in the history and traditions of any nation to explain why its particular form of communism (or fascism, or whatever) is the most wicked.

For example, arguing from certain strands in French history, one could say that the French habit of driving logical argument to its extremes and the glorification of *la Révolution* and "the people" make French Communism a most likely candidate for tyranny. In Germany, the combination of the spirit of Hegel, militarism, and the cult of efficiency would argue for an equally nasty form of German Communist despotism. In Romania, we need hardly look beyond the heritage of Vlad the Impaler, the spirit of the Ottoman janissaries, and the Iron Guard to explain why Ceausescu's now-toppled dictatorship was the worst of them all.

So, while I am not disputing your point that the trigger to the rise of all these unpleasant forms of government was, or could be, the totalitarian doctrine of communism. I do believe that every nation has in it the capacity to turn any political idea into a particularly nasty—or an acceptable and civilised—dispensation. There are, it seems to me, strands in every nation's history that can be summoned to support this-or-that form of development—good or bad. But our problem with Bolshevism is that it chose, or perhaps saw itself forced to build on, the most retrograde elements in the Russian heritage.

ULAM I think we are really both saying the same thing. There *is*, as I've said, a Russian element in the Soviet form of communism. It stems from a particularly authoritarian conception of socialism in the nineteenth century, to which were added a very Russian form of xenophobia and Russian nationalism. Leninism inherited all these, and although Lenin thought of himself as a sworn enemy of great-Russian chauvinism, Russian nationalism nevertheless became a determining element of the Soviet system. Under Stalin it came out into the open as a strong Russian chauvinism.

But, with all that, I believe that the totalitarian character of Communist régimes stems from the basic tenets of communism itself. I do not disagree with you that suitable elements from the national past can be summoned to give it colour and legitimacy, but the basic impulse is the letter and spirit of Communist thought. Communism has to be tyrannical and imperialistic *because* it is communism.

Extracts from G. R. Urban, *End of Empire: The Demise of the Soviet Union* (Washington, D.C.: American University Press, 1993), pp. 155–159. Reprinted by permission of the publisher.

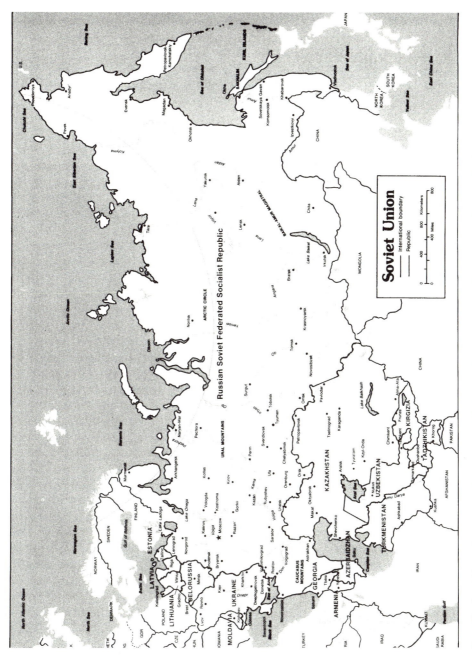

From *The Soviet Union*, third edition. Copyright © 1990. Reprinted by permission of Congressional Quarterly Books.

EASTERN EUROPE

Miles
0   100   200   300

Barents Sea

White Sea

UNION OF
SOVIET
SOCIALIST
REPUBLICS

FINLAND

Helsinki
Leningrad

Gulf of Finland

NORWAY
Tallinn
Moscow

SWEDEN
ESTONIA

Oslo
Stockholm

LATVIA
Riga

LITHUANIA
Minsk

Vilnius
Baltic Sea
BELORUSSIA
DENMARK
RSFSR

Copenhagen
Kiev

Warsaw
UKRAINE

Berlin
POLAND
Sea of
Azov

EAST
GERMANY
MOLDAVIA

Kishinev

Prague

WEST
GERMANY
CZECHOSLOVAKIA
Black Sea

Budapest

Vienna
RUMANIA

AUSTRIA
HUNGARY
Bucharest

From *The Soviet Union*, third edition. Copyright © 1990. Reprinted by permission of Congressional Quarterly Books.

Glossary of Selected Terms

Alpha Team. An elite Soviet counter-terrorism unit that was part of the KGB, but became a separate entity in 1991, following the collapse of the USSR. The Alpha Team was responsible for the attacks on civilians in the Vilnius Massacre (January, 1991) in Lithuania. Its leaders, however, were sympathetic to Boris Yeltsin during the August 1991 coup attempt, and refused to obey KGB orders to storm the Russian Republic's White House—center of Yeltsin's resistance to the coup.

Apparatchiks. Senior members of the Communist Party of the Soviet Union who held the most important positions within the Soviet government and who received substantial material benefits in return for their loyalty.

Berlin Blockade. A road and rail blockade of the western part of Berlin by Soviet forces on Stalin's orders (July 1948–May 1949) to attempt to pressure the United States, the United Kingdom, and France into dropping plans to merge their post-World War II occupation zones into a state of West Germany. The blockade was one of the major crises of the Cold War, and it failed due to the massive American, British, and French airlift (250,000 flights brought food and supplies into the city).

CIS. The Commonwealth of Independent States, which was formed in December 1991 to replace the USSR. Member states are independent but have agreed to the creation of a post-Soviet "common market" within their borders, as well as a unified military and nuclear command structure. Members include Armenia, Azerbaidjan, Belarus, Kazakhstan, Kirghizstan, Moldova, Russia, Tajikistan, Turkmenistan, Ukraine, and Uzbekistan.

Client State. A state dependent politically, economically, and military upon the assistance of a more powerful state, and frequently willing to assist in carrying out the foreign policy objectives of its powerful ally. The Warsaw Pact countries, for example, were clients of the more powerful USSR.

Cold War. A struggle lasting 1945–1989 (or to 1991, the end of the USSR) between the USSR, its Communist client states in the Warsaw Pact and its overseas allies, against the U.S. and the countries of the NATO alliance. It was characterized by a few cases of open warfare—usually between one of the superpowers and a client or ally of its rival (as in the case of Korea, Vietnam, and Afghanistan). For some of the period, the Cold War was characterized also by fears of imminent nuclear war, and each side spent a great deal of time and money preparing for an anticipated global confrontation—a World War III—that never occurred.

Collectivization. Soviet policy of forcing peasants throughout the USSR onto government-owned collective farms, a plan devised by Stalin and carried out in a brutal manner in the 1930s. Millions of peasants died in the process from starvation or in the labor camps of the Gulag Archipelago. Collectivization was an effective means of exercising state control over agricultural labor, but it caused great harm to the productive capacity of the USSR.

Command Economy. The centralized, planned system of economy of the USSR from 1929 onward, in which governmental planning agencies attempted to exercise complete control over the Soviet market (and, by extension, that of their client regimes as well). The Soviets established quotas regulating the output of industrial and agricultural sectors of the economy. It proved to be unprofitable, and Gorbachev's perestroika attempted to reform the system by introducing capitalist elements.

Communism. Totalitarian system of governmental, economic, and social organization based upon the writings of the philosopher Karl Marx (1818–1883). The ideal of Communism is a classless and stateless society in which industrial workers (the proletariat), whom Marx alleged are enslaved by Capitalism, can completely control their destiny. Marx believed that traditional religion and many aspects of culture would wither away under Communism. Socialism, in which the state controls the political, economic, and societal mechanisms in the name of the workers, is considered a temporary, transitional phase on the path to Communism. Stalin claimed that the USSR had attained Socialism in 1936. Several Communist governments were created in the twentieth century, such as the USSR, by members of Communist parties and sympathetic military leaders, who claimed to rule on behalf of the proletariat.

CPRF. The Communist Party of the Russian Federation, the largest and most important of the post-Soviet Communist parties operating within the CIS. In 1995 it had approximately 500,000 members, and in that year it won 22 percent of the seats in the Russian Parliament. Its presidential candidate, Gennady Zyuganov, narrowly lost the primary to Boris Yeltsin in 1996 but lost badly to Yeltsin in the subsequent runoff.

CPSU. The Communist Party of the Soviet Union, which was formed from the Bolshevik faction of the Russian Social Democratic (Communist) Party and ruled the Soviet Union from 1917 to 1991. At its height in the 1980s it had about 19 million members, but after the August 1991 coup attempt against General Secretary (and President) Mikhail Gorbachev by party hard-liners, it was dissolved and its property was sold.

Cuban Missile Crisis. High point of Cold War confrontation between Warsaw Pact and NATO (October 16–27, 1962). Caused by Soviet leader Nikita Khrushchev's placement of intermediate-range nuclear missiles in Cuba aimed at the U.S., at the request of Cuban Communist leader Fidel Castro. American President John F. Kennedy blockaded Cuba to force Castro to return the missiles to the USSR. Both sides threatened nuclear war, and World War III could have broken out at any moment. The crisis was defused by secret negotiations on October 26 and 27. The Soviets withdrew the missiles from Cuba, and the U.S. also withdrew missiles from Turkey.

Destalinization. Policy initiated by Soviet leader Nikita Khrushchev at the Twentieth Congress of the CPSU in February, 1956, in which the political legacy of Joseph Stalin was minimized within the USSR (somewhat of a de-emphasis on the Gulag Archipelago, and a slight lessening of governmental controls on the arts and sciences).

Détente. Diplomacy conducted between the USSR and the U.S. which aimed to preserve the balance of power between the superpowers and reduce the risk of nuclear war. The Strategic Arms Limitation Treaties, SALT I (1972) and SALT II (1979), are examples of détente.

DRA. The Democratic Republic of Afghanistan, a Communist client of the USSR that was founded with Soviet assistance in 1978. When the DRA was in danger of falling to Muslim rebels (the *mujahidin*) in 1979, Soviet leader Leonid Brezhnev sent in Soviet military forces to prop it up. The DRA fell to the *mujahidin*, however, after the withdrawal of Soviet forces in 1989.

Glasnost. Mikhail Gorbachev's policy of political openness within the USSR beginning in 1986. The policy involved ending Soviet government censorship in the press and in cultural activities, and reevaluating the policies of past Soviet leaders. New publications appeared, and the government tolerated debate about perestroika.

Gosplan. The Soviet state planning commission, founded in 1921, that was responsible for charting the USSR's economic course by establishing Five-Year Plans for industrial production.

Gulag Archipelago. Group of concentration camps scattered throughout the USSR in which millions of political prisoners (people deemed to be ideological deviants) perished due to exposure, overwork, undernourishment, or outright murder. One of the more brutal coercive elements of the Soviet system.

Iron Curtain. Term coined by Winston Churchill in 1946, to describe an imaginary line in central Europe, behind which lay the Communist states dominated by the USSR—the future Warsaw Pact countries.

KGB. The Soviet political police, founded in 1921 by Felix Djerzhinsky. Originally called Cheka (1917–1922), the organization underwent many name changes: GPU (1922–1924), OGPU (1924–1934), NKVD (1934–1943), NKGB (1943–1946), MGB (1946–1953), MVD (1953–1954), and KGB from 1954. Its duties involved locating and eliminating all actual (or potential) sources of dissent within the USSR, as well as foreign espionage and domestic counterintelligence activities. The KGB still exists, but has been split into two divisions—

a Central Intelligence Service and a Russian Security and Internal Affairs
Ministry (an inter-republic security service). The number of personnel has
been reduced from 500,000 to about 40,000.

Khalq. A faction of the People's Democratic Party of Afghanistan, founded in
1965 by Nur Muhammad Taraki. Its name means "people." It was more
openly Marxist than its Afghan Communist rival, Parcham. Its quarrels with
Parcham weakened the DRA and set the stage for the Soviet invasion of
Afghanistan in 1979.

Komsomol. The All-Union Leninist Communist Union of Youth, formed in 1918
for purposes of indoctrinating Soviet youth. Its members were between 14
and 28 years of age. More than 70 percent of CPSU recruits came from Komsomol ranks.

Korean War. Lasting from 1950 to 1953, the war started when Communist North
Korea, a Soviet ally, invaded South Korea, and United Nations forces, led by
the United States, came to the aid of South Korea. It became a major crisis
of the Cold War, when the Communist Peoples' Republic of China entered
the war on behalf of North Korea. Stalin, however, decided against direct
intervention in the conflict and the USSR played a secondary role, providing
supplies for the North Koreans.

Kremlin. Headquarters of the government of the USSR.

Mujahidin. Afghan Muslim "holy warriors," whose struggle against the Communist
DRA led to the intervention of the Soviet army in Afghanistan in 1979. The
mujahidin, who were supplied with weapons by the United States and NATO,
as well as by fellow Muslims, held the Soviet military at bay for ten years and ultimately won a victory when Gorbachev ordered the withdrawal of Soviet
forces. The *mujahidin* were not a conventional army but were organized into
several factions that followed individual imams (religious leaders).

Mutual Verification. The need to monitor nuclear disarmament and testing policies
between the superpowers in the SALT I and SALT II treaties led to the idea
that each side should be able to inspect the nuclear military facilities of their
opponent. Mutual distrust between the superpowers, however, led to the demise of the idea of mutual verification.

NATO. The North Atlantic Treaty Organization is a military alliance formed in
1949 whose original members consisted of the United States, Canada, Iceland,
the United Kingdom, France, Portugal, Italy, Belgium, the Netherlands, Luxembourg, Denmark, and Norway. Formed in the aftermath of the Berlin
Blockade, the alliance was ostensibly anti-Soviet.

NEP. The New Economic Policy was formulated by Lenin in 1921 to revive the
sagging Soviet economy by allowing the reintroduction of certain capitalist
elements into the economy, such as private land ownership and small-scale
privately-owned workshops. It was successful in making the Soviet economy
more productive, but only lasted until 1929, when Stalin replaced it with the
First Five-Year Plan.

New Style Calendar. The Russians adopted the Julian calendar at the time of Peter
the Great in 1700. The Bolsheviks later adopted the more accurate Gregorian

calendar on January 31, 1918, and decreed that the next day was February 14. This was to make the Russian calendar come into alignment with that of most of the rest of the world. Some histories date the events of the Russian Revolution by the Old Style (Julian) calendar which was then in use, while others prefer to use the New Style (Gregorian) calendar.

Oblast. A large subdivision of a Soviet republic, comparable to a province.

Parcham. A faction of the People's Democratic Party of Afghanistan that formed in 1965 and was led by Babrak Karmal. Its name means "banner." Although it was favored by the Soviets, it was less openly Marxist than its rival, Khalq, and tried to present itself as a moderate reformist party. Its quarrels with Khalq, however, led to *mujahidin* victories and Soviet intervention.

Perestroika. Mikhail Gorbachev's program of economic restructuring of the USSR. Perestroika began in 1985 and was intended to make the Soviet economy profitable through market reform. Gorbachev expected perestroika to bring about a better standard of living for Soviet citizens and thus bolster weakening popular support for the Soviet system. Glasnost was a part of perestroika, as was the slow democratization of Soviet politics.

Plebiscite. A vote in which a population can directly decide a political issue such as independence.

Plenum. Plenary meeting of the CPSU Central Committee, held at least twice a year.

Politburo. The most powerful body within the CPSU and the Soviet government, its 13 voting members aided the party general secretary in shaping the USSR's domestic and foreign policies.

PRC. The People's Republic of China, a Communist state founded in October 1949 by Mao Zedong. The USSR and the PRC signed a mutual assistance pact in 1950, which caused fears in the West of a global and unified Communist threat. However, the two states came to see themselves as rivals in east Asia and fought an inconclusive war in 1969 over border disputes. The PRC has outlasted the USSR.

Presidium. An all-powerful body elected by the Supreme Soviet, its thirty-eight members served collectively as the legal arbiter of the USSR, interpreting law and even ratifying diplomatic treaties.

Procurator. A kind of overseer and ombudsman within the Soviet legal system who supervised criminal investigations, authorized arrests, regulated prisons, and heard citizen complaints.

Propaganda. Important to the USSR from the very inception of the regime, propaganda serves to influence public opinion and regulate thought on a particular issue. The widespread promotion of the officially-sanctioned ideology of the CPSU was handled by Agitprop, a bureau of the CPSU Central Committee. Agitprop carefully regulated discussion of politics, history, economics, and a host of other topics. Propaganda infiltrated every aspect of Soviet life, as government censors monitored the written and spoken word in every incarnation.

Proxy Regime. A proxy regime is a client regime of a greater power that is willing (often for economic as well as ideological reasons) to assist the greater power in attaining its foreign policy objectives. A proxy state might go to war on behalf of a superpower ally. Several of the Warsaw Pact countries, as well as Cuba and Vietnam, were considered to be proxy states of the USSR during the Cold War.

Purges. The elimination of political opponents within the CPSU by high-ranking party leaders. Most victims of purges were charged with ideological deviance from the official beliefs of the CPSU. A purged victim was frequently executed, and, at a minimum, sentenced to a term in a Gulag prison camp. Stalin was responsible for the most widespread purges in the history of the USSR, in the mid-to-late 1930s, when millions of Soviet citizens perished.

Raion. An administrative area equivalent to a city district.

Rasputin Scandal. The scandal which contributed to the discrediting of the tsarist regime in 1915–1916, derived from the influence within the government wielded by religious charlatan Gregory Rasputin, who urged that many reliable ministers of the government be dismissed simply because he viewed them as rivals.

Rehabilitation. The restoration of the reputation of an individual previously purged by the Soviet system. In many cases, however, this was done posthumously because the state had executed the purge victim. Thus, it benefitted the survivors of the victim by reinstating a pension or simply clearing the family name. The first such cases derived from Khrushchev's destalinization of the mid-1950s, and applied only to party members victimized by Stalin. In the Gorbachev era, however, it became possible for non-party members to have their reputations restored as well. Cases of rehabilitation reinforced the opinion among the Soviet populace that the Soviet system was severely flawed.

Russification. The promotion of Russian ethnicity, language, and culture over that of other national groups within the USSR. While the Soviets officially claimed that the USSR was a multinational state, the degree to which members of non-Russian ethnic groups succeeded in the Soviet system depended upon fluency in Russian and an ability to adopt, or adapt themselves to, Russian culture.

SALT I and II. The Strategic Arms Limitation Treaties signed in 1972 (SALT I) and 1979 (SALT II) by Soviet leader Leonid Brezhnev and, respectively, American presidents Richard Nixon and Jimmy Carter. Conceived in the atmosphere of détente, the treaties were supposed to limit the number of new weapons each side could test and produce, but problems relating to mutual verification hindered any possibility of success. The December 1979 Soviet invasion of Afghanistan ended the ratification procedure for SALT II in the U.S. Congress.

Socialism. Intermediary step along the path to Communism in the ideology of Communism. The Socialist state is brought about by revolution, and theoretically signifies the "dictatorship of the proletariat and peasantry," in which the state controls the means of production, as well as all aspects of politics and culture in the name of the workers. See also Communism.

Sputnik. The world's first artificial, or man-made, satellite launched into Earth's orbit by the USSR on October 4, 1957. It began the space race between the USSR and U.S. and demonstrated the early technical lead held by the USSR.

Supreme Soviet. Elite legislative branch of the Soviet government, consisting of about 1,500 members, and divided into two equal chambers, the Soviet of the Union (whose members were chosen by the population), and the Soviet of Nationalities (whose members were chosen by national republic leaders and regional leaders).

Third World. Term used to describe the various countries of the world whose economies are developing towards more sophisticated conditions, and which are located outside of either Europe or the Americas (the conventional "Old World" and "New World," respectively). Seen as a battleground between Communism and capitalism during the Cold War.

Totalitarianism. Form of government originating in the 20th century in which all political and military power is monopolized by a small elite, and in which no opposition to the established order is tolerated. The difference between totalitarianism and other authoritarian regimes is the degree to which the totalitarian regimes can exercise power over every aspect of life of the citizenry. Soviet and Chinese Communism are examples of totalitarianism, as is the fascism of Nazi Germany and Imperial Japan during World War II.

USSR. The Union of Soviet Socialist Republics, the Communist state formed by the Bolshevik revolution of 1917. Its government was controlled by the CPSU, and it lasted until 1991. The USSR was divided into 15 Soviet Socialist Republics: Armenia, Azerbaidjan, Belarus, Estonia, Georgia, Kazakhstan, Kirghizstan, Latvia, Lithuania, Moldavia, Russia, Tajikistan, Turkmenistan, Ukraine, and Uzbekistan. The USSR's leaders were Vladimir Lenin (1917–1924), Joseph Stalin (1924–1953), Nikita Khrushchev (1953–1964), Leonid Brezhnev (1964–1982), Yuri Andropov (1982–1984), Konstantin Chernenko (1984–1985), and Mikhail Gorbachev (1985–1991). The USSR was dissolved in December 1991 after the failed August coup attempt against Gorbachev by CPSU hard-liners. It has been replaced by the CIS.

Virgin Lands Program. Initiated by Nikita Khrushchev in 1953–1956, it brought new areas under cultivation in Central Asia as a means to improve the productivity of Soviet agriculture.

Warsaw Pact. Military alliance between the USSR and its East European client states—Poland, Hungary, Czechoslovakia, East Germany, Romania, and Bulgaria established by Nikita Khrushchev in May, 1955. Albania was a member until 1968. The USSR trained the officers in each of the East European armies, and closely monitored each of the armies. It provided a kind of Communist buffer zone for the USSR and a counterbalance to NATO, until it dissolved during Mikhail Gorbachev's tenure in 1989.

Annotated Bibliography

The annotated bibliography is divided into sections historically (beginning with the origin of the Soviet system), and the final section is video material.

THE ORIGIN OF THE SOVIET UNION

Lane, David S. *The Roots of Russian Communism: A Social and Historical Study of Russian Social Democracy, 1898–1907.* University Park: Pennsylvania State University Press, 1975. Provides a good overview of the formative years of the Communist Party in Russia.

Lewin, Moshe. *Lenin's Last Struggle.* New York: Monthly Review Press, 1978. A seminal work on Lenin's efforts to prevent the growth of an overly large bureaucracy in the Soviet system and his attempt to stem the growing power of Stalin.

Lincoln, W. Bruce. *Passage through Armageddon: The Russians in War and Revolution.* New York: Simon and Schuster, 1986. A massive and masterful examination of World War I and the Bolshevik takeover.

Pipes, Richard, ed. *Revolutionary Russia.* Cambridge, MA: Harvard University Press, 1968. An authoritative source on the activites of the revolutionaries.

Ulam, Adam B. *The Bolsheviks.* New York: Collier Books, 1968. A judicious assessment of the party, its goals, and its methods.

Von Laue, Theodore H. *Why Lenin? Why Stalin? Why Gorbachev?* New York: HarperCollins, 1993. A short but insightful essay on the major transformations of Soviet government from the beginning to the end of the system.

Wolfe, Bertram D. *Three Who Made a Revolution.* New York: Dial Press, 1964. A penetrating analysis of the leaders of the Bolshevik revolution.

THE SOVIET POLITICAL SYSTEM

Baradat, Leon. *Soviet Political Society*. Englewood Cliffs, NJ: Prentice-Hall, 1989. A lucid explanation of the inner workings of Soviet politics.

Black, Cyril E. *Understanding Soviet Politics: The Perspective of Russian History*. Boulder, CO: Westview Press, 1986. A good overview of the evolution of the Soviet system within the context of Russian political thought.

Brown, Archie, ed. *Political Leadership in the Soviet Union*. Bloomington: Indiana University Press, 1990. A good collection of readings about the paths to power in the Soviet system.

Conquest, Robert. *The Soviet Political System*. New York: Praeger, 1968. A reliable study of Soviet government.

Hazard, John N. *The Soviet System of Government*. Chicago: University of Chicago Press, 1968. A useful explanation of the structure of Soviet government.

Hough, Jerry F., and Merle Fainsod. *How the Soviet Union Is Governed*. Cambridge, MA: Harvard University Press, 1979. A lucid assessment of the mechanisms of Soviet power.

Lewin, Moshe. *The Making of the Soviet System*. New York: Pantheon, 1985. An insightful analysis of the apparatus of Soviet government.

Narkiewicz, Olga A. *The Making of the Soviet State Apparatus*. Manchester, U.K.: Manchester University Press, 1985. An authoritative essay on the inner workings of the Soviet system.

THE LEGACY OF SOVIET REPRESSION

Conquest, Robert. *The Great Terror: A Reassessment*. New York: Oxford University Press, 1990. Judicious reassessments of the causes, course, and consequences of the Great Terror.

———. *The Great Terror: Stalin's Purge of the Thirties*. New York: MacMillan, 1968. An analysis of the Soviet purges during the Stalin period.

———. *Harvest of Sorrow: Soviet Collectivization and the Terror-Famine*. New York: Oxford University Press, 1986. An examination of the human cost of the Soviet collectivization of agriculture during the Stalin years.

———. *The Nation Killers: The Soviet Deportation of Nationalities*. New York: MacMillan, 1960. An important study of the Soviet repression of national minorities within the union during World War II.

Dolot, Miron. *Execution by Hunger: The Hidden Holocaust*. New York: W. W. Norton, 1985. A gripping study of the terrible consequences of Soviet collectivization in the 1930s.

Heller, Mikhail, and Alexander Nekrich. *Utopia in Power: The History of the Soviet Union from 1917 to the Present*. New York: Summit Books, 1986. An interesting interpretation of the evolution of the mechanisms of Soviet tyranny.

Malia, Martin. *The Soviet Tragedy: A History of Socialism in Russia, 1917–1991*. New York: Free Press, 1995. A thorough examination of Soviet ideology and the conventional Soviet justifications for coercion.

Medvedev, Roy. *All Stalin's Men*. Garden City, NJ: Anchor Press–Doubleday,

1984. A skillful exploration of the Stalinist system and the men who made it work.

———. *Let History Judge: The Origins and Consequences of Stalinism*. New York: Columbia University Press, 1989. An authoritative assessment of the legacy of Stalinism in the USSR.

Pipes, Richard, ed. *The Unknown Lenin: From the Secret Archive*. New Haven, CT: Yale University Press, 1996. A volume in the Yale University Press "Annals of Communism" series, which identifies the totalitarian trends of early Soviet politics through previously unknown documents by Lenin.

Solzhenitsyn, Alexander. *The Gulag Archipelago, 1918–1956*, 3 vols. New York: Harper and Row, 1973–1978. The definitive study of the Soviet Gulag system, from the perspective of a former inmate. Also available in a one-volume abridged edition, edited by Edward Ericson (New York: Harper and Row, 1985).

SOVIET LEADERS AND POLITICAL TRENDS
BEFORE GORBACHEV

Bialer, Seweryn. *Stalin's Successors: Leadership, Stability and Change in the Soviet Union*. New York: Cambridge University Press, 1980. A good assessment of the means by which Stalin's immediate successors (Khrushchev and Brezhnev) rose to power in the Soviet political system.

Breslauer, George W. *Khrushchev and Brezhnev as Leaders: Building Authority in Soviet Politics*. Winchester, MA: Allen and Unwin, 1982. A sound analysis of how Khrushchev and Brezhnev wielded power within the Soviet system.

Dallin, Alexander, and Thomas H. Larson, eds. *Soviet Politics since Khrushchev*. Englewood Cliffs, NJ: Prentice-Hall, 1968. Dated but judicious essays on the Soviet system from the time when Brezhnev held a position of unchallenged supremacy.

Deutscher, Isaac. *Stalin: A Political Biography*. New York: Oxford University Press, 1966. A good examination of the methods behind the apparent madness of Stalinism.

Doder, Dusko. *Shadows and Whispers: Power Politics inside the Kremlin from Brezhnev to Gorbachev*. New York: Random House, 1986. A journalist's analysis of the inner workings of Soviet politics.

Dornberg, John. *Brezhnev: The Masks of Power*. New York: Basic Books, 1974. A good look at Brezhnev from the time when he was at the height of his power.

Fireside, Harvey. *Soviet Psychoprisons*. New York: W. W. Norton, 1979. An important look at the misuse of psychiatry as a coercive tool of the KGB under Brezhnev, and the creation of a new kind of Gulag.

Friedman, Robert O., ed. *Soviet Jewry in the Decisive Decade, 1971–1980*. Durham, NC: Duke University Press, 1985. Good essays on the conditions of Soviet Jewry during the era of détente.

Hoffmann, Eric P., and Robbin F. Laird. *The Politics of Modernization in the Soviet Union*. Ithaca: Cornell University Press, 1982. An interesting interpretation of the evolving technological infrastructure of the Soviet Union.

Hough, Jerry F. *Soviet Leadership in Transition*. Washington, DC: Brookings In-
    stitution, 1977. An examination of the changes in and continuity of Soviet
    political priorities during the late Brezhnev period.
Kelley, Donald R., ed. *Soviet Politics in the Brezhnev Era*. New York: Praeger,
    1980. An authoritative collection of readings about Brezhnev.
Kerblay, Basile H. *Modern Soviet Society*. New York: Pantheon, 1983. A compre-
    hensive study of the Soviet population from the beginning of the Soviet
    regime through the Brezhnev era, examining subjects as varied as educa-
    tion, work, marriage, religion, crime, and mobility.
Medvedev, Zhores. *Andropov*. New York: W. W. Norton, 1983. A biography of
    the fifth leader of the Soviet Union.
Rancour-Lafferiere, Daniel. *The Mind of Stalin*. Ann Arbor, MI: Ardis, 1988. A
    recent assessment of the forces behind Stalinism.
Strong, John W. *Soviet Union under Brezhnev and Kosygin: The Transition Years*.
    New York: Van Nostrand Reinhold, 1971. An overview of Brezhnev's con-
    solidation of power and his political relationship with Alexei Kosygin, chair-
    man of the Council of Ministers.
Tucker, Robert C. *Stalinism: Essays in Historical Interpretation*. New York: W. W.
    Norton, 1977. An authoritative collection of various perspectives on Stalin-
    ism and its legacy in the USSR.
Voslensky, Michael. *Nomenklatura*. New York: Doubleday, 1985. An important
    study of the power held by the apparatchiks within the Soviet system.
Wolfe, Bertram D., ed. and trans. *Khrushchev and Stalin's Ghost*. New York: Prae-
    ger, 1957. A translation and analysis of Khrushchev's destalinization speech
    of 1956.
Wolin, Simon, and Robert M. Slusser, eds. *The Soviet Secret Police*. New York:
    Praeger, 1957. Traces the evolution of the primary means of repression
    within Soviet society.

SOVIET FOREIGN POLICY AND THE COLD WAR

Blight, James G., and David A. Welch. *On the Brink: Americans and Soviets Re-
    examine the Cuban Missile Crisis*. New York: Hill and Wang, 1989. A recent
    study of the most dangerous moment of the Cold War, and a good example
    of how glasnost enabled Soviet historians to fully come to grips with the
    past.
Byrnes, Robert F., ed. *After Brezhnev: The Sources of Soviet Conduct in the 1980s*.
    Bloomington: Indiana University Press, 1983. An assessment of Soviet for-
    eign policy trends in the late Brezhnev years.
Caldwell, Dan. *American-Soviet Relations: From 1947 to the Nixon-Kissinger
    Grand Design*. Westport, CT: Greenwood Press, 1981. An overview of su-
    perpower relations during the first three decades of the Cold War.
Caldwell, Lawrence T., and William Diebold. *Soviet-American Relations in the
    1980s: Superpower Politics and East-West Trade*. New York: McGraw-Hill,
    1980. An examination of the economic aspects of the competition between
    the superpowers in the late Brezhnev period.
Dawisha, Karen. *Kremlin and the Prague Spring*. Berkeley: University of Califor-

nia Press, 1984. A lucid explanation of the forces behind the Czechoslo-vakian revolt of 1968 and the Soviet intervention.

Edmonds, Robin. *Soviet Foreign Policy 1962–1973: The Parody of Super Power.* New York: Oxford University Press, 1975. An interesting interpretation of the aims and results of the Brezhnev doctrine, written at the height of Brezhnev's power.

Gelman, Harry. *The Brezhnev Politburo and the Decline of Detente.* Ithaca: Cornell University Press, 1984. A study of shifts in Soviet policy away from détente.

Katz, Mark N. *The Third World in Soviet Military Thought.* Baltimore, MD: Johns Hopkins University Press, 1982. An important examination of Soviet strategic objectives in the Third World during the Brezhnev period.

Lettis, Richard, and William E. Morris, eds. *The Hungarian Revolt.* New York: Scribner's, 1961. A good sourcebook on the Hungarian revolt of 1956.

Lewis, William J. *The Warsaw Pact: Arms, Doctrine, and Strategy.* New York: McGraw-Hill, 1982. An authoritative assessment of Warsaw Pact capabilities from the late Brezhnev period.

Low, Alfred D. *The Sino-Soviet Dispute.* Madison, NJ: Fairleigh Dickinson University Press, 1978. An overview of the Sino-Soviet conflict that erupted into war in 1969.

Pipes, Richard E., ed. *U.S.-Soviet Relations in the Era of Detente.* Boulder, CO: Westview Press, 1981. A comprehensive collection of readings about superpower relations in the Brezhnev era.

Rubinstein, Alvin Z. *Soviet Foreign Policy since World War II.* Boston: Little, Brown, 1983. A textbook on the evolution of Soviet foreign policy during the Cold War years.

Steele, Jonathan. *Soviet Power: The Kremlin's Foreign Policy—Brezhnev to Andropov.* New York: Simon and Schuster, 1983. A good look at Soviet foreign policy priorities through the transition period from Brezhnev to Andropov.

Ulam, Adam B. *Dangerous Relations: The Soviet Union in World Politics, 1970–1982.* New York: Oxford, 1982. An important study of Brezhnev's foreign policy objectives.

———. *The Rivals: America and Russia since World War II.* New York: Viking, 1971. An authoritative work on superpower relations through the first half of Brezhnev's tenure.

Weeks, Albert L. *The Troubled Detente.* New York: New York University Press, 1977. An examination of problems inherent in the relations between the superpowers.

Yanov, Alexander. *Detente after Brezhnev: The Domestic Roots of Soviet Foreign Policy.* Berkeley, CA: Institute of International Studies, 1977. A dated but useful analysis of the sources of Soviet conduct in the Brezhnev period.

PERESTROIKA AND ITS BACKGROUND

Beichman, Arnold, and M. S. Bernstam. *Andropov: New Challenge to the West.* New York: Stein and Day, 1983. A good examination of Andropov's domestic and foreign policy objectives.

Bialer, Seweryn. *The Soviet Paradox: External Expansion and Internal Decline.* New York: A. A. Knopf, 1986. An assessment of Gorbachev's imperial dilemma.

Butson, Thomas G. *Gorbachev: A Biography.* New York: Stein and Day, 1985. A readable (but dated) narrative of Gorbachev's rise to power.

Colton, Timothy J. *The Dilemma of Reform in the Soviet Union.* New York: Council of Foreign Relations, 1986. A perceptive examination of the internal difficulties facing the Gorbachev reform process.

Daniels, Robert V. *The End of the Communist Revolution.* London: Routledge, 1993. An authoritative overview of perestroika.

Doder, Dusko, and Louise Branson. *Gorbachev: Heretic in the Kremlin.* New York: Viking Press, 1990. A thorough examination of Gorbachev's objectives and his method of government.

Gunlicks, Arthur B., and John D. Treadaway, eds. *Soviet Union under Gorbachev: Assessing the First Year.* New York: Praeger, 1987. Various early interpretations of Gorbachev and his impact.

Hazan, Barukh. *From Brezhnev to Gorbachev: Infighting in the Kremlin.* Boulder, CO: Westview Press, 1987. A study of the evolution of Soviet policy and the rise of Gorbachev.

Hosking, Geoffrey. *The Awakening of the Soviet Union.* Cambridge, MA: Harvard University Press, 1991. A reliable overview of changes wrought by Gorbachev in the Soviet Union prior to its collapse.

Joyce, Walter, Hillel Ticktin, and Stephen White, eds. *Gorbachev and Gorbachevism.* London: Frank Cass, 1989. Excellent essays on the motives and results of the perestroika process.

Kaiser, Robert G. *Why Gorbachev Happened: His Triumphs and Failures.* New York: Simon and Schuster, 1991. An insightful examination of Gorbachev's ideas for reform.

Kerblay, Basile H. *Gorbachev's Russia.* New York: Pantheon, 1989. A perceptive look at the political and social context of perestroika.

Lewin, Moshe. *The Gorbachev Phenomenon.* Berkeley, CA: Paragon House, 1988. A short but important assessment of the social and institutional factors that led to perestroika.

McCauley, Martin, ed. *Gorbachev and Perestroika.* New York: St. Martin's Press, 1990. An important collection of readings on perestroika from various perspectives.

———. *The Soviet Union under Gorbachev.* New York: St. Martin's Press, 1987. A good collection of studies on the early part of the Gorbachev era from a variety of perspectives.

Millar, James R., ed. *Cracks in the Monolith: Party Power in the Brezhnev Era.* Armonk, NY: M. E. Sharpe, 1992. An authoritative collection of essays on the background of perestroika in the Brezhnev era.

Miller, Robert F., John H. Miller, and Thomas H. Rigby, eds. *Gorbachev at the Helm: A New Era in Soviet Politics?* London: Croom Helm, 1987. An early collection of essays on the prospects of perestroika.

Niiseki, Kinya, ed. *The Soviet Union in Transition.* Boulder, CO: Westview Press, 1987. A collection of essays on perestroika from various viewpoints.

Nove, Alec. *Stalinism and After: The Road to Gorbachev*. London: Unwin Hyman, 1989. An important study of the institutional roots of perestroika.

Owen, Richard. *Comrade Chairman: Soviet Succession and the Rise of Gorbachev*. New York: Arbor House, 1987. An analysis of the factors accounting for Gorbachev's rise within the Soviet system.

Parker, John W. *Kremlin in Transition*, 2 vols. Boston: Unwin Hyman, 1991. A thorough and judicious assessment of the Gorbachev era.

Shtromas, Alexander, and Morton A. Kaplan, eds. *The Soviet Union and the Challenge of the Future*. New York: Paragon House, 1989. One of the most all-embracing multi-author volumes on perestroika, including essays on both the Soviet Union and the Soviet client regimes.

Walker, Martin. *The Waking Giant: Gorbachev's Russia*. New York: Pantheon, 1986. An early assessment of changes wrought by perestroika in the Soviet Union.

Zemtsov, Ilya. *Chernenko—The Last Bolshevik: The Soviet Union on the Eve of Perestroika*. New Brunswick, NJ: Transaction Books, 1989. An insightful examination of the Soviet Union on the threshold of perestroika.

Zemtsov, Ilya, and John Farrar. *Gorbachev: The Man and the System*. New Brunswick, NJ: Transaction Books, 1989. An overview of Gorbachev and perestroika at mid-point.

"INSIDER" PERSPECTIVES ON THE GORBACHEV ERA

Boldin, Valeri. *Ten Years That Shook the World: The Gorbachev Era as Witnessed by His Chief of Staff*. New York: Basic Books, 1994. An explanation of the inner workings of the Gorbachev reform process by Gorbachev's chief of staff.

Medvedev, Roy, and Giulietto Chiesa. *Time of Change: An Insider's View of Russia's Transformation*. New York: Pantheon, 1989. Discussions between Medvedev (a former dissident) and Italian journalist Chiesa on a wide range of topics, including glasnost, Chernobyl, Afghanistan, and the USSR's nationalities crisis.

Pozner, Vladimir. *Eyewitness: A Personal Account of the Unraveling of the Soviet Union*. New York: Random House, 1992. An interesting account written by a former American-Russian supporter of the Soviet system, whose views evolved along with the system.

Sakharov, Andrei. *Memoirs*. New York: A. A. Knopf, 1990. Important observations about the repressive nature of the Soviet system and the meaning of reform, from the Soviet Union's most notable dissident and nuclear scientist.

Shevardnadze, Eduard A. *The Future Belongs to Freedom*. New York: Free Press, 1991. Perspectives written by Gorbachev's foreign minister and an important proponent of perestroika.

Sobchak, Anatoly. *For a New Russia: The Mayor of St. Petersburg's Own Struggle for Justice and Democracy*. New York: Free Press, 1992. The case history of how the mayor of St. Petersburg was affected by perestroika and glasnost.

Yevtushenko, Yevgeny A. *Fatal Half Measures: The Culture of Democracy in the Soviet Union*. Boston: Little, Brown, 1991. A collection of essays spanning the years 1968–1990, by one of Russia's leading poets (and formerly a prominent dissident).

Zaslavskaya, Tatiana I. *The Second Socialist Revolution: An Alternative Soviet Strategy*. Bloomington: Indiana University Press, 1990. Insights from a prominent economist involved in perestroika reforms.

GLASNOST AND SOVIET SOCIETY

Cerf, Christopher, and Marina Albee, eds. *Small Fries: Letters from Soviet People to Ogonyok Magazine, 1987–1990*. New York: Summit, 1990. Letters from Soviet citizens to one of the major glasnost publications provide a good study of the concerns of average citizens during the era of perestroika.

Davies, R. W. *Soviet History in the Gorbachev Revolution*. Bloomington: Indiana University Press, 1989. An important study of how glasnost enabled Soviet history to be reexamined in an objective fashion, following almost seven decades of propaganda disguised as history in the Soviet Union.

Dizard, Wilson, and S. Blake Swensrud. *Gorbachev's Information Revolution: Controlling Glasnost in a New Electronic Age*. Boulder, CO: Westview Press, 1987. An exploration of the convergence of new freedoms and new technology in the Soviet Union during the Gorbachev era.

Jones, T. Anthony. *Perestroika: Gorbachev's Social Revolution*. Boulder, CO: Westview Press, 1989. An overview of the societal changes brought on by glasnost in the Soviet Union.

Korotich, Vitaly, ed. *The Best of 'Ogonyok': The New Journalism of Glasnost*. London: Heinemann, 1990. A selection of articles reflecting glasnost—from one of the major glasnost publications, chosen by its editor.

Lane, David S. *Soviet Society under Perestroika*. Boston: Unwin Hyman, 1990. A perceptive analysis of the transformation of Soviet life in the Gorbachev era.

Laqueur, Walter. *The Long Road to Freedom: Russia and Glasnost*. London: Unwin Hyman, 1989. An important work by a leading expert on the development of glasnost.

———. *Stalin: The Glasnost Revelations*. New York: Scribner's, 1990. An important study of the horrors of the Stalin era, revealed in the Gorbachev era by previously secret Soviet archives.

Melville, Andrei, and Gail W. Lapidus. *The Glasnost Papers: Voices on Reform from Moscow*. Boulder, CO: Westview Press, 1989. A study of the impact of the new freedom of expression on Soviet politics and society.

Miller, William Green, ed. *Toward a More Civil Society? The USSR under Mikhail Sergeyevich Gorbachev*. New York: Harper and Row, 1989. A collection of readings on the problems inherent in the attempt to bring democracy to the Soviet Union.

Shlapentokh, Vladimir. *Public and Private Life of the Soviet People: Changing Views in Post-Stalin Russia*. New York: Random House, 1990. One of the most important social histories of the Soviet Union, assessing developments over a period of almost 40 years.

————. *Soviet Ideologies in the Period of Glasnost: Responses to Brezhnev's Stagnation*. New York: Praeger, 1988. A particularly insightful study of the range of attitudes held by the Soviet leadership in the Gorbachev era.

THE ECONOMICS OF PERESTROIKA

Aslund, Anders. *Gorbachev's Struggle for Economic Reform: The Soviet Reform Process*. Ithaca: Cornell University Press, 1988. An authoritative work on the economic reform process in the Soviet Union under Gorbachev, written by an economics expert who has served as an advisor to the Russian Federation government of Boris Yeltsin.

Aslund, Anders, and P. R. G. Layard, eds. *Changing the Economic System*. New York: St. Martin's Press, 1993. A comprehensive collection of essays on the problems inherent in the transition to capitalism in the Soviet Union and the Russian Federation.

Becker, Abraham Samuel. *Gorbachev's Program for Economic Modernization and Reform*. Santa Monica, CA: Rand Corporation, 1986. A thorough but dated analysis of perestroika from the beginning of the reform process.

Berliner, Joseph. *Soviet Industry from Stalin to Gorbachev*. Ithaca: Cornell University Press, 1988. A look at the long-term trends in Soviet industry through mid-point of the Gorbachev era.

Campbell, Robert W. *The Failure of Soviet Economic Planning: System, Performance, Reform*. Bloomington: Indiana University Press, 1992. An assessment of why Gorbachev failed to reform the Soviet planned economy.

Davies, Robert W. *The Soviet Economy in Turmoil*. Cambridge, MA: Harvard University Press, 1989. An assessment of the relative successes and failures of perestroika at mid-point in the Gorbachev era.

Desai, Padma. *Perestroika in Perspective: The Design and Dilemmas of Soviet Reform*. Princeton, NJ: Princeton University Press, 1990. A thorough analysis of Gorbachev's economic plans and the problems of reforming the Soviet economic system.

Hewitt, Ed A. *Reforming the Soviet Economy*. Washington, DC: Brookings Institution, 1988. An overview of the economics of perestroika.

Hough, Jeffrey F. *Opening Up the Soviet Economy*. Washington, DC: Brookings Institution, 1988. An assessment of the results of economic reforms made under perestroika, from mid-point in Gorbachev's tenure.

Kontorovich, Vladimir, and Michael Ellman, eds. *The Disintegration of the Soviet Economic System*. London: Routledge, 1992. Important studies that interpret the ultimate failure of perestroika to bring about the changes that Gorbachev desired.

Millar, James R. *The Soviet Economic Experiment*. Urbana: University of Illinois Press, 1990. An overview of Gorbachev's economic reforms.

Moskoff, William. *Hard Times: Impoverishment and Protest in the Perestroika Years*. Armonk, NY: M. E. Sharpe, 1993. An important study of the social distress brought about by the phasing out of economic guarantees to Soviet citizens in the Gorbachev era.

PERESTROIKA-ERA FOREIGN POLICY

Clark, Susan L., ed. *Gorbachev's Agenda: Changes in Soviet Domestic and Foreign Policy*. Boulder, CO: Westview Press, 1989. A good collection discussing domestic and foreign priorities in the era of perestroika.

Clemens, Walter C. *Can Russia Change? The USSR Confronts Global Interdependence*. Boston: Unwin Hyman, 1990. A perceptive examination of the changing role of the Soviet Union in world politics in the late Gorbachev era.

Gelman, Harry. *Gorbachev's Policies toward Western Europe: A Balance Sheet*. Santa Monica, CA: Rand Corporation, 1987. An early (and therefore somewhat dated) assessment of Gorbachev's attitudes toward the western European countries and NATO, written prior to the collapse of the Warsaw Pact; provides context for the subsequent evolution of Gorbachev's views on the ending of the Cold War.

Hammond, Thomas T. *Red Flag over Afghanistan: The Communist Coup, the Soviet Invasion, and the Consequences*. Boulder, CO: Westview Press, 1984. A good overview of the Afghan War, written about five years into the conflict.

Holden, Gerard. *The Warsaw Pact: Soviet Security Policy and Bloc Politics*. New York: Blackwell, 1989. A useful study of pre-collapse Soviet attitudes on eastern Europe, published (ironically) during the year of the breakup of the Warsaw Pact.

Jacobsen, Carl G., ed. *Soviet Foreign Policy: New Dynamics, New Themes*. New York: St. Martin's Press, 1989. A collection of readings on the impact of perestroika on foreign policy, published prior to the collapse of the Warsaw Pact.

Laird, Robbin F., and Susan L. Clark. *The USSR and the Western Alliance*. Boston: Unwin Hyman, 1990. A look at the changing relationship between the Soviet Union and the NATO countries in the aftermath of the Warsaw Pact.

Lynch, Allen. *Gorbachev's International Outlook*. Boulder, CO: Westview Press, 1989. An examination of the foreign policy of the perestroika era, before the end of the Warsaw Pact.

Rubinstein, Alvin Z. *Moscow's Third World Strategy*. Princeton, NJ: Princeton University Press, 1988. Shows the shifting concerns of the Kremlin leadership with regard to Third World countries before the termination of Soviet subsidies to client regimes.

THE COLLAPSE OF THE WARSAW PACT

Ash, Timothy Garton. *The Magic Lantern: The Revolution of '89 Witnessed in Warsaw, Budapest, Berlin, and Prague*. New York: Random House, 1990. An excellent essay on the collapse of Communism in Poland, Hungary, East Germany, and Czechoslovakia.

Banac, Ivo, ed. *Eastern Europe in Revolution*. Ithaca: Cornell University Press, 1992. An authoritative collection of readings on the process of the collapse of communism in eastern Europe.

Dawisha, Karen. *Eastern Europe, Gorbachev, and Reform: The Great Challenge.* New York: Cambridge University Press, 1990. A thorough overview and analysis of the ending of the Soviet domination of eastern Europe brought about by Gorbachev's policies.

Gati, Charles. *The Bloc That Failed: Soviet–East European Relations in Transition.* Bloomington: Indiana University Press, 1990. An assessment of the end of the Soviet external empire in eastern Europe.

Gwertzman, Bernard, and Michael T. Kaufman, eds. *The Collapse of Communism.* New York: Times Books, 1990. An excellent collection of *New York Times* articles on the changes in the Soviet Union during the Gorbachev era and the collapse of the Warsaw Pact.

REFORM OF THE SOVIET POLITICAL AND LEGISLATIVE SYSTEMS

Barry, Donald D., ed. *Toward the Rule of Law in Russia? Political and Legal Reform in the Transition Period.* Armonk, NY: M. E. Sharpe, 1992. A collection of essays on the political and legal legacy of perestroika through the collapse of Communism.

Brown, Archie, ed. *New Thinking in Soviet Politics.* London: MacMillan, 1992. A collection of essays on the transformation of the Soviet political process brought on by perestroika.

Hazen, Barukh A. *Gorbachev's Gamble: The 19th All-Union Party Conference.* Boulder, CO: Westview Press, 1990. Analysis of the 1988 party gathering in which many of Gorbachev's political reforms were unveiled.

Huber, Robert T., and Donald R. Kelley, eds. *Perestroika-Era Politics: The New Soviet Legislature and Gorbachev's Political Reforms.* Armonk, NY: M. E. Sharpe, 1991. A collection of essays on Gorbachev's transformation of Soviet legislative and political procedures, and their implications for the future of the Soviet Union.

Kiernan, Brendan. *The End of Soviet Politics: Elections, Legislatures, and the Demise of the Communist Party.* Boulder, CO: Westview Press, 1993. An overview of how Gorbachev inadvertently caused the demise of the Soviet system.

McFaul, Michael, and Sergei Markov. *The Troubled Birth of Russian Democracy: Parties, Personalities, and Programs.* Stanford, CA: Hoover Institution Press, 1993. A thorough assessment of the political parties and processes in Russia brought on by perestroika.

Rees, E. A., ed. *The Soviet Communist Party in Disarray: The XXVIII Congress of the Communist Party of the Soviet Union.* New York: St. Martin's Press, 1992. An authoritative collection of readings on the Twenty-Eighth Party Congress (1990) of the CPSU, in which Yeltsin and others resigned from the party.

Rieber, Alfred J., and Alvin Z. Rubinstein, eds. *Perestroika at the Crossroads.* Armonk, NY: M. E. Sharpe, 1991. An excellent collection of essays on the crisis of perestroika.

Rigby, T. Harry. *The Changing Soviet System: Mono-organizational Socialism from*

Its Origins to Gorbachev's Restructuring. Brookfield, MA: Elgar, 1990. An exploration of the evolution of the monolithic structure of Soviet government from its beginning through the Gorbachev era.

Sharlet, Robert. *Soviet Constitutional Crisis: From De-Stalinization to Disintegration.* Armonk, NY: M. E. Sharpe, 1992. A study of the evolution of the Soviet constitution, and the importance of the idea of the rule of law in the Gorbachev era.

THE NATIONALITIES CRISIS OF THE LATE SOVIET PERIOD

Bialer, Seweryn, ed. *Politics, Society and Nationality inside Gorbachev's Russia.* Boulder, CO: Westview Press, 1989. An authoritative collection of essays on the nationalities problem from the period when the union began to fall apart.

D'Encausse, Helene Carriere. *The End of the Soviet Empire: The Triumph of the Nations.* New York: HarperCollins, 1993. A narrative and analysis of the national minority problems in Central Asia, the Caucasus, the Baltic, and Russia, as well as the various diasporas created by the collapse of the union.

Dunlop, John. *The Rise of Russia and the Fall of the Soviet Empire.* Princeton, NJ: Princeton University Press, 1993. A look at the rise of a new Russian nationalism and the end of the Soviet Union.

Lapidus, Gail, and Victor Zaslavsky, eds. *From Union to Commonwealth: Nationalism and Separation in the Soviet Republics.* New York: Cambridge University Press, 1992. A comprehensive collection of readings on the breakup of the union from various perspectives.

Laqueur, Walter. *Black Hundred: The Rise of the Extreme Right in Russia.* New York: HarperCollins, 1993. An important examination of the rise of right-wing Russian nationalism and anti-Semitism, including the Pamyat organization and Vladimir Zhirinovsky.

Motyl, Alexander, ed. *The Post-Soviet Nations—Perspectives on the Demise of the USSR.* New York: Columbia University Press, 1992. A thorough and insightful collection of essays on the former Soviet national republics and the breakup of the Soviet Union.

Nahaylo, Bohdan, and Victor Swoboda. *Soviet Disunion: A History of the Nationalities Problem in the USSR.* New York: Free Press, 1990. An overview of the nationalities crisis.

Urban, G. R. *End of Empire: The Demise of the Soviet Union.* Washington, DC: American University Press, 1993. A collection of conversations about the demise of the Soviet Union between Urban, a Soviet and Russia specialist (and former head of Radio Free Europe), and leading historians and politicians (including Otto von Hapsburg and Milovan Djilas).

THE AUGUST 1991 COUP ATTEMPT

Black, J. L. *Into the Dustbin of History: The USSR from Coup to Commonwealth, August–December, 1991.* Gulf Breeze, FL: Academic International Press, 1993. An insightful overview of the August coup attempt.

Goldman, Marshall I. *What Went Wrong with Perestroika*. New York: Norton, 1991. An analysis of the problems of perestroika.

Gorbachev, Mikhail S. *The August Coup: The Truth and the Lessons*. New York: HarperCollins, 1991. An important explanation of the causes, course, and consequences of the coup attempt, from the perspective of Mikhail Gorbachev.

Loory, Stuart H., and Ann Imse. *Seven Days That Shook the World*. Atlanta, GA: Turner Publications, 1991. A good photographic and textual record of the attempted coup by CNN reporters who were on the scene in Moscow.

Miller, John. *Mikhail Gorbachev and the End of the Soviet Power*. New York: St. Martin's Press, 1993. A reliable post-collapse assessment of the attempted coup.

Remnick, David. *Lenin's Tomb: The Last Days of the Soviet Empire*. New York: Random House, 1993. A perceptive study of the end of the Soviet period.

Sixsmith, Martin. *Moscow Coup: The Death of the Soviet System*. London: Simon and Schuster, 1991. A riveting first-person account of the events of August 1991, with an overview that places the events in context.

THE POST-SOVIET PERIOD OF RUSSIAN HISTORY

Boettle, Peter J. *Why Perestroika Failed*. London: Routledge, 1993. A lucid discussion of the forces responsible for the collapse of Communism in Russia and the effect of these forces on post-collapse developments.

Colton, Timothy J., and Robert Levgold, eds. *After the Soviet Union: From Empire to Nations*. New York: Norton, 1992. An excellent collection of essays on the post-Soviet nations and their political, economic, and military relationships.

Krasnov, Vladislav. *Russia beyond Communism: A Chronicle of National Rebirth*. Boulder, CO: Westview Press, 1991. An interesting early assessment of problems facing the new Russia.

Solomon, Susan Gross, ed. *Beyond Sovietology: Essays in Politics and History*. Armonk, NY: M. E. Sharpe, 1993. An important collection that explores new themes in Russian studies since the collapse of Communism.

White, Stephen, Graeme Gill, and Darrell Slider, eds. *The Politics of Transition: Shaping a Post-Soviet Future*. New York: Cambridge University Press, 1993. A superb collection of readings on the present condition of Russia and the future of the country.

VIDEOS

Capital Cities/ABC Video Enterprises. "Dateline: 1985—Moscow" (23 mins., 1989). A volume in ABC's *The Eagle and the Bear* series; provides historical background to Mikhail Gorbachev's election as general secretary, and points out that Gorbachev was "the only leader of the USSR to have been born and raised entirely under Communist rule."

Capital Cities/ABC Video Enterprises. "Dateline: 1987—The Summit" (23 mins.,

1987). A volume in ABC's *The Eagle and the Bear* series; explores the history of U.S. Soviet summit meetings from 1955 to 1987.

Capital Cities/ABC Video Enterprises. "Red Star Rising—The Dawn of the Gorbachev Era" (60 mins., 1989). Provides context for perestroika and glasnost.

Capital Cities/ABC Video Enterprises. "Dateline: 1980—Afghanistan" (23 mins., 1989). A volume in ABC's *The Eagle and the Bear* series; looks at the causes, course, and consequences of the Soviet invasion of Afghanistan.

Capital Cities/ABC Video Enterprises. "Dateline: 1989—Hungary" (23 mins., 1990). A volume in ABC's *The Eagle and the Bear* series; explores Soviet-Hungarian relations from the revolt of 1956 through the breakup of the Warsaw Pact in 1989.

Capital Cities/ABC Video Enterprises. "Dateline: 1989—Prague" (23 mins., 1990). A volume in ABC's *The Eagle and the Bear* series; explores Soviet-Czechoslovakian relations from the 1968 Prague Spring revolt through the collapse of the Warsaw Pact in 1989.

Capital Cities/ABC Video Enterprises. "Dateline: 1989—Romania" (23 mins., 1990). A volume in ABC's *The Eagle and the Bear* series; explores Soviet-Romanian relations through the fall of Ceaucescu's regime in 1989.

Capital Cities/ABC Video Enterprises. "The Week That Shook the World" (65 mins., 1991). Detailed coverage of events of August 19–25, 1991.

CNN Video. "The New Russian Revolution" (47 mins., 1991). A detailed look at the August coup attempt and its background, reasons for its failure, and the subsequent collapse of the Communist Party.

The Idea Bank. "Living in Russia Today" (25 mins., 1997). A survey of contemporary, post-Communist, Russian society and culture. It provides glimpses into the daily lives of average citizens.

Index

About the Author

WILLIAM E. WATSON is Lecturer in the Departments of History and Political Science at Drexel University and at LaSalle University. He is co-author (with Alexander V. Riasanovsky) of *Readings in Russian History* (1991).